ASIL N.

and the rise a

POLLY P

ASIL NADIR
and the rise and fall of
POLLY PECK

DAVID BARCHARD

LONDON
VICTOR GOLLANCZ LTD
1992

First published in Great Britain 1992
by Victor Gollancz Ltd
14 Henrietta Street, London WC2E 8QJ

A Gollancz Paperback Original

© David Barchard 1992

The right of David Barchard to be identified as author
of this work has been asserted by him in accordance with
the Copyright, Designs and Patents Act 1988

A CIP catalogue record for this book is available
from the British Library

ISBN 0 575 05206 6

Photoset in Great Britain by
Rowland Phototypesetting Ltd, Bury St Edmunds, Suffolk
Printed and bound in Great Britain by
Butler and Tanner Ltd, Frome, Somerset

For İffet and Halit

Contents

1 · Tuesday 7 August 1990

'May we come in?'

The chairman looked up from his desk at the two men hovering in his doorway beside his private secretary. The elder was his most senior lieutenant, the company's financial director for the last four years, soon to step up to deputy chief executive. The younger, a fairish, slightly-built man in his middle forties, was due to be his successor in a few weeks' time. The chairman was not altogether sure why they had asked for a slot in his diary on this particular morning, except that it had something to do with cash-flow forecasts, but he beamed at his new director with the sort of charming smile which comes only in the uncomplicated first stages of any working relationship.

The mood in the chairman's office on the first floor of 42 Berkeley Square was beguiling rather than intimidating. This was no ordinary room. It was a chamber of wonders – an 'Aladdin's cave', some people called it, with furnishings which had cost more than £1 million. Even the walls were edged with gilt gesso, but the most remarkable thing about the room was that somehow it was neither obtrusive nor ostentatious. 'I hate anything flashy,' the chairman would say. 'I work best with nice things around me.' Indeed, visitors to his office reported that it radiated a calm assuredness far beyond normal late-twentieth-century London corporate opulence. The collection of valuable objects in it might have graced one of the great country houses for centuries. But in fact it had all been put together over the previous three years from the showrooms of Mayfair.

The chairman was relaxed and on good form. He began this meeting as he began all others of its kind, by sliding into the slightly formal gentle personal inquiries and polite jokes which always preceded his business discussions. Perhaps, on this occasion, he particularly wanted to strike the right note with his new finance director, Reg Mogg. Had they both had good evenings? How were their wives and families? What did they think of the worsening situation in the Gulf? Yes, it was definitely bad news. How was Reg Mogg settling down in the company? Did he like his office and was he being given everything that he needed? It was a combination of sensitive personal interest and restless optimism that had turned many heads and charmed many sceptics over the years. Employees would leave Asil Nadir's presence with a sense of elation which afterwards they found difficult to explain.

This particular meeting of the three senior executive directors was taking place against a mildly sombre background. Polly Peck was one of the best-known large corporations in Britain with operations all over the world from Chile to Japan. It was a global empire and the first-floor room stuffed with antiques at 42 Berkeley Square was its heart. From an eighteenth-century English desk on which miniature golden tortoises crawled, Asil Nadir ran a company which had grown in less than a decade from an ailing firm of backstreet dressmakers into a worldwide conglomerate which no longer had much to do with women's dresses or the textile business. Asil Nadir now owned more than two hundred subsidiary companies in thirty countries. There were over eighty trading subsidiaries. The previous year Polly Peck had been admitted into the select group of one hundred leading British companies on which the main Stock Exchange share index was based.

This vast empire had been created out of virtually nothing. From rotting oranges in the abandoned groves of North Cyprus in the mid-1970s, Asil Nadir had built up one of the three largest fresh fruit businesses in the world with turnover of £572 million in the first half of 1990 alone. He was also a growing force in the world of consumer electronics. He had worked with dazzling speed and imagination over the previous decade to create the group, which was recognised to be largely his personal achievement. Almost from the beginning it had been the acknowledged star performer on the Stock Exchange where it now had a market value of £2 billion. Its latest set of remarkable results had produced pre-tax profits of £161 million in the previous year on turnover of £1,162 million, to the delight of the shareholders.

The largest shareholder was the chairman himself, who still owned more than a quarter of the company. He had been rewarded by becoming a vastly wealthy man, the thirty-sixth richest person in Britain, according to one computation. Nor was he merely immensely rich himself: he changed the lives of all those around him, and was beginning to have an increasingly powerful gravitational effect on the whole Eastern Mediterranean world.

In Turkey and Northern Cyprus he was a colossus whose economic power showed clear signs of transforming not just the business life, but also the politics and the culture of the two countries, fusing them into the mainstream of modern European commercial life for the first time. In his airline, newspapers and magazines (part of a business empire he owned outside Polly Peck) he was acknowledged to be raising standards of style and quality to heights never before locally achieved. Like a latter-day Midas, he seemed to be transforming Northern Cyprus, the country of his birth, from a poor country into a prosperous one in a mere handful of years.

Asil Nadir enjoyed his Midas image and the status and mystique that came with it, boasting that he was perhaps a billionaire. If that was an exaggeration, he had undoubtedly managed to join the ranks of the super-rich in less than two decades after arriving in London's East End as a teenage immigrant. His family were friends with royalty. His younger son was at Eton. In Istanbul he lived in an eighteenth-century wooden palace on the Bosporus in which Princess Margaret sometimes stayed. When he travelled, he did so in his personal jet, jokingly called Polly One by his friends.

His admirers saw him as a mixture of Aristotle Onassis and Henry Ford. His enemies disliked and distrusted him, but the sceptics were never able to dissuade his admirers, and in the previous twelve months his credibility had been growing steadily. His rise had made many of his admirers rich, not to mention an ever-widening circle of lieutenants and camp followers. For loyal shareholders, it seemed to be a case of faith being rewarded. Anyone who had bought £1,000 worth of the company's shares when Asil Nadir had taken it over, ten and a half years earlier, would now own more than £1 million of stock.

Yet something was slightly wrong. At the beginning of August 1990 the company's share price had been 453p, close to its all-time high, but during the previous week the market, perhaps unsettled by Saddam Hussein's invasion of Kuwait, had started to turn against it and it had dropped by 5 per cent in as many days. All the advances of the earlier part of the year were in danger of being wiped out. Yet the chairman, studying the ebb and flow of the market's mood on the row of screens in his office, remained optimistic. He always was. In his view, the market undervalued his shares and the sceptics would be proved wrong in the end.

Such things do indeed happen to the shares of most large companies from time to time. They, and the market, usually take them in their stride, knowing that an upturn will also come sooner or later. There was no particular reason for a company which seemed to be at the peak of its fortunes to feel uneasy if the investors cooled towards it for a week or two. In the past, when Polly Peck had been a much smaller company, it had survived far worse storms. No doubt some of the recent spate of selling was profit-taking around the time the share price peaked. This was understandable at any time, but especially so now that the market was battening down in anticipation of a war in the Gulf. In any case, the directors' mood during the summer had been more cautious. Instead of favouring new acquisitions, the Polly Peck board had spent much of its time discussing a withdrawal from one or possibly two of the group's lines of business.

Now the courtesies drew to a close. The chairman's expression indicated that the moment had arrived for his visitors to explain what was on their minds.

There was a cough and the rustle of papers amongst the coffee cups. The older man, David Fawcus, made the introduction and did most of the talking. In the course of going over the company's accounts and doing some entirely standard cash-flow forecasts for the company over the next few months he had spotted one or two areas which seemed to need attention now, although there was nothing unduly alarming. He showed the chairman his calculations about the flow of forthcoming payments to the banks over the months ahead.

'It is now early August. There seem to be a number of bank loan facilities coming up for renewal or rolling over,' he said. 'In all, it looks as though we may need to repay about £25 million by the end of October. This is money which falls due anyhow. But we could use some extra cash.'

This was the sort of request that the chairman had heard many times before during the ten years he had controlled the company. Unruffled, he murmured that if it was necessary, of course he would be able to find the money. 'So we need £25 million in all?' he asked.

'Not quite,' came the reply. Both directors drew breath and moved on to the second stage of their campaign.

'It is more likely to be about £50 million that is required,' said David Fawcus. 'You should bring back more cash than you need in the short term.'

The chairman looked thoughtful as he listened.

David Fawcus went on: 'The banks are becoming nervous in view of what has been going on in the last week or two. As I am sure you are aware, there have been a lot of rumours about the company in the press this summer – talk of acquisitions, tax problems, share-dealing and that sort of thing – and it seems to have got worse in the last few days. I think we should do something to put the media's nervousness to rest.'

'What do you suggest then?' said the chairman. He was wearing his glasses as he studied the figures and they gave him a strangely vulpine look. 'How do you think we ought to counter this nervousness?' He looked up expectantly from his notes, but he must have known what was coming.

'I have a suggestion,' said Fawcus. 'If we get back about £50 million from the company's cash holdings in Cyprus, we could put all the banks' fears to rest very easily. If we hold a fair amount on deposit in London, word will soon get around and breed confidence. It will also give us sufficient funds to pay off any facilities that the banks want repaid. The more cash you provide us with early on, the less we will actually need. If you can provide £50 million in cash, we may not even need any of it as most of the facilities will probably be rolled over.'

The chairman considered the idea. For one of the UK's largest quoted companies, £50 million was not such a large sum in relation to a balance sheet of over £1 billion. On the other hand, £50 million is a lot of cash by anyone's standards. It was not far short of a third of Polly Peck's entire published pre-tax profits in the previous year. Transferring large cash balances to the UK and then holding them there on deposit was in any case not something which the group had done before.

If a well-managed company has £50 million in cash, this is likely to be locked up earning interest in time deposits rather than stashed away in a short-term account, but it was still not uncommon for companies to keep cash deposits of that size on call in London, particularly with banks from which they had large loans. And like all companies, Polly Peck quite often experienced moments when it was squeezed for cash – sometimes very severely so. For the past year it had been very heavily indebted, after buying in rapid succession first Del Monte Fresh Fruit in the USA and then Sansui in Japan. Total borrowing was around £1.2 billion, but it had been cleverly carried out. No single bank was in a position to push the company around. In fact there was no sign that this large burden had become unmanageable, though it did make the group more vulnerable to market rumours and meant that it had to go carefully. But trading in the current year was said to be very good indeed. A day or two earlier the chairman had told the press that profits were set to leap from £161.4 million in 1989 to perhaps £250 million in 1990 – a jump of more than 50 per cent.

So there should not have been much to worry about. It was just that, as the finance director said, the flow of payments through head office in London required careful monitoring and likely difficulties needed to be pinpointed well in advance.

Both directors were hoping for a decisive reply from their chairman, and – as always – they got an answer that seemed reassuring. 'Right,' he said. 'I'll get £25 million back this week and £25 million next week and then it'll all be over.' He smiled benignly. 'Will that do, gentlemen?'

It would, of course, do very well – provided he actually produced the money. In the meantime there was little more to say.

The chairman rose to say goodbye to his visitors. The meeting came to an end with more cordialities and a slight sense of relief and anti-climax on the part of the two directors. The office doors closed behind them and the chairman turned to the telephone to answer a waiting caller. The screens beside him blinked with the movements of the market. The share price was still moving down a little, but it was defi-nitely nothing to worry about.

This was also the end, though neither the chairman nor his directors knew it, of normal times at Polly Peck. Only five days would pass until all three met again for an extended discussion, but this time at the first of many emergency board meetings.

No one could have guessed that all this wealth and power was in fact far more precarious than it looked in early August 1990. In less than twelve weeks, Polly Peck would slide into disaster. A £2-billion company would be reduced to rubble. Before the end of the year its chairman would find himself in Brixton prison without enough money to buy a packet of cigarettes, and facing a bankruptcy petition for more than £60 million.

But on the morning of 7 August, all that lay in the future and things seemed perfectly straightforward. All that was needed was to unlock £50 million from the company's abundant cash holdings in Cyprus, where bank deposits were earning interest at far higher levels than in the UK. Once that money was brought back to the UK, the slight clouds of the summer would disperse.

2 · A Cyprus Childhood

'We had an eighteenth-century childhood. Things were very quiet in Cyprus in those days. Nothing eventful ever happened and there was no sign that we could see that Asilkan, any more than the rest of us, would grow up to do extraordinary things,' says one of Asil Nadir's childhood friends in Famagusta.

Talking to his secretaries and assistants in his sumptuous Berkeley Square office years afterwards, Asil Nadir would often reminisce about his Cyprus childhood. 'I had a harsh upbringing,' he used to say, and would tell stories of being beaten. But his relationship with both parents was extremely close, combining respect, affection and perhaps just a hint of fear, throughout the rest of his life.

Asilkan Nadir was born at Lefke in 1941 while his father was on duty in the north of the island, but the family moved to Famagusta on the southern coast while he was still a baby, and remained there for the rest of their days in Cyprus. He was named Asilkan – 'Noble Blood'. The name, chosen by his mother, was taken from the closing lines of Atatürk's address to Turkish youth, to be found on every Turkish classroom wall, in which the founder of the Turkish Republic appealed to children of future generations to defend his legacy. The closing words of his speech are: 'The strength for this task is inherent in the noble blood flowing through your veins.' Safiye and İrfan Nadir were children of the Atatürk era, hence, no doubt, their slightly unusual choice of name for their only son. Throughout his childhood, he was known to his friends as Asilkan, shortening the name to Asil only after he left Cyprus.

Asilkan was the second child of İrfan and Safiye Nadir, born two and a half years after Meral, their eldest daughter. In the early 1940s, there can have been little about the family to suggest that they would one day become the island's wealthiest inhabitants. Born in Paphos on the west coast of Cyprus in 1918, İrfan was the grandson of a sailor, known in the family as 'the navigator'. Other members of the family were farmers, growing vines, a typical crop for Turkish landowners. In Cyprus Turks grew the grapes; the Greeks made the wine from them. Each autumn the two sides bargained fiercely about the sale of the crop, but somehow a deal was always struck.

İrfan himself spent the early years of his adult life as a *zaptiye*, the Ottoman equivalent of a gendarme or police constable, a title which survived
in Cyprus under British rule. He left the force under a slight shadow in
1947, when Asil was six, probably for engaging in business on the side.
But his years in the service had a lasting legacy: early on he had met Safiye,
the daughter of one of his colleagues. As a junior officer, İrfan had been
sent by her father, the head of his station, on errands which involved taking
things to and from his home. There were more than half a dozen children
in the house, but the young Safiye caught İrfan's eye and he determined
that she should become his bride. In due course, he persuaded her father
to let him marry her and the wedding was arranged.

More than forty years later, when he lay on his deathbed in Cyprus
in 1985, İrfan recorded his life's memories on tape. Perhaps some day
they will be published and bring him more clearly into focus. He is
remembered in Famagusta as a very hard-working and active man, with
a streak of cunning. He was always hungry for new opportunities and
chances to improve the family fortunes. He was fond of giving the
impression of being a hard man, but those who knew him well reported
that he was not as stern as he looked: he would give in quite easily
when asked for a favour. But he was undoubtedly a strict father, and
particularly so to Asilkan, his only son.

His wife, Safiye, was a determined, well-organised woman, proud of
her family, but eager to work at the same time. Throughout most of the
Nadirs' years in Famagusta in the 1940s and 1950s she ran a grocer's
shop. Today she still lives in Famagusta, close to relatives and friends
from the years before the family emigrated to Britain, even though Asil
Nadir generally prefers to stay in Kyrenia, the picturesque main resort
in Northern Cyprus.

Outwardly Famagusta in the first two decades of Asil's life was a
sleepy community of about 15,000 inhabitants, of whom perhaps only
4,000 were Turks. Its port had lain on the main sea route between
Europe and the Middle East since the days when the Crusaders lost Acre
in 1291, and inside the walled part of the town were many reminders of
its medieval prosperity.

Under British colonial rule, the town had changed only little since
Ottoman days. The mass tourism business did not yet exist. Shipping
was still the mainstay of the local economy: it was by far the busiest port
in Cyprus, while its farmers grew cereals, potatoes and oranges, of which
Famagusta was then one of the island's largest producers. After World
War II, it became one of the most rapidly growing towns on the island,
with almost all the development being concentrated in Varosha, the new
town along the coast.

By the standards of larger countries than Cyprus, Famagusta may have been little more than an overgrown village, but like everywhere else on the island, its small population was divided between several cultures and languages. The two main groups were of course the Greeks and the Turks. Though the two communities lived together, they did not mix much. 'There was an invisible barrier between us at the best of times,' recalls Özer Raif, a Famagusta businessman who grew up close to the Nadir family.

Apart from Greeks and Turks, and the ruling British, there were also Maronites, Latins and other minorities. The 4,000 Turks lived mostly inside the vast honey-coloured bastions of the Venetian town walls, conforming to the standard Ottoman practice whereby Muslims lived mostly within the walls of a city and non-Muslims outside them. Even so, each Sunday, the bells of Aya Kserinos, a Greek Orthodox church inside the walls, pealed out in the Turkish quarter.

Turkish Famagusta was much less developed economically than the Greek part of the town. Under the Ottoman Empire, trade and manufacturing had been left by the Muslims to the Christian and Jewish minorities. The Turks had been farmers, soldiers, policemen (as İrfan Nadir was). Today the people of Famagusta are a hard-working, unaffected community in which everyone knows – and is usually somehow related to – everyone else, and there are few social distinctions.

In this respect Turkish Cyprus is very different from mainland Turkey, polarised between a huge peasant population and a wealthy and sophisticated metropolitan élite. The sharp sense of social distinction which pervades life on the mainland is missing in Cyprus. 'There seem to be no classes in Cyprus,' says Ayşegül Nadir, the girl from Istanbul who was to become Asil Nadir's wife. Another Istanbul lady puts it more precisely: 'Cyprus is a very *petit-bourgeois* place.'

Then as now, the Nadirs saw themselves as a hard-working middle-class family. The children were brought up to despise unnecessary ostentation or displays of wealth. They saw this as one of the main differences between themselves and the business families of Istanbul and Anatolian towns, for whom conspicuous consumption in the form of lavish entertainment and a life-style laden with expensive clothes and possessions was very important. Even if one does not have a lot of money in Turkey, it is important to try and look as if one does.

The difference persists today. Most of the Nadir family in the UK live close to each other in comfortable but distinctly middle-class houses on the outskirts of London. Nevertheless the Nadirs were slightly untypical. They may have disliked flashiness but they did want to become rich and they were all conspicuously hard-working. Though Safiye's

grocery was inside the walls of Famagusta, as soon as they could afford
to the family moved out of the old town to a home at number 11, Herod
of Attica Street in the new part of town. The house, built of concrete
blocks, still stands in what is now called Kocatepe Street, renamed in
the wake of the 1974 invasion after a Turkish battleship which was
accidentally sunk during the fighting. The property was enlarged when
the Nadirs lived there in the 1950s, but after 1974 the street was settled
by displaced Turkish immigrants from the south of the island and it
went somewhat down in the world. A few years later, the Nadirs bought
the larger house next door at number 13, again expanding it.

It was a mildly daring choice of place to live. It was not altogether
surprising that economically active Turkish families like the Nadirs
chose to move outside the city walls, where Turks had lived in Ottoman
times. But Herod of Attica Street was strongly Greek. There was only
one other family of Turkish neighbours nearby. As a result, the Nadir
children grew up speaking good Greek. Asil Nadir's earliest childhood
friends were Greeks called Loizo, Kogo, Andrea and Fritzi. The children were too young to be aware of the differences between them, but
this was in any case still an age of innocence on Cyprus, the last years
of World War II and the beginning of the post-war era. Politics and
nationalism were only just beginning to cast their shadows.

During the years of Asilkan's infancy, intercommunal politics were
overshadowed by the war, but beneath the dilapidated exterior of
colonial Cyprus forces for change were stirring. In 1931, the Greeks
had demonstrated against British rule, calling for union with mainland
Greece. The British had clamped down hard on the entire population,
making no distinction between Greeks and non-Greeks. Coffee-houses,
regarded as seed-beds for nationalist agitators, were shut down, and
flags and maps of Turkey and Greece were forbidden. The restrictions
were resented, while the Turkish minority began to feel nervous about
what the future might hold.

Safiye's father had been particularly affected. During the 1931 Greek
nationalist uprising, he had been a gendarme in an area near Nicosia
which was almost entirely Greek. As a result the police station he was
in at Paralimera had come under attack and was burned down. He was
transferred to another district, but never forgot the experience. The
authorities subsequently decided that Turkish gendarmes should not be
posted to districts which were predominantly Greek.

In 1947, when Asilkan was six years old, politics erupted in earnest
when the Greeks staged a May Day rally in defiance of the British.
Some Turkish workers joined in the demonstration, attracted perhaps
by its slogan, 'Eight hours work, eight hours sleep, and eight hours

leisure'. But the demonstration ended with a petition to the colonial authorities calling for union with Greece, and the Turks felt they had been cheated.

They set up an organisation to protect the rights of the Turkish minority. Its leading figure, Dr Fazıl Küçük, was a distant relative of Safiye Nadir, though such connections are not uncommon in the small world of Turkish Cyprus. Dr Küçük, an old-style communal leader rather than a modern party politician in the full sense of the word, would lead the Turkish Cypriots throughout the 1950s, becoming the first – and so far the only – vice-president of Cyprus under the 1960 constitution.

Around this time, while Asilkan was learning his ABC, İrfan was taking his first steps in business. His ventures were unpredictable and sometimes short-lived. Neighbours, perhaps unfairly, put his failures down to losses at the poker table. He drank Bell's whisky, though not to excess, had an eye for pretty women, and liked experimenting with new businesses. One day he hoped he would find something which would make the family truly rich. By the mid-1950s he had already made it rather wealthier than any other trading family in the Turkish community in Famagusta, but he pursued a whole variety of trades before he eventually found his métier in the East End rag trade in London a dozen years later. His first line of business was selling chemical tests for marsh gas in the mines. Later he imported balloons into Famagusta, novelties which astonished little Asilkan's friends. 'Things were very basic here in those days. It was a big event for us children to see balloons for the first time,' one of Asil Nadir's childhood friends recalls.

Safiye stuck to a more established line of business. The grocery she ran in the old town was in Princess Elizabeth Street (today İstiklâl Caddesi), beside the Maronites' houses. She gradually learned to direct her business towards the most lucrative end of the market, the British families in the town. It was here, beside his mother in her shop, that Asilkan acquired the work ethic which was to stay with him all his life. Years afterwards he would say that his first introduction to business had been selling newspapers at the age of six. In the Eastern Mediterranean, where children routinely work alongside their parents in the family business, this was not all that unusual, but it set the pattern for a childhood in which family business took priority over close friendships with schoolmates.

During the week, İrfan was out of the house for most of the day, usually not returning until late, but on Sunday mornings between nine and eleven, he would gather the three children together in their parents' room and tell them stories. These were stories which he had made up himself, and though the children at the time thought he was telling them only for fun, they would realise as they grew up that each tale was designed to teach a certain moral. There might be the story of three sons who worked together and, by staying local to each other, would save themselves. At the end of the story would come the moral: 'A single stick can be broken easily, but a bundle of sticks is impossible to break.' The emphasis on solidarity and unity is very Turkish and many Anatolian children have grown up hearing this proverb.

There was also a strong undercurrent of piety. İrfan told his children that God forgives sinners who work very hard. 'If you work hard, it is as good as praying. God forgives us because we are working so hard, even if we do not go to the mosque. It does not matter, we are working very hard and we keep ourselves pure inside. We don't wish bad things for anyone,' he would say.

Before meals, the children would say an old Anatolian Turkish grace which they had learned as Scouts, which to European ears contains uncanny echoes of the 'Our Father'. It ran: 'O God who is in heaven, give us this day our bread as you give it to the birds and the animals and forgive us the bad things that we do to others and protect us from all bad things.' Sometimes the gulf between Muslims and Christians is narrower than either side is aware.

İrfan's emphasis on diligence and self-improvement, and the harsh family discipline which went with it, grew naturally out of the Muslim traditions of the *esnaf* – small-town traders or artisans. But it also had Anglo-Saxon roots. The works of Samuel Smiles, the Victorian advocate of self-help, thrift and diligence, had long been available in Turkish and found an admiring readership among Turkish small businessmen in the towns of Anatolia.

The Nadir children accepted their parents' constant discipline, and the corporal punishment which came with it, but they could see that they were treated more strictly than many of their friends. They belonged to a strongly patriarchal culture. There was no question of openly defying their parents or resisting their authority, although in childhood there were many occasions on which they whispered their resentment at their harsh upbringing to each other in secret. There was nothing they could do to change it, however, and in time they would all accept the mould, more or less as their parents wanted.

Certainly there was little opportunity to play off one parent against the other as there might have been in another family. Safiye Nadir was universally acknowledged to be a tough and single-minded lady, very committed to the traditions of her community: 'a true old Ottoman lady' is how her friends describe her today. She saw to it that the grocery shop made a steady profit, which sometimes had to be used to help İrfan's more risky business lines out. Work also meant that she sometimes had to leave her children unattended. Once, when Asilkan was a small baby in swaddling clothes, she left him alone in the shop while she went out on an errand, only to experience a moment of panic when she returned an hour later to find that the bars of the shop window had been forced apart and the baby removed. A search revealed that he had been taken by soft-hearted neighbours who were upset to hear the baby crying alone.

The three children grew up to look strikingly like their parents, with proud aquiline noses, Mediterranean olive complexions and dark hair. Asilkan was to be taller and more willowy than his father, but there was still an unmistakable resemblance between father and son. Early photographs of Asilkan show him as a solemn Cypriot child, a far cry from the whiz-kid photographs of the 1960s and 1970s with their Afro hairstyle and pop-star smile. Nothing about him as yet suggested that the course of his life would be any different from that of other Famagusta children.

Asilkan's school-days began at Nahide hanım's nursery school, where he stayed until he was seven years old. Perhaps it was at this time that he first began to hear about the political troubles of the island, for Nahide hanım, from whom he learned the alphabet, was a somewhat controversial figure locally. Her husband Kazım worked in the Greek municipality and was known as the first Communist in Turkish Famagusta.

At school Asilkan turned out to be hard-working, diligent, rather serious. At seven he went with his friends Eşref Çetinel and Hüseyin Cavit to the Gazi İlkokulu (primary school) where he began reading. Contemporaries noticed that from an early age he played with only a few children and did not mix very easily with those he did not know. 'He was rather introverted,' recalls one of his classmates at both nursery school and primary school, perhaps surprisingly in view of his later career.

Asil and Meral were given a sound musical education from an early age. They were sent to an Italian music master when still at primary school. The Italian was very strict and if they played a wrong note, he would rap them on the fingers with his ruler. Despite this Asil persevered. He decided to learn the violin – the difficult instrument – while Meral chose the more conventional piano. He studied it for six years, taking the Royal Academy of Music exams each year and reaching the sixth grade. He and his sisters would spend any spare time they had at

home playing music or listening to it on records and the radio, and
he did not abandon the habit of playing the violin for relaxation until
after he married Ayşegül, who seems to have thought it slightly
ridiculous.

As Asilkan and his companions grew up, they became more aware of
the complexities of the community they lived in. By mainland standards,
the Turkish Cypriots were not especially devout when it came to matters
of religion, but each Friday the children were forced, rather unwillingly,
to attend prayers in the mosque. Around the age of seven, Asilkan would
have been circumcised in accordance with Turkish Islamic custom.
When his own sons underwent this operation many years later, Asil
Nadir would follow the customs of the mainland, throwing a vast party
to celebrate the event. In Cyprus, however, the occasion passed without
much ceremony. His parents gave just a small party at home.

Down the road from the Nadirs' house was the English cemetery,
shaded by cypress trees. As the children explored this, they came into
contact with a British colonial culture which they only gradually came
to understand. The cemetery contained the graves of British airmen,
killed in a forgotten air accident near Famagusta in the pre-war period.
From time to time there would be new funerals. The mourners would
bring accordions and pipes and the sound of music and singing would
waft through the cypress trees. Meral would take Asilkan, then not yet
five years old, to watch and listen from the road. They were drawn to
these occasions by the music – the chanting of hymns to the strains of
the accordion. The sounds were sweet but puzzling to Turkish Cypriot
children who had no idea of what hymns were.

In these and other ways, Asilkan and his friends gradually discovered
that they were growing up as members of a religious and ethnic minority
living in a colonial society. On the walls of the primary school and the
Namık Kemal Lycée which Asilkan attended afterwards were portraits
of King George VI and his daughter Princess Elizabeth. Each morning,
God Save the King was played in school.

These manifestations of England were largely taken for granted. The
British were not disliked and there was little conscious resentment of
their rule among the Turks. But the schools Asilkan went to were
Turkish schools, partly supported by mainland Turkey. The text-books
the children read were suffused with Turkish nationalism, and on
Turkish national days, patriotic poems would be read out and speeches
declaimed, pledging undying attachment to the Turkish motherland
across the water and the need to fight colonialism. Namık Kemal, the
first great Turkish nationalist of modern times, had been imprisoned in

the former Venetian Palace in Famagusta in the 1870s and his bust stood outside the sixteenth-century building which had been used as a prison under Ottoman rule.

None of this nationalist rhetoric mattered very much until 1954, when Asilkan was thirteen. There was little political activity on the island and the Nadir family lived peaceably in their mixed community. But in 1954 the Cyprus emergency began as the Greek Cypriots launched a campaign for Enosis – union with Greece – and within a few years, it became clear that British rule on the island was not going to last for ever.

Meanwhile, İrfan had been trying his hand at a succession of businesses. He rented out bicycles at 4 pence each in the Maronitler area of the old town. Then he opened a music shop, the only one in Famagusta, where he sold guitars, trumpets, and sheet music, but opportunities were limited and eventually in the mid-1950s he decided to sell it off. He found a potential purchaser in a local Greek, Charalamboulos Hambi: to make sure that the sale went through, İrfan tipped a number of local Turks a shilling to come into the shop and make purchases while he was showing the prospective buyer around. He also bought and sold text-books for primary and junior school and his children would spend the evenings before the start of the school year assembling sets of text-books for sale. He bought novels by famous authors, too, and operated a small bookshop which served as a lending library as well for fiction and poetry.

His next business was a pastry shop, the Europe Pastahanesi, the family's first venture into the food and leisure industries. It was a bold undertaking, not because food was involved – soon afterwards İrfan had a catering business and a hotel management contract as well – but because the *pastahane* was situated in the Greek part of Famagusta and seems to have been in part an unsuccessful enterprise in a predominantly Greek Cypriot milieu.

The pastry shop was swiftly followed by an altogether different line – a bus service, running from the British army camp to town, and using double-decker buses. Its customers were national servicemen, increasingly pleased to have local friends in Famagusta whom they could trust. By now Asilkan was old enough to work alongside his father, talking constantly with him about his views on life and business, and beginning to imbibe something of his entrepreneurial ambitions. But he worked only in the evenings. His parents were determined that he should do well at school, and during the daytime he went to the Namık Kemal Lycée. It was basically a Turkish school, similar to Turkish lycées on the mainland, though a little Greek and rather more English was taught.

If Asilkan had been Greek, he would have gone to the Greek high school, which the Turks felt was better endowed and equipped because it was subsidised by the Church.

Some of Asilkan's teachers were seconded from mainland Turkey. There was Sıtkı Özkay, the music teacher, who was himself a violinist and taught Asilkan the instrument from the age of fifteen. He was a fairly good student, who had no difficulty in passing exams, but he was not particularly interested in sport (though he was captain of the soccer team) or the arts, apart from music. His concentration on business was already beginning to show. His contemporaries seem to have felt that he did not mix enough with his own age group, his spare time being taken up by work with his parents.

Yet he had something of the showman in him. The areas where he shone at school were in music and debating. The schoolboy Nadir is remembered by his contemporaries mainly as an accomplished violinist and singer. In fact his teachers thought he might make a career out of music, and when the time came for him to choose a university it was suggested that he might consider going to the Ankara Conservatory to study music. Had he taken that course, Asil Nadir might well have ended up not as a world-famous businessman but as the lead violinist in the Presidential Symphony Orchestra, playing to Ankara audiences at the City's Friday evening concerts.

At the lycée there were also teachers from Britain, and they were the first English people that Asilkan got to know well. Not surprisingly, these 1950s' expatriate schoolmasters were not perhaps the most shining examples of what Britain had to offer. There was Mr Brush, who, as his name suggests, had a large moustache, and shocked his pupils by drinking Scotch whisky and beer night and day, and Mr Underwood, who rumour had it was a wealthy man, with shares in a petrol company in Arabia, almost certainly the first time that Asilkan encountered share-owning as a form of wealth. Few Cypriots owned shares. Their assets were in small businesses or farms.

Once a week Asilkan and his friends would be taken by İrfan to Hadji Hambi, the Greek cinema in Varosha. He had tickets for a box from which they watched swashbuckling adventure films, like *The Black Arrow* and *The Pirate Prince*, on cinemascope. The excursion was the highlight of the week, and also one of the relatively few occasions when Asilkan mixed with his friends. İrfan, like many another stern father in Turkey or Cyprus, did not like his son to be idle or go around the town without his permission.

İrfan himself had other hobbies. One was horse-racing, an interest shared by his son. At various times İrfan owned three race-horses which ran at the race course at Nicosia. The first was Arrivederci; later came two horses with Turkish names, Alev (Flame) and Bora (Gale). However, İrfan suspected that the horses were nobbled by the Greek trainers on the course. Once, when Arrivederci disappointed him by losing, he inspected the horse's mouth and concluded from the foam in it, that the horse had been doped.

A little later came a serious distraction from parental discipline in the form of Asilkan's first girlfriend. Her name was Rose and she was Anglo-Indian, the daughter of a British warrant officer who was serving on the island. She was sixteen years old, and her family had a large house at the end of the road where the Nadirs lived, on the way to the south-west gate of the old city. They had an Opel car, something which was sufficiently unusual to attract attention.

Asilkan's native language was Turkish (more exactly, the *patois* Turkish of the island which people from Istanbul did not find easy to understand), but he spoke better-than-average English, as well as passable Greek, because he had many opportunities to practise while speaking to the customers in his mother's shop. So it was quite easy for him to make the transition from the world of his family and the Turkish community to that of Rose and the British service expatriates.

The friendship was extremely unwelcome to İrfan, even though he himself had a fondness for the ladies, and Asilkan was ordered not to speak to Rose. The veto had little effect, although one of the worst moments of Asilkan's teenage years came one day when his father returned unexpectedly to Famagusta from a trip out of town, and discovered him in Rose's home. He was soundly whipped for his disobedience.

What was the objection to the friendship? Probably not that Asilkan was forming friendships with the British, more that Cyprus was a conservative society; teenage dating was frowned upon, for marriages in both communities were generally arranged by parents. But İrfan was again untypical in this respect: he was strongly against arranged marriages and none of his children had one. Perhaps his main objection to Rose was that Asilkan's friendship with her was a distraction from his work.

Safiye feared that if Asilkan started having girlfriends, he would end up by marrying out. Turkish parents did not like their children to marry foreigners, especially non-Muslims. Rose was definitely not what İrfan and Safiye had in mind for their daughter-in-law. İrfan may also have already sensed that his son was the sort of boy who would get married very young, as he himself had done. In this department of his life, however, more than in any other, Asilkan would go his own way. The friendship with Rose continued until she left Famagusta three years later.

In his late teens, Asilkan had to have an operation on his nose. He had tripped and fallen on his face while walking. He and his friends joked that he had been given an Elvis Presley nose, but a slight respiratory problem was to stay with him after the operation.

By the second half of Asilkan's teenage years, politics had become inescapable. First there was the emergency. Quite apart from the fear of violence, it meant curfews which got in the way of normal existence. When Meral Nadir took her A levels, she had to have special permission to go to the examination centre in a British army jeep.

As the Greek Cypriot campaign for union with Greece grew stronger, the Turkish Cypriots produced their response: partition of the island, with Turkey being given the northern coastline – more or less what eventually happened in 1974. In the Namık Kemal Lycée, '*Ya taksim ya ölüm*' – 'Partition or death' – became the rallying-cry among Asilkan's classmates. The Turks represented just under a fifth of the total population of the island, although they believed – on tenuous evidence – that they had once been in the majority before the British arrived. Certainly they had a strong sense of having been the masters at one time.

Turkish Muslim culture and Greek Orthodox civilisation did not mix easily, and the Turkish Cypriots had no illusions about what their fate would be if Cyprus became part of Greece. They knew they were likely to go the way of the Turkish minority on Crete, another large Mediterranean island which had once belonged to the Ottoman Empire. Crete had had a larger Muslim Turkish (though mostly Greek-speaking) minority than Cyprus, just under a third of the population. Crete had passed into mainland Greek rule by stages between the 1890s (when intercommunal fighting broke out on Crete, and British battleships prevented the Ottoman Empire from coming to the aid of the Turkish population) and 1913.

The Turks on the island of Crete had been forced to leave in successive waves amid massacres of their families which somehow went unreported in history books written by Europeans. By 1923, the Turkish Cretans had all gone. Even though they were a Greek-speaking people and remained so when resettled in Turkey, there had been no place for them in Greece. Would things be any different in Cyprus? No one at the Namık Lycée thought so.

The Greek Cypriots regarded Cyprus simply as a Greek island rather than the homeland of two communities. If 80 per cent of the population wanted something, they argued, they should have it and not be blocked by one-fifth of the population. If the Turks did not like what the majority chose, they could leave, as they had done in Crete. Even promises by moderates to respect the rights of the minority seemed to suggest that Cyprus was not the real home of the Turkish Cypriots and to contain a hint of possible expulsion. 'The Turks of course must have their safeguards, whether they choose to stay in Cyprus or go back to their homeland,' wrote Charles Foley, editor of the English-language *Times of Cyprus*, notably supportive of the Greek Cypriot cause, in the second half of the 1950s.

Though they probably did not know who they were, the Nadirs rubbed shoulders every day with some of the fiercest loyalists of EOKA, the Greek Cypriot guerrilla movement. One of the most famous of them lived nearby for several years. The stringer of the *Times of Cyprus* in Famagusta in the mid-1950s was Nicos Sampson, later a leader of several EOKA units around Nicosia, and nearly executed by the British. Later still, in July 1974, he would be briefly installed as a puppet president of the island by the Greek dictators in Athens in the interval between the overthrow of President Makarios and the Turkish invasion.

Even in British Cyprus, the Turkish Cypriots had a strong sense of being second-class citizens by comparison with the Greeks. Though they saw themselves as the former rulers of the island, they were obviously economically backward compared to the Greeks, and much less close to European standards. 'We still feel it,' says one of Asil Nadir's primary school classmates. Now they began to feel not only underprivileged but also physically threatened. They suspected, too, that the Greeks wanted to ensure that they remained poor and backward so that the number of Turkish Cypriots emigrating would continue. Since the 1930s emigration to Turkey and Britain had created a sort of Turkish Cypriot diaspora, with at least a third of all Turkish Cypriots living outside Cyprus. The Nadirs would one day be the best-known family of this diaspora community.

Since 1945, the Turkish Cypriots had chosen political leaders for their community to represent the minority. The British colonial authorities quite liked the Turks, whom they regarded as more dependable than the Greeks. But as Britain prepared to pull out of Cyprus, the Turkish Cypriots began to look increasingly to Turkey, only 40 miles away across the sea from Kyrenia, though at that time still a very inward-looking and underdeveloped country. Their attempts to rouse public opinion to their plight on mainland Turkey eventually succeeded, thanks to the support of *Hürriyet*, Turkey's largest-selling daily paper in those days.

Across the island, Turkish and Greek Cypriots polarised into hostile and mutually fearful communities. Tensions were strongest among young men of Asilkan's age, regarded by both communities as their warriors.

On 3 October 1958, Famagusta briefly hit the international headlines with a particularly horrifying murder when Mrs Catherine Cutliffe, the wife of a Royal Artillery sergeant and a mother of five, was killed by EOKA gunmen who shot her in the back while she was leaving a Famagusta dress shop. Four people, including a British soldier, died in the fighting between troops and Greek Cypriots which followed her killing, and scores of people had to be treated in hospital.

The Turkish schoolboys of Namık Kemal Lycée – some of them still only fourteen years old – were hired as special constables to help the British maintain order. They were paid 2 shillings a day for their work, the same amount as a civil servant earned. In return they were given a uniform and a Greener riot pistol and supervised traffic coming into and out of the town as well as tipping off the authorities when EOKA militants were spotted.

Several of Asilkan's classmates took on this work for the British, but he himself declined it, just as he seems to have turned down most time-consuming activities outside the family businesses. One reason for the refusal may have been that İrfan and Safiye, as business people, felt less inclined than other Turkish Cypriots to expose themselves to political risk in the service of the colonial authorities. İrfan's businesses were very vulnerable to Greek Cypriot ill-will, and as British power waned, it was clear that the economic future of the island would lie with the Greeks.

İrfan Nadir had been thinking for some time of joining the growing number of Cypriots who were leaving the island to seek their fortune in London. He was approaching forty and had a wife and three children to support, although they were all by now in their teens. In another year or two Asilkan would be in university. Meral, the eldest child, was not inclined to business. She liked music and by now was studying English literature at Ankara University. She chose to become a teacher, a career in which her mother had qualified but had never taken up. But Asilkan wanted to make money.

By this time İrfan was coming under some pressure. He was not a very political man and his career suggests that he had originally been quite willing to live in an ethnically mixed community. He had opened shops in the Greek quarter of Famagusta. But now he began to receive death threats and anonymous letters. One day in the summer of 1958, the tyres of his buses were slashed. There was little doubt about who had done it, and it was a pointer to what would probably lie ahead for

Turkish businessmen under Greek rule. İrfan told Safiye that there was no future for the family on the island. She wanted to stay in Cyprus more than he did, but she recognised that the island's political troubles made this impossible.

In 1959, İrfan finally decided to move to London. The next question was what line of business he should take up when he settled there. He was not going as a pauper. The family had a number of businesses and though they were beginning to run down by 1959 as the end of British rule on the island came into sight, he could sell them – and the house in Herod of Attica Street – and raise a certain amount of capital.

İrfan selected the textiles business, the valve through which immigrants had always entered the British economy, as the best opportunity for the family in London. It was not a line of which he had much experience, but it was one in which other Cypriots, mostly Greeks, were already well established in London. 'İrfan had seen that he had no future on the island and so he decided to go. There were those who went early on because they were direct targets for EOKA and those who left along with the British. İrfan bey belonged generally to the second category,' says one of Asil Nadir's childhood contemporaries.

Like most immigrants in London, İrfan began in the East End, staying in the home of Zekiye hanım, an old Famagusta friend, who was then living in Kingsland Road, Dalston. In time-honoured fashion he went ahead of the rest of the family. Safiye remained in Famagusta while Meral was in Ankara. Asilkan was just about to finish school, but Bilge, the younger daughter, still had some years to go.

İrfan was followed in a few months by Fehim Nevzat, a young family friend who was to marry Bilge a few years later. Fehim Nevzat's elder brother İlker, who studied law in the UK and became a solicitor, would become Polly Peck's head on Cyprus until the autumn of 1990.

In Famagusta Safiye continued to run the family businesses on her own. Unlike İrfan whose English was quite good, she spoke only broken English and always felt much more at home in Famagusta. London was to be only a relatively short-lived episode in her life rather than a permanent new home.

In Cyprus, Turkey and Greece reached agreement in February 1959 with a deal under which the island would become an independent state. It looked as though, despite everything, the Greeks and the Turks had finally managed to bury their differences and there would be no partition of the island. A conference in London at Lancaster House later in the year designed a bicommunal state, guaranteed by Britain, Greece and Turkey, with a complicated constitution which gave the island a Greek president and a Turkish deputy president. Both had powers to veto cabinet decisions. The Turkish Cypriot minority, though just under 20 per cent of the population, was given the right to 30 per cent of the civil service and the police, and 40 per cent of the island's armed forces. It was an arrangement that might have worked had the two sides liked and respected each other, and had there been some strong international neutral presence to hold the ring between them after the British departure.

On 16 August 1960, the Venetian walls of Famagusta castle reverberated to the sound of HMS *Ajax*, a Royal Navy battleship moored off Famagusta, as it blew its siren in the warm Cyprus night air to mark the arrival of independence. Özer Raif, among the crowds of celebrators on the shore, looked at the new flag and the portrait of Makarios. 'I thought, this is my president. But only the next day he made a statement that he headed the first Greek government in Cyprus.'

Asilkan was not there on that night of independence festivities. In 1959 he had flown to England for the first time and spent some weeks there, during which he had the long-delayed operation on his nose which his parents seem to have thought it would be wiser to have done in England. He attended some courses, but his sights were now on Istanbul and a university education.

The Nadirs had formed their own judgment about what the post-independence constitution would mean in practice for Cyprus. Asilkan had followed his father to London, and though he used his diploma from Namık Kemal Lycée to go to Istanbul University, his links with the island of his childhood ended abruptly, except through a few continuing connections with friends such as Hüseyin Cavit and Mustafa Salih. Classmates at the Namık Kemal Lycée would not see him again for almost thirty years.

One reason for his absence may have been the strong possibility that he would be drafted to do military service. But going into business in London was not so much an evasion as an alternative. The Turkish Cypriot authorities recognised that the role of the London Turkish Cypriots, sometimes referred to as 'economic commanders' in the battle for national survival, was important in its own right.

At any rate, there now came a clear break in his life. For whatever reason, though Asil Nadir visited Istanbul frequently in his early adult years, he did not go back to Cyprus for just over two decades. When he returned in the early 1980s, it would not be on a sentimental journey, but a promotional business trip taking out analysts to see what Polly Peck was doing on the island.

By then he would be going back not to the Famagusta of his childhood, but to a new wholly Turkish Famagusta where Greeks, Maronites and Latins no longer lived. By then the rather unexceptional if very hardworking Famagusta schoolboy would have long since evolved into the youthful chairman and chief executive of Polly Peck, the whiz-kid and star of the London business world with the miracle touch.

3 · Istanbul and London

For almost all his life, Asil Nadir has lived in close daily contact with the rest of his family, caught up in the stern discipline of maintaining first the family businesses and then his own company. By contrast, his three years as a student at the Faculty of Economics in Istanbul were spent almost entirely out of contact with his parents. Even phone calls between London and Turkey were difficult in the early 1960s.

During his student years the hard-working and intelligent but not very remarkable Famagusta schoolboy developed into a man who combined restless energy, fierce ambition and a legendary ability to charm – and who began speaking openly of his dreams of becoming a millionaire. He would also return to England a married man with a young bride to support – a convent schoolgirl, rather than a beauty queen as the legend has it. She would help propel his life and career in a totally new direction.

İrfan and Safiye's first years in England were spent moving into the London rag trade and achieving relative prosperity within two or three years. From their temporary address in Kingsland Road they moved rapidly up the London housing market. By 1963 they were living in some style in a semi-detached house in Romford, Essex, though their work still took them to London's East End each day.

The name of the family company in the mid-1960s was Nadir Modes, later changed to Nadir Fashions. It was one of many hundreds of small businesses set up in the miles of dingy nineteenth-century houses north of the City. The Turkish Cypriots were following an earlier wave of Greek Cypriot immigration and would themselves be followed by migrants from mainland Turkey in the 1970s and 1980s until Dalston and Stoke Newington eventually became London's first-ever Turkish quarter.

The Nadirs set their sights higher than most immigrants. They had been prosperous even in Cyprus and they were not beginning quite at the bottom of the pile now, bringing business experience and some family money with them from their homeland.

They worked fairly close to the centre of London, in the frontier zone where the East End looks across to the City, and they lived as far out as they could, rather than in the huddled immigrant quarters. Safiye disliked living in the densely-populated heart of a large city and wanted to be closer to the open country. In any case İrfan found the humidity of central London affected his chest.

In due course Asil Nadir was to meet people who made their living in the City and would gradually discover what the stock market (something unknown in Cyprus) was and how it could literally transform the fortunes of a small company. But in 1960 all that lay a long way in the future.

Running a textiles workshop required different skills from those needed to run a family store, but Safiye rapidly acquired them. It was she who would run the Nadir factories in London in the 1960s and early 1970s and later manage the family's operations in Cyprus. A tough and effective task-master, a stickler for detail and something of a perfectionist, she was determined to see her son make the best of himself. In fact both parents were eager for Asil to go to university. Neither of them had had the chance of a university education, though Safiye had qualified as a teacher.

Asil Nadir finished his Famagusta lycée education just at the point when the family were setting up in England and it would have been most useful for his father to have had him there. Despite this, it was clear to İrfan that his son must get a university education. The only question was whether he should go to a British university or a Turkish one. Armed with his lycée diploma from British Cyprus, he could have attempted either. A British university degree might improve the prospects of the family, who were very conscious that they were starting in London with everything to do. On the other hand, by studying in Turkey, Asil would reinforce his Turkish identity and strengthen the family's links with Turkey.

There were some other points in Turkey's favour, too. Asil's elder sister, Meral, and her husband, Güner Kâşif, were by then living in Istanbul, in a flat in Cihangir close to Taksim Square: Asil could lodge with them. And his lycée diploma from Famagusta entitled him to a place at Istanbul University. Studying there, he would acquire the standard Turkish of educated mainlanders. He would also have the chance to break away from the discipline and restrictions of his family home for a time.

In interviews given in his Polly Peck days, he would look back on his student years as a period of relative poverty, when he sometimes went hungry for lack of money. In fact, by Turkish student standards of that time, he must have been unusually affluent, for by his second year he owned a turquoise-blue twin-seater MG-A sports car which he had driven out from England. It was İrfan Nadir's reward to his son for doing well in his first-year exams – and a clear indication of the continuing prosperity of the Nadirs even during their first year or two in England. In Istanbul, the car enabled Asil to stand out from almost everyone else he knew. Private passenger cars were still uncommon in Turkey in the 1960s, where horses were still often to be seen on the streets of big cities.

The year 1960 had been a turning-point for Turkey as it was for Cyprus, though for very different reasons. Asil Nadir's student career began in the aftermath of a revolution, one in which students seemed to have played a leading part. In May 1960, a committee of generals and colonels, backed by the universities and much of the urban middle class, deposed Adnan Menderes, the prime minister, on the grounds that he was trying to set up a dictatorship. A new liberal constitution was introduced, although the credentials of the new regime were blotted when it placed Menderes on trial in a military court on very slender charges of corruption and then hanged him – an event which occurred at the beginning of Asil Nadir's second year at university. The execution caused particular distress among Cypriots, for Menderes had been the prime minister who only two years earlier had negotiated the independence settlement on Cyprus. His foreign minister, Fatin Zorlu, an indefatigable diplomatic campaigner for the Turkish Cypriots, perished with him.

At the same time powerful forces of social and economic change were unlocked. When Asil Nadir arrived in Turkey in 1960, it was still an overwhelmingly agrarian country. Within a year or two, a disorganised but rapid process of industrialisation would get under way, based on selling locally produced goods to a heavily protected home market. The fortunes made then would become the Istanbul 'old money' which would look fearfully on Asil Nadir's industrial investments in the late 1980s.

There were also new political currents. Socialism and Marxism, banned in Turkey for decades before 1960, emerged as the leading creeds of students and intellectuals. If Asil Nadir had gone to Istanbul University two or three years later, he would almost certainly have been caught up in the fierce student radicalism of the mid-1960s. Cypriots, however, tended to be a little shy of the politics of the mainland. Meral Kâşif recalls watching the 1960 revolution from a much more detached perspective than her mainland classmates in Ankara. 'As Cypriot students we kept ourselves to ourselves,' she remembers.

For a Cypriot who had grown up under British rule and within a partially British system of education, finding his way around on the mainland was not an easy matter for Asil. In his first year at Istanbul University, he stuck mostly to his books, working very hard and doing well in his examinations. He had relatively few friends: one was Hüseyin Cavit, his Famagusta school-friend who was to follow him to London and become a doctor; another was İsfendiyar, also Cypriot, who would later work for Asil in Polly Peck.

In his second year, Asil's life began to take new directions. The first sign of the changes ahead came when he set up his own pop group. Music was of course an important part of his life, and he had always played the guitar as well as the violin at the Famagusta lycée. The violin now gave way to the electric guitar. The schmaltzy pop music of the early 1950s had been replaced by rock and roll – Elvis Presley, Cliff Richard and Adam Faith. After his visit to London, Asil was up to date with the latest pop music. He loved to sing the songs of Elvis and Cliff Richard, and as a competent guitar player and singer forming a pop group was a fairly natural step for a student in the early 1960s. The group was called the Asiller – in English, the Asils. The other members included İskender, a teenager from Büyükada, the island in the Sea of Marmara off Istanbul from which Ayşegül also came, and Nino, a member of Istanbul's large Jewish minority, who also lived on the island.

The Asiller seems to have been only a fairly brief phase in Asil Nadir's life. If he really needed the income he got from singing, perhaps it was only for a brief period until İrfan sent the next instalment of cash from London. But he made his mark. Thirty years later, lawyers in Istanbul still remember him singing in the canteen of the Istanbul Bar Association. He also seems to have played the drums for a while and to have worked in the band at a restaurant in Tepebaşı, under the shadow of the Galata Tower. He was not only interested in Western pop music. He met Erol Büyükburç, the most famous Turkish pop singer of the time, whom he persuaded to give him some tips on singing Turkish music.

But it was as the leader of the Asiller that Asil Nadir first met his future wife, Ayşegül Tecimer, around Christmas in 1961. Ayşegül, the daughter of a fairly wealthy Istanbul family, was then fifteen and studying at Notre Dame de Sion, a convent girls' school in the city. Having a strongly outgoing personality, she had been picked by her classmates to present a show for the school's Christmas party. (According to Ayşegül Nadir, it was specifically a Christmas rather than a New Year's party, even though Turks, being Muslims, do not celebrate Christmas.) She had arranged for Erol Büyükburç to be the star turn at the concert, and two other groups had been asked to perform as well. One of them was the Asiller, invited because Ayşegül knew İskender from Büyükada, and İskender introduced her to Asil.

Their first encounter was strictly business: Asil had some tough bargaining to do. Since the Asiller were amateurs, Ayşegül thought that they should play first in the concert, rather than take the more important billing next to a nationally famous pop singer. Faced with the possibility of getting the worst billing, Asil launched negotiations with Ayşegül to be promoted to the second-best spot in the show, immediately before Büyükburç. 'He wasn't aggressive. On the contrary, he did it in a sweet way,' recalls Ayşegül.

That afternoon (school parties for Turkish teenagers take place in the afternoon rather than the evening), the convent girls of Notre Dame de Sion were treated to the sound of Cliff Richard hits, 'Travelling Light' and 'Living Doll', sung on stage by Asil. 'He had a very good voice,' recalls Ayşegül. 'He still has.' He had also brought his car. 'He had this lovely car parked outside the school that all the girls were admiring,' she says.

The next day, their mutual friend İskender got in touch to ask if Ayşegül would like to take a drive up the banks of the Bosporus in Asil's sports car. She agreed, though it was a very short trip because she had to be home before dusk. 'Can I call you again?' Asil asked as they parted, and Ayşegül told him to do so. They had begun dating, which for Istanbul convent girls in those days was considered a little advanced.

Ayşegül's family, the Tecimers, were very different from the Nadirs. They were a self-consciously metropolitan family, used to living in the cosmopolitan society of Istanbul and enjoying a good deal of unearned wealth. Even their international and cultural horizons were different. Like all well-to-do Turks of their generation, the Tecimers regarded French rather than English as the main world language.

They were also conscious of being a family with a history. The Tecimers traced their origins through a generation or two in the Caucasus back to Central Asia in the late Middle Ages. Ayşegül's grandfather and great-uncle had come to Istanbul around the turn of the century from the Eastern Black Sea town of Rize where the family acquired the fair hair and green eyes of the Eastern Black Sea people, which they like to attribute to distant Viking ancestors. Though Ayşegül, with her chestnut-coloured hair, was fair by Mediterranean standards, she was darker than most of her family.

The Tecimer menfolk had traded with Czarist Russia in tobacco and furs, and when they settled in the Ottoman capital, they were already wealthy. In the last century the family – like most notables in Ottoman

Turkey – had a traditional surname, Hacıyusufzade ['the sons of Pilgrim Yusuf'], but in Atatürk's day they dropped this oriental-sounding name in favour of Tecimer, a newly invented 'pure' Turkish word for businessman.

As the friendship between them deepened, Asil began to promise Ayşegül that he would do great things for her. Even at the age of fifteen, Ayşegül felt that she wanted the best of everything out of life, the best clothes, the best antique furniture around her. One afternoon they drove up the Bosporus to have tea in a café by the yacht harbour near Emirgan. They gazed across at a particularly splendid vessel. 'I am going to buy you one of those one day,' Asil said.

'You're joking,' said Ayşegül.

'You'll see. I promise you,' said Asil.

Within a few weeks, they were both talking to their families about getting married. Meral, who got on well with Ayşegül, quizzed her about why she wanted to marry so young and give up her education halfway. She recalls Ayşegül saying that she was fed up with her convent school. 'I don't want to go to school any more, so I am going to get married.'

The next step was to inform the Nadir parents in London. This fell on Meral, for Asil felt that the announcement would come best in a letter from her. His sister was not very enthusiastic about undertaking the task. 'Isn't it a bit soon? How long have you known the girl?' she asked. None the less she duly relayed the news to the Nadir family home in Romford. Not surprisingly, İrfan and Safiye were furious at first, but gradually they changed their minds. If their son wanted to get married, they would go along with it, even though they would have much preferred a girl from Cyprus. İrfan did not believe in arranged marriages, and who could tell whom Asil would eventually marry if he returned to London by himself? Besides, there was no way of making the young couple change their minds.

The Tecimer family now had to contend with the fact that their fifteen-year-old daughter had fallen in love with someone about whom they knew nothing. 'I remember my uncle saying, "Who is he? Where does he come from? All we know about him is that he has a very nice car,"' recalls Sevim Tecimer, Ayşegül's cousin. 'The car was a great social success in Istanbul. At that time, no one had ever seen a car like that here. Today it wouldn't catch anyone's eye, but in those days it did, all over the city.'

There were considerable differences between them. Ayşegül was little more than a child and by her own account had enjoyed a very easy life. The element of harshness in Asil's upbringing, its constant emphasis on hard work and discipline, mildly appalled her. She saw – and to some extent still sees – Asil as someone who missed out on his youth because of the tight controls imposed by his parents. 'The poor boy hadn't had a chance to develop socially,' she says.

Asil was invited over to the family home on Büyükada, where the Tecimers spent most of the summer. He was, they thought, little more than a child himself, only just out of his teens. Their alarm mounted when it very quickly became apparent that the two really were determined to get married.

In Turkey custom obliged Asil, or rather his family, to seek Ayşegül's father's consent for the wedding. This was not just a traditional convention. Because Ayşegül was so young, more than just politeness was required: her father had to give his formal permission before the marriage could legally take place. At first Hasan Tecimer was deeply reluctant to agree. 'Money was not the important thing. What mattered was that the groom was completely unknown to us,' says Sevim Tecimer.

But Ayşegül quickly let the rest of the family know that if her mother and father did not agree to allow her to get married to Asil, she would run away with him. Reluctantly, and after a good deal of argument, they finally gave way and Ayşegül made her farewells to her friends at Notre Dame de Sion.

Towards the end of May, there was a little ceremony at the Tecimers' flat when Meral arrived, as the head of the Nadir family in Turkey, to drink tea with the bride's family and formally request her hand in marriage on behalf of Asil. In fact the two families had already reached agreement, and the meeting was largely symbolic, but for the family it was an important Turkish custom.

Meral and her husband Güner were offered tea by the Tecimer parents, served from a silver Ottoman tea-service in a drawing-room full of antique furniture, where priceless Hereke carpets, the finest in Turkey, adorned immaculate floors of polished wood. Once the preliminaries were completed and the necessary courtesies and enquiries exchanged, Ayşegül appeared and made Turkish coffee for the visitors, a ceremony which, like many Turkish girls with a modern outlook, she probably performed with mixed feelings as a necessary stage on the way to the marriage registry.

Asil realised from the outset that Ayşegül was likely to be more expensive than most wives. He promised her that he would always maintain her at the standard of living to which she was accustomed. No doubt many students make similar pledges. Asil was one of the very few who would turn out to be capable of making his promises come true.

On 2 June 1962 Ayşegül and Asil celebrated their engagement with an engagement party at the Istanbul Hilton, by far the most splendid setting in the entire country for such a reception. It was followed on 16 September 1962 by a registry office wedding: in Turkey all weddings are civil ceremonies.

İrfan and Safiye flew out to Istanbul for the wedding and met their future daughter-in-law for the first time at the airport. Bilge was unable to come and Meral and Güner Kâşif had by now left Istanbul. The Nadirs and their future daughter-in-law recognised at first sight that they were people from very different worlds. Ayşegül was not long past her sixteenth birthday, little more than a child, used to a life of luxury. İrfan was just into his forties, but the gap between them seemed immense, not least because at this stage the fun-loving Ayşegül had no interest in making money, only in sophisticated ways of spending it.

The wedding was a much less grand occasion than the reception for the engagement. 'Although they were well-off, my parents were not willing to do much because this marriage was against their wish, and his parents were not in a position to help that much,' says Ayşegül. Her grandmother let the young couple live in a flat she owned in the centre of the city, but they somehow had to find money to survive.

'Their father, Hasan Bey, said, "Wait and see. It may not last. They may split up,"' says a member of the Tecimer family. 'Ayşegül was a very young girl and no one knew much about the bridegroom's family. People in Istanbul generally knew very little about Cyprus at all in those days. So there seemed to be little point in throwing a grand society wedding.'

After the wedding, Asil and Ayşegül drove across Europe in the turquoise sports car. Asil Nadir loved driving, and if the car ran into any problems he was also a good mechanic. The young couple went first to Greece, where they stayed a night or two in Salonica and Athens, before driving up through Italy to the south of France, to Saint-Remy and Saint-Tropez, returning via Venice and Yugoslavia.

In most of the places where they stopped they knew no one, which Ayşegül hated. But they had a few introductions from her father, including one in France to Hayri İpar, then one of Turkey's best-known businessmen, who kept a home on the Riviera. Asil fell into conversation with him about business. To his other guests, İpar declared himself impressed. 'This boy is going to turn out to be a fantastic businessman one day, he is going to be very very rich,' he predicted over dinner.

It was an auspicious remark, for Asil Nadir had by now decided to give up his studies in Istanbul and return to London to join his parents in the family business. In the normal course of things, he would have had to study for a final fourth year before taking his degree. After that he could perhaps have gone into business in Turkey, but he had decided against this. Istanbul was not yet the capital of an industrial business world but was still much closer to what it had been in the 1930s and 1940s, a decaying trade centre shorn of its former glory. There had never been any real doubt about Asil Nadir's career plans: he would work in the family business in London. So returning there without taking his degree made reasonable sense, even though being a university drop-out carried a mild social stigma in Turkey. Twenty-six years later, when he was nationally famous in Turkey, Asil Nadir would straighten the record by taking his final exams in Istanbul and becoming a graduate.

So, after ten months of marriage, in July 1963, Asil Nadir abandoned his studies just before the beginning of his fourth year at Istanbul University and returned to England with his wife. It is fairly clear that this decision was prompted by their parents, for the young couple seem to have run out of money. In any case Asil was determined to get under way with his business career and make money of his own. He and Ayşegül travelled back to London in the sports car.

Their prospects in England were highly uncertain. Asil warned Ayşegül, who was expecting a child in a few months' time, that at first at least she would face considerable difficulties. She was going at the age of sixteen to a country which previously she had only seen in films. 'Whatever he said was okay by me,' she recalls.

The only place to live was in the Nadir family home at Romford. In Britain, it was instantly recognisable as the sort of address to which people moved from successful businesses in the East End. To Ayşegül, brought up in Turkey with an education that looked to France, it was wholly unfamiliar.

The elder Nadirs may have hoped that Ayşegül would join the other members of the family in the business. If so, they were to be disappointed. Ayşegül never worked in the formal sense of the word, and was not drawn towards business. In adult life, a different sort of vocation eventually emerged when she took a fine arts course and became an expert on antiques, editing a book on Ottoman *fermans*, the decorated imperial decrees which are prized by collectors.

Safiye, her new mother-in-law, was a strong personality, but she seems to have been unable to direct Ayşegül into the industrious lifestyle favoured by the rest of the family. There were other differences, too. Ayşegül and her relatives, who later came to stay, all spoke the polished Turkish of Istanbul. The Nadir family usually conversed in

Cypriot *patois* Turkish which Ayşegül initially found unfamiliar and hard to understand. She tried to encourage Asil to talk to her in Istanbul Turkish. İrfan Bey by now spoke very good English, but Safiye could still only manage broken English. Bilge and her husband Fehim were also living under the same roof for a while: their sights were concentrated on a career in the textiles business.

For Ayşegül these first years in England were inevitably difficult. Asil had begun working in the East End. He quickly developed a business life there and was beginning to make friends in the City. He worked long hours and was away for most of the day. Ayşegül, the teenager who had given up school for marriage in a foreign country, sat alone in her Romford bedroom, listening to the only thing she could understand on the radio: French programmes. But as time passed, she too evolved. She made her way to the West End and discovered Bond Street, with its antique shops and fashion houses. 'I couldn't spend any money, but at least I could look at beautiful things,' she remembers.

At Nadir Modes, the Nadirs' business at this time, dresses were stitched together in a small workshop by about a dozen workers. İrfan employed Greek Cypriots as well as Turkish Cypriots. In this he was not particularly unusual. Many Turkish Cypriot businessmen, especially those in textiles, continued to have close business links and long-standing friendships with Greek Cypriots. They would pride themselves on speaking Greek as well as any Greek. Most of the time the disputes and hostilities in the Mediterranean had little meaning in London. Asil even went by a Greek name, Vasil, when talking to Greeks.

Asil's return was good news for his father in many ways. The two men could talk together for hours and agreed on most things; they were both intensely ambitious and eager to become rich as soon as possible. But there were differences. The Turkish Cypriots in London quickly found their own business style and stuck to it, while Asil, who was more educated than his father, was infinitely more adventurous. He had developed a clear penchant not just for elegance but for showiness, unlike the more modest taste favoured by the rest of the Nadir family. As the years went by, he began to feel the need to be something more in life than just his father's lieutenant.

Not long after Ayşegül and Asil came to London, the post-independence settlement in Cyprus collapsed amid fighting between the two communities at Christmas 1963. Far away in London, the Nadirs watched on television as British troops returned to the island, this time as peace-makers. It seemed to vindicate their decision to move to Britain, since the Turks now became outcasts in their own country, living in enclaves. The rest of the world recognised only the Greek Cypriots, and the Republic of Cyprus became, at least as far as the Turkish on the island were concerned, a straightforwardly Greek entity which did not recognise their existence or entitlement to separate communal arrangements.

The Nadirs had not been impressed with the 1960 Cyprus Republic which seemed to discriminate against Turkish middle-class professionals such as themselves. They found that they could not get jobs. Güner Kâşif, Meral's husband, went in for an engineering post in the civil service. Although he was a graduate with good professional qualifications, he lost the job to a Greek Cypriot with no degree. He and his family drew their own conclusions.

Safiye had flown home to Cyprus to spend Christmas with Meral, her husband and their little son, Tolga, unaware that hostilities were about to erupt. When fighting began, Meral realised that she and her family were in danger and would probably find themselves fleeing home in a few days. She and Güner both carried their passports, birth certificates and degree diplomas with them wherever they went. If they had to leave in a hurry, at least they would have their most essential documents with them and would be able to get jobs somewhere.

They were not mistaken. A day or so after the troubles began, Greek Cypriot soldiers – a mixture of their local neighbours and soldiers from mainland Greece – burst into their home and ransacked the house, shouting that they would kill them immediately if any guns were found. The Kâşifs were not interested in politics and no guns were found, and so they were taken hostage instead and their house was burned down, along with all their possessions.

After a few days' captivity they were released in a prisoner exchange. Safiye had kept enough money to buy tickets for a flight to London. On the way, the plane stopped at Athens, and they spent some hours there terrified that they would be arrested again by the Greeks. 'In time of war all these things happen. I am not blaming anyone for anything,' says Meral, but her life was never the same again. From then on she lived in London, where her husband made his career, and her children would grow up more British than Cypriot. Three years would pass before she even visited Cyprus again.

The Kâşifs had to be squeezed into the Nadirs' Romford home, along with Ayşegül and Asil, but a few weeks later, Güner got a job in an engineering company and Meral landed a teaching post through the simple method of identifying a suitable school and walking in to ask if any teachers were needed. They moved to Surrey.

On 15 June 1964, Birol, the elder son of Asil and Ayşegül, was born. The name – it means 'Be the One' – was chosen by Hasan Tecimer.

With the arrival of the baby, the Romford house was definitely over-crowded and Ayşegül and Asil moved out to a flat at Lancaster Gate, the sort of area which Ayşegül felt they were entitled to live in. But this new home rapidly proved too expensive for them: after six months they had to return to live with the Nadir parents at Romford. İrfan and Safiye willingly opened their home to them again, but it was an awkward moment.

Some small fissures were already beginning to show in the marriage. Asil did not like the way that Ayşegül, craving a little luxury, and feeling she simply could not stay at Romford with the baby all the time, would return to her family home in Büyükada several times a year, and stay for a month or more.

To resolve matters, Asil was now saving hard for the down-payment on a flat. The rag trade was a severe taskmaster, however. The Nadirs had made one important breakthrough by this stage in their quest to become big-time business people: they had discovered that they could earn a steady income with reduced overheads by farming out clothes to outworkers for cut-and-sew work, and as a result, their business was beginning to grow faster. But making money was still a slow, hard task, taking up long hours, and at the end of the day, cash trickled in only in small amounts.

In the evenings, the Nadirs would talk about the vanished comforts of their life in Cyprus and their home in Famagusta. It seemed much easier to them than the hard grind of an immigrant family's existence in the East End. Part of the problem was that they had only a small circle of friends compared to the teeming life they had known in Cyprus. As for Ayşegül, she knew a few mainland Turks living in London but she was eager to widen her circle. The Nadir family had little time for such ambitions.

By early 1965 Asil had enough money to rent a small two-bedroom flat in a council tower block in South Woodford. He had worked desperately hard for months, rising at dawn to go around the markets, in order to save the cash to furnish it. The Nadirs stayed there for two years, by when they were able to afford a nanny to look after Birol. They also began to dine out frequently in the West End after a trip to the cinema, probably the only entertainment Asil Nadir truly enjoyed. His favourite actor was Steve McQueen.

İrfan Nadir still dominated the family business, but for some time Asil Nadir, still only twenty-four years old, had been trying to strike deals on his own and build up his financial base outside the family. In 1965, the time seemed to be right to venture into business on his own. He opened up his own showroom at 20 New Road, opposite the family business, where he was able to hire one or two workers. Boutique and dress shop owners began to visit him.

Things went sufficiently well during the first year for Asil and Ayşegül to feel by 1967 that they could afford a mortgage. They bought their own flat in Woodford High Road where they again stayed for two years: their next move – in 1969 – would be to the Bishop's Avenue in Hampstead.

By then Nadir Fashions, as it was renamed, had given way to Wearwell as the main family business. Wearwell was a much bigger and faster-growing enterprise than any that had come before it, and though both Irfan and Asil ran it, Asil now played the more important role. Within three years its shares would be traded on the Stock Exchange. At last the Nadir family had found a business which would take them out of the small business world for ever.

Wearwell grew out of Nadir Fashions, but it had a much clearer concept behind it, selling to retailers through a large and, by the standards of the day, glamorous showroom, relying on a team of outworkers for production. Asil Nadir received visitors at a desk in the showroom, which was his first office. It was here that he met Richard Strong of Strong and Fisher, the man who went on to bail out Wearwell in the mid-1970s and would become a director of Polly Peck.

As for the new house in Hampstead, Ayşegül would probably have liked to live somewhere more central, but Asil hankered after a home with a pool and a garden, and they were persuaded by Turkish Cypriot friends to buy the Bishop's Avenue house. 'It's a famous road, Millionaires' Row,' they said. The move from a council flat in Woodford to Millionaires' Row was astonishingly rapid. The house – Asil named it 'Turquoise' – cost £30,000. The purchase was made possible by the rapid growth of Wearwell's business.

Although as yet Asil and Ayşegül knew almost no one socially, the new house, where they were to stay for a decade, was ideally suited for entertaining on a grand scale. Ayşegül, who was still only twenty-three, had lived almost like a schoolgirl for the past six years, counting each day until she could go back to Istanbul. Now she had the chance to become a hostess in her own right. 'Asil does not like entertaining guests, but Ayşegül always did. Over the years she gradually got him used to a more outgoing social life, but it was a long struggle,' says one visitor to their home in the 1960s.

The difference in their life-styles was omnipresent. When morning came, Asil Nadir would rise as early as six or seven and creep away to work, leaving Ayşegül to lie in late. Yet to the people who met them they seemed a happy and well-matched couple. While they still did not give as many parties as Ayşegül would have liked, they now came into contact with far more people, and began regularly to entertain Asil's business friends, English and Turkish Cypriot, to dinner. For a while, in his early thirties, Asil Nadir's life at home and at work was more or less the conventional existence of any successful London businessman. But although he had arrived in Millionaires' Row, he was not yet a millionaire. The next few years would see him turn the dream into reality.

4 · The Turquoise Millionaire

Asil Nadir will go down in history as the man from Polly Peck. But before his name and that company were ever linked, he had a business career stretching back more than a decade and a half. It was Wearwell, the East End clothing wholesaler in Tower Hamlets, that launched his stock market career and made him into a millionaire. Wearwell was set up in 1968 and floated in 1972. Asil Nadir's first million pounds of personal assets came in the form of Wearwell shares. In June 1984, eleven years after it was listed on the London Stock Exchange, Wearwell disappeared, swallowed up inside Polly Peck. But during its decade as a quoted company, Wearwell followed a roller-coaster career strangely similar to that of Polly Peck in the 1980s, albeit on a much smaller scale. It was rather like a different novel written by the same author: a few years of striking initial success were followed by a stage at which Asil Nadir overreached himself and came within a hair's-breadth of going bankrupt after a bout of reckless acquisitions.

The Wearwell story, of course, had a different ending from that of Polly Peck in 1990. Asil Nadir and Wearwell were saved when a backer emerged to bail them out, and by the end of the 1970s, Nadir seemed to have regained everything that he had lost. When he launched his bid for Polly Peck in February 1980, the reputation he had made for himself at Wearwell helped send the new company's share price shooting up. 'I don't know whether "hairy" is the right word for the Wearwell years,' says one friend of Asil Nadir, 'but it was a very unnerving time, Asil has very great nerve and thinks very clearly about where he wants to go. That is what enabled him to survive that decade.'

Wearwell's original method of operating was very simple. Asil and İrfan Nadir would go out and buy rolls of finished cloth and then farm out pieces of cloth to outworkers in shops in the East End rag trade to be made up into dresses. Wearwell also took on sidelines, such as sheepskin coats and suedes, which brought it into contact with Strong and Fisher, the Northampton leather and tanning firm whose chief executive, Richard Strong, was destined to play a crucial part in its fortunes.

'Wearwell was the perfect example of a Nadir company,' says a friend who worked with Asil Nadir in these years. 'Low stock turnover and enormous margins. The stock turn-around was always tight. How is it possible in the garment-making business to have 20 per cent profit margin? Answer: sell to Libya, good uniforms and other clothes, and your stock turn-around is one. God help you if you have a bad debt.'

In the early years Wearwell did not look to exotic markets such as Libya. The company was a continuation of Nadir Fashions. Retailers would buy direct from Wearwell through showrooms and, sometimes, by mail order. Buyers came in, bought a few dresses, and paid for them in cash.

As payment was always in cash, the company enjoyed a healthy cash flow. Stocks were always kept as small as possible. In the beginning this was because the Nadirs and Wearwell did not have the capital to buy up a large stock. Later, they realised that by concentrating on selling a stream of garments as fast as possible through showrooms, they also avoided the risk of having to sell off unpopular lines at a discount.

It sounds a pretty pedestrian sort of business and in many respects it was. But in some ways, Wearwell was conspicuously different from most of its competitors. For a start, it was much more showy. It had eye-catching showrooms and boasted that its workers operated in spacious and comfortable conditions. Its headquarters in Commercial Road, in London's East End, were a deconsecrated Church of England church, converted into business premises by Armağan Tekvar, Asil Nadir's architect.

Above all, Wearwell was a family company. Its last set of published accounts shows İrfan as its president, and Asil as its chairman and chief executive. Among the other directors were Güner Kâşif and Fehim Nevzat. Bilge Nevzat was also on the board. The only Anglo-Saxon name was that of Richard Strong of Strong and Fisher.

Safiye Nadir was not on the board of directors, though she followed the affairs of the company closely. She ran the workshops and small factories which made up dresses and other clothes with a stern hand. 'Cut-and-sew' was one part of the operation where, if things were badly run, it was least easy to make a profit, but Safiye became legendary for her efficiency. Later in the 1970s, she was able to switch the factories out of London to Cyprus where labour costs were much cheaper, thus enabling her to fulfil her wish to live on the island once more.

Stoy Hayward, the accountancy house which subsequently audited Polly Peck, were selected as auditors for Wearwell. Anil Doshi, the Indian accountant who later was widely regarded as the brains behind Polly Peck's expansion, was finance director and deputy chief executive, though he also had his own accountancy business outside Wearwell.

Doshi had the head for figures which Asil Nadir himself lacked. As finance director, when propositions were put to merchant bankers, it was Doshi who would provide the figures including the forecast earnings. It was also through Doshi that Wearwell negotiated deals to supply the House of Fraser and the Co-op with sheepskin coats, although its main line continued to be cash and carry.

Despite his outstanding gifts with numbers, however, Doshi lacked Asil Nadir's skills at communications and making allies. Bankers who talked with Asil Nadir and Doshi in the 1970s tended to feel a certain indulgent affection for Asil, even if they chose not to do business with him in the end, but on the subject of Doshi they were more reserved. The City followed them in this. Although those who had dealings with him report that Doshi was modest, amusing, shrewd and good-natured – provided that one was working alongside him rather than as a rival – he was if anything more distrusted than Asil Nadir by the City. Doshi himself bitterly suspected that he was the target of racial prejudice. Perhaps the truth of the matter was that Anil Doshi seemed to be less of a visionary and more in command of detail than Asil Nadir. But the business relationship between the two men was a sort of symbiosis, sometimes spilling over into their domestic lives. When the Nadirs moved house, they passed on much of the furniture and fittings to Doshi.

In its early days Wearwell grew relatively slowly, and for a number of years İrfan and Asil Nadir must have been unsure whether their latest business venture would prove any more lasting than its predecessors in Nicosia and Dalston. Nevertheless, Wearwell soon began to grow. In 1968, five years after Asil and Ayşegül had come to London from Istanbul, Wearwell reported pre-tax profits of £10,000 – a relatively modest amount, even for those days, but a figure which signalled that the Nadirs had graduated from the world of groceries and small traders. For the first time they were beginning to enjoy the trappings of serious wealth. Business guests would be entertained at home, for almost the only period in Asil's married life: when the Wearwell flotation was getting under way, the brokers were invited up to Hampstead to discuss details.

Things were also going less well at home, however. Asil and Ayşegül's marriage had always been tempestuous, partly because Ayşegül expected a way of life which most people – certainly the frugal Nadirs – would have regarded as well beyond their reach, but now it moved into its stormiest period yet.

In late 1971 Asil Nadir bought a country house and a farm at East Grinstead, in Sussex, with all the trappings required for life as a country gentleman. Several members of the family, notably his father İrfan, loved horse-riding, and Ayşegül's family, visiting from Istanbul, were also impressed. But Ayşegül herself was infuriated that she had not been consulted on the purchase (it coincided with one of the times she had been away) and Asil himself found that he had little or no time to spend at the house, so a few years later it was sold off again. He remarked airily to friends that he had had his fill of horses and stud farms, although towards the end of the 1980s he would return to country life on a grander scale when he bought Baggrave Hall in Leicestershire and began raising champion cattle there for county competitions.

In the evenings, Ayşegül and members of her family visiting London would drag Asil out to dine and dance at clubs in the West End. He was a reluctant dancer, but he enjoyed playing the tables in the casino. 'He always won. Always. No matter where he placed his bet. It was weird,' recalls a relative of Ayşegül's, but she adds, 'He didn't like going out. The three of us would go out together, Ayşegül loved dressing up to go out, but Asil didn't enjoy it. You expect young people to love going out, but he didn't.'

Then came the discovery that Asil Nadir was taking an interest in other women and was having an affair. Ayşegül was furious. Up until now in their marriage, the Nadirs had managed to resolve the great differences in their temperaments, tastes and backgrounds. But with another woman in the picture, Ayşegül was unforgiving. 'I married him only for love, for nothing else,' she says. 'When you have this sort of experience it is very difficult to accept. If I had had other motives, I could have turned a blind eye like some other wives do. Even when he was at his very richest, I was still not motivated by financial or material interests. To me he exists as the man I fell in love with and whom I still love very much, not as some money machine.' She announced that she was suing for divorce. The Bishop's Avenue household began to break up.

The love affair was no casual romance for Asil Nadir. It would last for many years, and in an interview in 1990 before the crash, Nadir was to acknowledge it as one of the most fulfilling experiences of his life. In the 1980s he went on to have two sons, and although they are being brought up as English rather than Turkish children, they are recognised by Asil's mother's side of the family. Pictures of her English grand-children are to be seen in Safiye Nadir's home at Famagusta and she is believed to have made provision for them in her will.

Yet this relationship never developed into a second marriage. Perhaps Asil Nadir felt that he was past the age when he could make the necessary adaptation easily. Certainly the love affair was a belated echo of the course his life might well have taken if he had married an English girl

during his early years in England and become more overtly anglicised
as a result – a pattern followed by many of his generation among Turkish
Cypriot immigrants, particularly students. Safiye Nadir would certainly
have been unhappy if her son had married outside his own community,
but she would have gone along with it in the end.

On the other hand, perhaps if Asil Nadir had married an English-
woman early in his career, he would not have been driven to create a
worldwide conglomerate. Ayşegül, with her thirst for the best of everything in Belgravia and Bond Street, seems to have acted as a catalyst
upon him.

In 1972, after a decade of marriage, Asil and Ayşegül were divorced,
and Ayşegül moved out of Bishop's Avenue. She had missed completing
her education, but she was still only in her mid-twenties. The end of
the marriage gave her the opportunity to turn her hobby of visiting
antique shops and sales rooms into something more serious. She
enrolled at the Inchbald School of Design in Eaton Place for a year's
course in fine arts in the winter of 1973.

In June 1973, however, she returned to live with Asil. They had
remained in touch after the divorce and decided that life together,
however stormy, was better than life apart. They did not remarry and
there were more major upsets periodically, but they remained together
until 1985. On 27 June 1975 Serhan Nadir, their second child, was
born, into much more prosperous surroundings than his elder brother,
Birol. Serhan was destined to be sent to Eton, unlike Birol, who had
been educated at Highgate and then at Sussex University.

In the summer of 1973, not long after Ayşegül returned to live with Asil
Nadir, came the flotation of Wearwell on the London stock market.
Coopers & Lybrand, the accountancy house which would supply Asil
Nadir with project feasibility studies and tax advice in the years to come,
were the reporting accountants for the flotation. The company was less
than four years old and to some observers the flotation – which established Asil Nadir as a millionaire for the first time – looked premature.
However, Asil Nadir had long been fascinated by the Stock Exchange
and the way it worked. Good news sent the share price up, increasing
the value of the shares owned by the Nadir family. By 1974, Wearwell
had built up its original cash-and-carry business into a network of a
dozen showrooms throughout the UK, and its pre-tax profits for 1974/
75 were more than £1 million. Its garments, produced by outworkers in
small work-rooms in both London and Cyprus, were on sale in dress
shops across the south-east.

Asil Nadir was only thirty-two years old, but he had already become a very rich man, even though most of his wealth lay in his share certificates. With his 1960s-style long hair he looked more like a pop star than a successful businessman coming up to the threshold of middle age. He would keep his long hair and his youthful appearance for another decade until his hairline suddenly receded in his mid-forties.

This youthful, fun-loving image was one that Asil Nadir deliberately cultivated, although it was distinctly at odds with the workaholic reality of his daily life. Over two decades, Asil Nadir looks out from a succession of press photographs with a smile that acknowledges a frenzy of good fortune and rapturous applause. Almost certainly, the smile dated back to his student days as a pop group guitarist in Istanbul. By fostering a self-image of this sort (for many years, he seems to have released no press photographs of himself in any other mood), Asil must have been aware that he was cocking something of a snook at the more dour elements of City opinion among which a less festive expression would have helped build his credibility. Perhaps, however, it was more important to him that his public image should reflect his bright side rather than the side which was the reality for most of the time – the hard-working recluse, slaving away for long hours in solitude at his desk. At all stages of his life, from his schooldays in Famagusta to his Berkeley Square office, his Turkish friends and business acquaintances always tended to remember him as someone whose habit of incessant hard work detached him from normal social life.

It was at this time that Peter Jones and Geoffrey Bowman of L. Messel, the firm of stockbrokers which became the main advocate of Polly Peck in the early 1980s, first met Asil Nadir. The connection persisted after L. Messel was absorbed into Shearson Lehman in the mid-1980s. Jones and Bowman were to remain among his strongest supporters in the City for more than a decade, and in the early 1980s they were hailed as the main authorities on Polly Peck and its profitability. He is remembered as by turns voluble, enthusiastic, charming and persuasive, good at telling a story and pressing his case in a slightly excited manner. He spoke passable English, though his tongue still stumbled over certain words and expressions. 'If there was any uncertainty in your mind about what he was doing,' recalls one City friend who worked with him in those years, 'you would pay him a visit and find that he would generally persuade you. He could uplift people with his enthusiasm.' Sometimes, however, he responded badly to direct questioning, giving evasive answers and sounding more like a politician than a businessman, which sowed mistrust in the minds of others among his new City friends. In any case, he always intensely disliked confrontation.

The loyalties were soon to be put to the test. Although İrfan and Asil
Nadir believed that they were riding a wave, the success of Wearwell
was in fact more precarious than they realised. Nor was Asil's wealth
necessarily secure. The Wearwell flotation had made him a millionaire,
but his fortune was almost entirely tied up in the company's shares. If
Wearwell collapsed, it would take him down with it.

The mid-1970s was a turbulent period in both Britain and Cyprus.
Wearwell's Stock Exchange flotation was followed within months by the
1973 Arab–Israeli War and the sudden quadrupling of oil prices which
followed it. Not only was the UK swiftly plunged into a recession in
which consumers spent less money on women's clothing, but the cost
of transport went up. Small independent retailers suddenly became less
inclined to drive miles to a showroom to buy a few dresses for their
customers. This struck at the heart of the cash-and-carry concept on
which Wearwell was based, and its earnings began to slacken off.

In July 1974 came a shock of a different kind for the Nadirs and
other Cypriot families. In the middle of the month, the government of
Archbishop Makarios was overthrown by right-wing coup-makers
backed by the dictatorship of the Greek Colonels in Athens. Nicos
Sampson, the EOKA guerrilla who had been a contemporary of the
Nadirs in 1950s' Famagusta, was declared president, and the unification
of Cyprus and Greece seemed close. Britain was reluctant to invoke its
powers as guarantor of the 1960 settlement. Henry Kissinger and the
State Department, who had never liked the left-leaning Makarios,
appeared to be moving towards recognition of the Sampson regime.

It was an historical turning-point. On 19 July that year Turkey invaded
Cyprus and took possession of the northern 34 per cent of the island. By
February 1975, the Turkish Cypriots had set up their own state in Northern Cyprus, something that they could hardly have dreamt of a year earlier.
It was internationally unrecognised, but it was self-governing. For the first
time in more than two decades, Turkish Cypriots felt that they enjoyed
physical safety. They were also free to develop their own economy, powerfully assisted by the fact that the new Turkish Cyprus included many of
the best parts of the island, including the port of Famagusta, the tourist
resort of Kyrenia and the orange groves of Morphou.

The Nadir family followed the crisis and the invasion on radio and
television. They had been away from the island for more than a decade,
and their links with the leaders of the Turkish Cypriot community were
not particularly close, but these were still among the most powerful
moments in their lives.

While Cyprus was being transformed in the wake of the Turkish
invasion, Asil Nadir launched his own market offensive in London. He

had decided that the time had come to shift Wearwell away from cash and carry to a new strategy of building up mail order operations and supplying chain stores, as well as entering the menswear market. With retailers showing signs of deserting Wearwell's showrooms, the approach was logical, particularly if the company was to expand. But there were serious drawbacks. The company would have to build up much larger stocks than it had ever done before, and instead of generating cash instantly, it would be providing credit to its customers. Neither objection deterred Asil Nadir. By the end of 1975 Wearwell had borrowing of over £1.1 million, nearly three times shareholders' funds of £400,000.

The excursion into borrowing could not have been worse timed for it coincided with a severe banking crisis in Britain. When Wearwell's results for 1975 were published the following spring, they showed that the company had slipped into a second-half loss of £653,000. Much of it was bank borrowing. For several months Wearwell was in dire trouble. Some of Asil Nadir's growing band of admirers in the City were deterred. Giles Coode-Adams of L. Messel cooled towards Nadir, as did Panton Corbett of Singer and Friedlander, though he was to remain a family friend over many years. Both men had helped bring Wearwell to the market three years earlier. 'They felt let down by the burst of acquisitions and the problems they led to,' recalls one friend.

Barclays Bank started to tighten the conditions on its loans and Wearwell was plunged into a crisis which dragged on for months and looked likely to end in liquidation. It had too much stock. It found difficulty in paying suppliers.

The Nadirs were now forced to make economies as Asil struggled to cut costs and find the cash he needed. Ayşegül recalls that 1976 was a very difficult year for the family. They had to cut back on their staff in Bishop's Avenue and other household expenses. Were the Nadirs on their way back to Woodford?

Asil Nadir was in fact fighting for survival. Yet even in the privacy of his home he was cool and reassuring, and his self-confidence seems never to have faltered. 'Somehow I had total confidence in him. He had the power to convince people and make them believe that things would be all right,' Ayşegül recalls. Yet almost everybody, including members of his own family, blamed Asil for what had happened. He had lost the confidence of his father, his financial advisers and his brokers. Within the family there were fierce arguments, especially when a rival Nadir family business opened across the road. Only Anil Doshi and Güner Kâşif, Meral's husband, stayed with Asil at what was to be the darkest point in his career until the Polly Peck crash of 1990.

In fact, Asil Nadir's remarks to Ayşegül that they would somehow pull through turned out to be correct, but he was extremely lucky. Without a bail-out, his business career would almost certainly have ended at this stage.

Determined to stave off collapse, Asil Nadir shut down the mail order business, pruned most of the credit sales to large chain stores and halved Wearwell's 300 staff to achieve economies. These moves left the company in much better shape, but it was still living on the good will of its bankers. And soon the banks were trying to foreclose on their lending and Asil was unable to pay creditors such as Strong and Fisher, or even his insurance premiums. At this point, however, Wearwell got a substantial injection of new cash. Richard Strong rallied to Asil Nadir's cause. 'I used to sell suede to Asil and we used to have enjoyable and amusing haggles. In the leather industry, nobody is happy or has done a really good deal unless they have had a good haggle,' says Mr Strong. 'We used to meet in Commercial Road and thoroughly enjoy it. They were large contracts and they were very important contracts to Strong and Fisher.

'The board of Strong and Fisher, with my recommendation, decided that because he had such considerable property assets in Commercial Road, it was a commercial risk to ask him to convert our debt, of around £250,000, into equity. I remember very well Asil had lunch with me in the Savoy Grill at a corner table, and we haggled over lunch and eventually a debt for equity at 12½p and a rights issue were organised, arranged by the London Investment Trust and Strong and Fisher with Singer and Friedlander. They produced £2.5 million in cash and left Strong and Fisher with around a fifth of the shares. About 13 per cent was held by three investment trusts. Asil and the Nadir family now held a controlling stake of about 42 per cent.'

Once it became known that Strong and Fisher had converted its debt into equity and that Richard Strong was on the Wearwell board, Asil Nadir was able to get new credit from his suppliers and the banks began to relax slightly. A year later, Wearwell was able to get backing from National Westminster on the recommendation of a regional director. By now the company was moving back into the black and could put a convincing case to the banks.

Gradually profits growth was resumed, though it took several years to return to the £1 million mark. In 1977, the company made a modest profit of £332,000. By 1978, Wearwell was reporting profits of £751,000 on sales of £8 million and telling the market that it was poised for further expansion. In September that year, it had a £750,000 27-for-100 rights issue at 25p each in September 1978, the idea for which had been suggested to Asil Nadir by Richard Strong. Strong and Fisher now had 3 million shares or 20 per cent of the total equity, another strong signal of confidence to the market. Dialogue with old friends in the City gradually resumed, although with only a quarter of the shares traded on the market, Wearwell's fortunes on the Stock Exchange were erratic. A single purchase or sale could make a great difference to the price. At the end of February 1979, for example, one seller caused the price to tumble from 30p to 26p by unloading 130,000 shares.

Asil Nadir was more concerned about expanding his business. Where could fast growth come from? He began to eye export opportunities in the Middle East. He discovered some gaps in the market, though they tended to be the type of business about which existing traders and banks were hesitant. Libya under Colonel Ghadafi, for example, was a good customer for uniforms. Nadir flew out to Libya and negotiated a deal to supply £3.2 million worth of uniforms to Libya's school-girls. By the end of the decade, Wearwell was able to announce proudly that it was no longer an East End rag trade company aimed at housewives. It had an order book which stretched two years ahead and around 85 per cent of its production was sold in the Middle East.

Wearwell also had some property assets by now; these had helped convince Richard Strong of the viability of a rescue operation in 1975. It had acquired two buildings at Commercial Road in the East End, just outside the City, and at the end of 1980 looked forward to a 'capital profit' of £7 million by developing a 52,000-square-foot freehold site at 81/91 Commercial Road, beside its headquarters, for £2 million. In the event, the site seems to have been sold for just under half the anticipated £9 million, fetching only £4.4 million when it was eventually sold to Barclays Bank, still uncompleted, in 1981.

Around this time a second friendship also played an important part in restoring the fortunes of Wearwell. Peter Kleeman, the merchant banker from Singer and Friedlander who had advised Asil Nadir some months before the Wearwell flotation, had later lost contact with him. In the summer of 1973, Kleeman, who had left Singer and Friedlander the previous year, had sold his own stake in Wearwell, feeling (correctly, as it proved) that the company's shares were too high. In 1977, he decided to look up Asil Nadir and see how far Wearwell had succeeded in recovering. By now the business was picking up and Kleeman was encouraged to see that it owned its own premises and appeared to have definite property assets to underpin it. He began to buy Wearwell shares, which at the time stood around 15p.

Kleeman was greatly struck by Nadir's isolation. 'He had no brokers, he had no bankers,' he recalls. He persuaded Peter Jones and Geoffrey

Bowman of Messel's to revive their links with Wearwell, and relations with Singer and Friedlander were also restored. Some life assurance funds even began to invest in Wearwell despite its tiny size.

Not long after this, the Nadirs also began to think of tapping some of the economic potential of Northern Cyprus by shifting a little of their production there from the UK. Work in Cyprus could easily be supervised on the spot by Safiye or İrfan who now returned to live there. By 1979, Wearwell was sending about 15 per cent of its clothing output for machining on the island and the figure quickly rose to one-third. Garments made in Cyprus were shipped to London, then re-exported back to the Middle East for sale in Libya and other countries.

Wasn't this more expensive than doing the work in London? No, said Wearwell. The cost of machining a garment in London was £3. But if the company sent the material out to Turkish Cyprus, had the work done there and brought it back again, the unit cost was only 75p, enabling it to undercut the competition – though manufacturing time was increased by up to a month. For a while the garments were flown back to London from Cyprus by Turkish Airlines. Then a three-month strike early in 1980 forced Wearwell to shift to using containerised trucks. When 1979/80 profit figures came in at £1.6 million, Nadir blamed the strike for holding back the company's profit by over £300,000, although they were still more than double the previous year's figures.

By early 1980 Wearwell had become a significant company in the UK ready-wear industry, selling about a quarter of its total production to large retailers like House of Fraser, Littlewoods, Debenhams and Owen. The company had moved into its new offices in Commercial Road and Asil Nadir had a very grand penthouse for his office, with a veranda and shrubs, and a sparkling private kitchen. It was in this office that he wooed his business contacts, building up friendships and seeking allies for deals.

By the end of 1979, Nadir was talking of substantially increased trading, particularly in export markets, in the 1980s. His sights must already have been on Polly Peck and the acquisition which took place just over two months later. There was even talk of Wearwell dipping its toes in Latin-American markets. 'We are talking to the Hudson's Bay Company and want to expand the European end,' Asil Nadir told the *Evening Standard* on 23 November 1979. 'But our main thrust continues to be the Middle East. We will not make anything which would not sell equally as well in Bahrain as in Montreal,' he said.

His remarks about expansion coincided with a £2 million two-for-five rights issue at 34p a share. It was by no means the first. As with Polly Peck, Wearwell's shareholders had to put up with frequent cash calls.

The 1979 rights issue provoked grumbles that it came only fifteen months after the £750,000 27-for-100 rights issue at 25p each in September 1978, not least because Asil Nadir did not take up all his rights, leaving it to the other shareholders to fork out the cash. The message to shareholders was that the order book was so heavy that a cash injection to buy new machinery was inevitable and it could not be done by borrowing fresh money from the banks.

In November 1979, Wearwell had group borrowing of around £3 million, about two-thirds of shareholders' funds. It was certainly no time to be borrowing. The newly elected Conservative government of Margaret Thatcher had pushed the banks' base rate to 17 per cent, making even healthy businesses groan and driving many weaker ones out of existence.

On 14 January 1980, it was announced that the Wearwell rights issue had been 93.07 per cent taken up – a response which indicated overwhelming approval from shareholders. It was not the last time that they would face an appeal for cash. In December 1981, Wearwell went back to the market once more, for a third rights issue in three years. This time it raised £5.2 million from shareholders in an issue which was 93.89 per cent taken up by 21 January 1982. 'At least Mr Nadir is taking up his rights issue this time,' sighed Lex in the *Financial Times*.

Wearwell was beginning to collect some accolades. In the spring of 1980 it won the Queen's Award for Export Performance, and it collected the award for a second time two years later.

In September 1980, Richard Strong sold his 20 per cent stake of the company for £2.4 million. 'We took the stake back in 1975 when Wearwell was in trouble,' he said. 'Now we need the cash, about £2,400,000. There has been no argument and I shall remain on the Wearwell board.'

When Strong sold out, Wearwell's shares had climbed to 70p and it had earned pre-tax profits of £1.3 million in the first half of the year, with sales at £6.52 million. A year later, it doubled its profits again to £3.02 million for the year ending on 1 May 1981. Turnover moved up at a less astonishing but still spectacular rate, from £10.4 million to £16.07 million. The pre-tax margin had improved to nearly 19 per cent, thanks – the group said – to its increasing use of Cyprus as an assembly base, which cut costs by over 20 per cent.

The figure disappointed the City, which had been expecting profit to be around £4 million. There had even been talk of a pre-tax profit of £5 million. 'The sky is the limit,' Nadir was fond of saying, but the dividend – a second interim because Wearwell was working its way through a fifteen-month year – was lower than the previous year's final dividend.

Sceptics raised questions about the size and quality of the company's assets. How much money did it really have? The largest item on its balance sheet in 1982 and 1983, for example, described as debtors and prepayments, was said in the accounts to be mostly money due from trade debtors. This was £23.17 million in 1983, or the equivalent of 85 per cent of the balance sheet, an enormous proportion. A year earlier the same item in the Wearwell accounts had been equal to around 75 per cent of the balance sheet, also a very high percentage. What would happen, the sceptics asked, if Wearwell's trade debtors suddenly became unwilling or unable to pay what they owed the company?

Wearwell's remarkable profits growth coincided with its move deeper into foreign markets for textiles. At the end of July 1981, Asil Nadir announced that Wearwell was now exporting more than 90 per cent of its products. But when profits growth slowed down over the following twelve months, he explained that the company did after all share reservations often expressed in the City about the risks of trading with the Middle East.

'Now we are hoping that home sales will rise to about 30 per cent this year and hopefully to about 40 per cent in due course.' But at this stage his remarks about Wearwell attracted little attention. By then the market's eyes were glued to another and much more remarkable of Mr Nadir's companies: Polly Peck, which was expected to announce half-year profits of over £3 million in June 1982, compared to £2.1 million in the previous seventeen months.

In fact the July 1981 profit figures were almost Wearwell's last set of results. In February 1983 Nadir announced that the company would be absorbed into Polly Peck through a merger. In 1983 Wearwell announced pre-tax profits of £5.3 million. By Nadir standards the 29 per cent rise from the previous figure of £4.1 million was somehow unimpressive. Polly Peck was a star of a different magnitude from Wearwell.

By buying Polly Peck himself rather than through a listed company, Asil Nadir also stood to make a greater personal gain if things went as planned. Wearwell had made him a millionaire but it had certainly not brought him a fortune in cash. Its 1983 accounts disclose that he earned slightly above £25,000 in 1982 and 1983 – a modest salary for a man who claimed that the sky was the limit and lived in Millionaires' Row.

5 · The 1980 Take-over

Nothing about Polly Peck in the first few weeks of 1980 suggested that it was poised for Stock Exchange stardom, still less for a decade-long career as a global corporation in the fresh fruit and electronic businesses. Set against its later history, Polly Peck's origins look almost comically incongruous. Yet Asil Nadir always remained attached to Polly Peck's name (though he made little use of it in Turkey and Cyprus) and never dropped it despite periodic suggestions from others that he should do so.

The Nadir family had long known Polly Peck. Like Wearwell, it was another East End rag firm but with a slightly higher profile. In 1980 most English women knew Polly Peck as the brand-name of a company which made lingerie, dresses and baby wear. Just over twenty years old, the company had been set up by Raymond and Sybil Zelker, a husband-and-wife team, in 1959, around the same time that İrfan Nadir was also eyeing the UK textiles industry for opportunities. The Zelkers had judged their market correctly on this occasion and they were promptly rewarded. In its start-up year Polly Peck made a healthy profit of £75,655 out of dresses produced by a cutting-room in Tottenham in north London. This rose to £96,821 in 1960.

In the early 1960s Polly Peck continued to thrive and was able to develop several brand-names, including 'Miss Polly', a slightly down-market line with a lower price-tag. (However, the company never owned and had no connection with 'Pretty Polly' tights, which were made by Thomas Tilling.) Polly Peck sold both to wholesalers and directly through a dozen boutiques inside large department stores.

The Zelkers might have remained in control of Polly Peck for the rest of their days if they had not become more adventurous in the second decade of their company's life. For in the early 1970s, perhaps sensing that the days of the rag trade were now numbered, they took Polly Peck into property, aided by a new director, Michael Clore, a nephew of Sir Charles Clore, the property tycoon. This was a serious error. They took their decision while the property market was near the top. But the boom soon ended and the market turned against them, while at the same time the cost of borrowing rose.

Within a few years, the enlarged Polly Peck group was limping along
under an almost unmanageable burden of debt. In July 1975 it plunged
into the red and reported a year-end loss of £117,460. Even though it
made a profit of £222,000 on its fashion operations and its exports grew
by 42 per cent, a loss of £339,921 on property more than wiped away
all the gains from the rag trade. A month later the company's share
price tumbled from 5p to 3p after a block of 100,000 shares failed to
find a buyer on the Stock Exchange.

The Zelkers were defiant, however. 'There's nothing wrong here. I
am not panicking. We are going through a recession and eventually
everything will come good for our company,' Raymond Zelker told
reporters. But he and Polly Peck survived the decade mainly because
their main banker, National Westminster, did not pull the rug from
under them.

Unlike Wearwell, which had also tried to go into new lines of business
just at the time the recession of the early 1970s struck, no friendly new
shareholder arrived to bail out Polly Peck in the mid-1970s, and there
was no swift turn-around for the company. In 1976, trading in Polly
Peck shares was suspended for three months while Raymond Zelker
worked out a restructuring plan with the banks to reduce his company's
burden of debt from property.

But the rescue operation did not work. In 1978 Zelker tried again,
this time resorting to a more desperate remedy. His aim was to write
off half the company's capital in order to trim its debt burden, now over
£354,000. To achieve this, he turned the company's 10p shares into 5p
units. This meant that the company would probably not be able to pay
a dividend for many years, although that would not have made much
difference to those shareholders who had persisted with the company:
Polly Peck had not paid a dividend since 1975, a clear signal to the
market that it was on its last legs.

In 1979, the company was still in the red, losing £22,000. Nor did it
seem to be set on the way back to recovery. Between March and September 1979 it lost £29,000. By now Mrs Thatcher and the Conserva-
tives were in power and interest rates were once more rising sharply.
Many small businesses would be killed off in the months ahead. Outside
help was the last chance for the Zelkers and Polly Peck. But to whom
could they turn for backing?

That same autumn, Asil and Ayşegül Nadir were moving house, their
fortunes firmly in the ascendant now that Wearwell's crisis of the mid-
1970s was behind them. After a decade in Bishop's Avenue, Ayşegül
had finally persuaded Asil to move into central London. She had her

eye on a Georgian house in Cheyne Walk beside the river in Chelsea, but the deal fell through, complicating their departure from Hampstead.

It was while the preparations for the sale of their home were under way that Asil Nadir told Ayşegül he was planning a new business deal and would like her to entertain some guests to dinner at their home. These were Raymond and Sybil Zelker, who, by now almost desperate to find an outside backer for Polly Peck, were delighted that their quest had finally been rewarded with success. 'They were thrilled about selling the company,' recalls Ayşegül. The first approaches quickly turned into an enthusiastic dialogue about prices. The Zelkers worked as a close husband-and-wife team in these talks, just as they had done throughout their earlier career. On the eve of St Valentine's Day 1980 the telephone finally rang in the sales-room of Messel's, the brokers who acted for Wearwell. On the line was Asil Nadir's secretary, Jean Thomas. 'Mr Nadir would like you to call us when there is a Stock Exchange announcement about a company called Polly Peck,' she said rather mysteriously, and put the phone down. Half an hour later Extel, the Stock Exchange news agency, reported that Restro Investments of Jersey was offering 9p a share for Polly Peck. Raymond Zelker, Sybil Zelker and a third director, Derek Hughes, had promised to support the bid, which meant that a total of 57 per cent of the shares had already gone to Restro – whose main beneficiary was Asil Nadir. Until that point Restro had not owned any Polly Peck shares. The cost of the deal was £270,000, a figure described by Raymond Zelker as 'financially prudent given that the current economic downturn may last a while'.

Even in the City, the deal did not make headline news. It rated two or three paragraphs in some papers. Still, those in the textiles business were curious about what was going on. Was this the prelude to a merger with Wearwell? No, said Asil Nadir. The independent listing of Polly Peck would be maintained. His intention was to develop the company. Stockbrokers vaguely remembered that at the half-year, Raymond Zelker had spoken of widening Polly Peck's distribution network, including its 'shop within a shop' operations – there were now thirty-three of them – in department stores. Could this be it? the market wondered.

Nadir's offer price of 9p was well above the 7.5p price of Polly Peck shares on the morning of 13 February 1980 and it compared extremely favourably with the 5.5p which the share had been fetching only a few weeks earlier. Within hours of his purchase Polly Peck's shares began to rise, first modestly leaping to 12p and 13p, then moving up more steeply to 20p. 'Every man, woman, and dog has been buying the shares since the bid,' quipped wits on the Stock Exchange.

Years afterwards, when Polly Peck was a vast multinational conglomerate and seemed to be at the zenith of its fortunes, some of the group's
staunchest admirers would recall this sudden and unexplained upward
velocity in the share price as one detail in the company's history which
did not seem right. Actually, the jump may not have been as mysterious
as it seemed. For many days, there was only one buyer of Polly Peck
shares. Peter Kleeman says that he bought Polly Peck shares steadily
until they reached 20p. 'I was the only buyer. I bought for several weeks
until the price reached 21p and then I stopped. I bought 11.5 per cent
of the company.' He was buying, of course, on behalf of their clients,
each of whom invested one unit in Polly Peck. They would soon have
cause to be grateful that he had done so. 'Eleven and a half per cent of
the company was not a lot of money in those days,' he says. 'It was the
last time that you were able to acquire stock in the size of a shell deal.'

When Kleeman left off buying Polly Peck, another buyer, an American broker living in London, stepped in. Kleeman says that he bought
because he was a specialist in smaller companies and, knowing Nadir
quite well, recognised the growth potential of Polly Peck in his hands.
He himself became for a while the main outside investor in the company,
though he never participated in any of the rights issues which followed.
Years later, Polly Peck executives would talk of how anyone who bought
£100 worth of the shares at the time of the take-over would subsequently
have watched it grow to well over £1 million. Apart from Asil Nadir
himself and his family, Peter Kleeman seems to have been the only
person to whom this actually happened.

The rise in the share price had an immediate effect on the Zelkers.
They now found themselves committed to sell at a price which was well
below the current trading value of Polly Peck's shares. Some unpleasant-
ness swiftly ensued, with them advising other shareholders not to accept
the offer. But it was too late. By 14 March, Restro had won its bid for
the company in which it now owned a 58 per cent stake. Other shareholders sold out to Restro, giving Asil Nadir a total stake of around 60
per cent. A deal was thrashed out with the Zelkers, who were allowed
to retain their places on the board, Raymond Zelker remaining as
chairman.

As the share price soared, the market value of the company grew. Asil
Nadir's bid had valued it at £470,000. By June that year, with the share
price at 85p, the market value looked distinctly less paltry at £4.4 million.
Then, on 17 June, Nadir made his next move. Dealing in Polly Peck
shares on the Stock Exchange was frozen, pending an announcement
about the group's future. The market shuddered – this was likely to be
the prelude to the acquisition of another business and would mean that

investors who had chased the share price upwards would now almost certainly have to dip into their pockets to find cash for a rights issue. Nadir was silent. A spokesman for Messel's said, 'I cannot confirm whether this is an injection of assets, but it is an expansion of Polly Peck as a company, not of its traditional business.'

On 8 July, shareholders were put out of their misery. Asil Nadir announced that Polly Peck would be making a £1.56 millon two-for-five rights issue at 75p per share to buy Unipac. This was not a name with which British investors were familiar. It was explained that Unipac was a Turkish Cypriot company manufacturing packaging for agricultural produce. It was owned by Asil Nadir, but would now be bought by Polly Peck. The rights issue would enable it to start production of corrugated cardboard boxes by September 1980, at a cost of around £950,000, with a further £148,763 going to reimburse Asil Nadir for the company's cost.

If that all sounded rather remote to English investors pondering whether or not to pay 75p for shares which had been worth only 5p or 6p earlier in the year, Asil Nadir had a clear message about the bottom line. A revamped Polly Peck would be able to make £2 million pre-tax profits in its first year alone by sales in Northern Cyprus, provided that a packaging plant for Unipac could be bought and installed at its Famagusta premises. For the first time, Nadir came on to the Polly Peck board.

Shareholders had just over a month to make up their minds. But they do not seem to have had much difficulty in reaching a decision. Rejection of the offer would have been swiftly followed by the collapse of Polly Peck's share price. Acceptances poured in and the offer was 92.2 per cent taken up. So began Polly Peck's march to become a global corporation.

Where had the idea behind the rights of an investment in Cyprus originated? It partly derived from the growing involvement of the Nadir parents in Cyprus in 1974, but the plan to set up a packaging operation and go into the citrus fruit business was mainly the result of a chance meeting some time in 1977 at a friend's house between Asil Nadir and Radar Reshad, then the commercial officer in the Turkish Cypriot representative office in London. It was one of those meetings that changes the course of a life.

Reshad – who ended up as the director in charge of Polly Peck's fruit operations – was one of the few directors to remain on Asil Nadir's side throughout the years ahead until the final weeks of the company's life in 1990 and he did not leave until early in 1991. Behind Reshad, however, seem to have lain high-level figures from the Turkish sector of

Nicosia. A group of senior Turkish Cypriots believed that something had to be done to create an active fruit export business.

Turkish Cypriots had traditionally been farmers, soldiers and civil servants on the island. It was only in London that they had turned to commerce and industry. President Denktaş is a lawyer by training. Most of his career has been spent in international diplomacy. Not surprisingly, his administration's economic policy in the 1970s had been basically to copy what was done on the mainland, setting up governmental agencies and state-controlled industrial concerns, just like those favoured by successive right- and left-wing governments in Turkey before 1980. Yet five years after the 1974 invasion, the Turkish Cypriot economy was still languishing, even though the Greeks in the south of the island had made good nearly all the economic losses they had suffered in the war. The contrast was the more glaring because the Greeks had lost the best portions of the island and the rich northern territories were now in Turkish Cypriot hands.

Nowhere was this contrast more manifest than in the fruit business. Citrus fruit exports from Northern Cyprus had been in decline ever since the Turkish invasion of the island in 1974. The Turkish Cypriots had traditionally been growers of grapes, and growing citrus fruit called for quite different skills which few Turkish Cypriot farmers possessed in the mid-1970s. As a result, the oranges and lemons literally rotted on the trees for several years following 1974. Turkish Cypriots did not need to be told that they were losing a valuable opportunity. The fact stared them in the face each time they passed the groves of Güzelyurt, as Omorfo, the centre of the citrus plantations, was renamed by the Turks.

What made the situation worse was that the Turkish Cypriots were losing export revenues at a time when both Northern Cyprus and mainland Turkey were starved of hard currency. By now the Turkish Cypriots had established that they could sell exports to the rest of the world, even though they lived in an internationally unrecognised state. For the first year or two after the invasion, the legal status of Turkish Cypriot exports had been in doubt as the Greek Cypriots challenged the new Turkish Cypriot businesses in the courts. But in 1978, Faik Müftüzade, the Turkish Cypriot representative in London, successfully beat off a legal challenge from the Greek Cypriots with a court judgment that established that there was a *de facto* government in the north of the island and that British courts could not concern themselves with matters such as alleged trespass by Turkish Cypriots on the property of dispossessed Greeks in the north. The Turkish Cypriots began trading their produce in London, though usually under a Cyprus label.

Rescuing the orange groves was now a priority: the authorities in Northern Cyprus no longer felt that Cypfruvex, the state fruit and vegetable company, would be able to do the job by itself. Cypfruvex had got under way in the mid-1970s and in the 1980s was a successful business, but it suffered from several disadvantages. It was Cyprus-based, had little capital or know-how, and, being run by civil servants, was slow-moving and responded to the orders of politicians and the wishes of producers rather than to the needs of international markets.

Mainland Turkey recognised that its own exports in the 1960s and 1970s were held up by its inability to package them adequately. The Turkish Cypriots would somehow have to leapfrog the mainland. One solution was to import packaging from other countries in the region – Israel, perhaps. But the imports had to be paid for with foreign currency which neither Turkey, in a deep economic crisis during the late 1970s, nor the Turkish Cypriots possessed.

Clearly the solution was to build a special plant to make the cardboard boxes in which the oranges would be exported. But with both the Turkish and Turkish Cypriot governments unable to find money for the investment, an outside partner had to be found for the project to have any chance of going ahead. Asil Nadir was an obvious potential investor in the new project: he was about the only Turkish Cypriot millionaire in London.

Radar Reshad knew Asil Nadir from his childhood, but the two men were not in regular contact in the 1970s. Radar came from a village near Famagusta and he had been at the Namık Kemal Lycée in the town, though he was three years older than Nadir, whom he remembers chiefly for his singing in the choir. He had moved to England in the mid-1950s, almost immediately after leaving school, and had followed a career in business, before becoming a Turkish Cypriot official in the second half of the 1970s.

The conversation between Asil Nadir and Radar Reshad in their mutual friend's house was not a planned approach, but the project obviously interested Asil Nadir and he and Reshad exchanged several telephone calls to discuss it further. Then there was silence. Reshad assumed that Asil Nadir must have gone off the idea. One day he ran into Nadir's elder sister and expressed his disappointment. After Meral's reminder Asil Nadir did ring back, but it emerged that Reshad had failed to persuade him.

Various other potential foreign investors were sniffing around for business opportunities in Northern Cyprus. Several of them were privately judged by the Turkish Cypriots to be shady-looking, and none of them had Asil's supreme attraction of being of Turkish Cypriot background. So the Turkish Cypriot authorities approached Asil Nadir again. This time they simply asked him to see what the City thought of the people who had stepped forward to invest in the orange business. Asil Nadir reported back that they were not suitable people to do business with.

And there things might have ended, had the seeds of an idea not been growing in Nadir's own mind. Reshad recalls him saying that perhaps the Turkish Cypriots were on to something. He wanted the fruit business to be handled through a separate company from Wearwell. Just why he did so is not altogether easy to explain. Unwillingness to allow Wearwell to venture into unfamiliar activities cannot have been the whole explanation, for the company did in fact venture into the citrus and paper trade, just as Polly Peck was to do.

In 1982 it sold £2.9 million worth of citrus fruit, earning profits of £198,954 on the business. A year later, citrus sales were down to £2.72 million, with profits of £179,608. The paper business was £1.42 million in 1982 and £2.05 million in 1983, earning profits of £237,000 and £395,383 respectively. Wearwell was plainly much less good at the citrus trade than Polly Peck. In 1983, 12.4 per cent of its turnover came from citrus, but less than 4 per cent of its profits.

Nor was opposition from the Wearwell board the main reason why Asil Nadir decided to buy Polly Peck. Richard Strong says he firmly believed that Wearwell rather than Asil Nadir himself should have bought Polly Peck, views which he made known at the time.

More than that is hard to say, for Wearwell, like Polly Peck, did not give detailed information on its subsidiaries in its accounts but broke them down only by activity and geographical markets. The Middle East – apparently excluding Turkey and Cyprus – accounted for about 64 per cent of Wearwell's turnover and 69 per cent of its profits in 1983.

One theory explaining Asil Nadir's decision to launch his new citrus business in Cyprus through Polly Peck was that İrfan Nadir disapproved of the new venture and insisted that Wearwell be kept well out of it. Perhaps, after the near-disaster in the mid-1970s, he was mistrustful of his son's latest venture. Nadir himself told journalists soon afterwards that after Wearwell's disastrous history of acquisitions in the 1970s, he had sworn never to make another purchase with the company. Now he began to move fast. Reshad and his wife were twice invited to dinner with the Nadirs.

The site chosen for Unipac was a shed on the Famagusta waterfront. At first glance it was extremely unprepossessing. It had stood unused since the gunfire stopped in August 1974 and it was abandoned by its Greek Cypriot owners. When journalists described it as bullet-scarred,

Polly Peck retorted that there were actually only six bullet-holes in the building, 'dating back to the partition troubles of 1974'. The roof of the building next to it was open to the sky, unrepaired in the six years since it had been torn apart in a rocket attack. Outside in the harbour were the hulks of several sunken vessels. The Turkish Cypriot authorities offered the premises to Nadir at a nominal rent and with a tax holiday of up to eight years. Once the factory came on stream, the import of cardboard boxes into the north of the island would be banned, thus ensuring the profitability of the new operation. When Asil Nadir bought Polly Peck, he commissioned a feasibility study from Yakitory of Finland and began purchasing second-hand machinery to fill the shed. His hope was that the plant could be got working in just over six months, so that it would be ready with packaging for the 1980 citrus crop from September onwards.

The rights issue did not seem to check the rise in the Polly Peck share price, which soared by an extraordinary 2,708 per cent from 5.3p at the end of 1979 to 168p during 1980. Observers grew increasingly puzzled. 'It seems that the market prefers a mystery tour to a known destination. The only problem is establishing whether the ticket to ride is appropriately priced,' wrote one journalist. Sceptics about Asil Nadir and Polly Peck not only felt that there was little to justify the optimism over the prospects for the cardboard box factory in Famagusta. Their doubts were soon fuelled by the peculiar events surrounding Nadir's purchase of a second rag-trade company, Cornell Dresses, in what seemed almost a parody of the Polly Peck take-over. Cornell's share price soared from 14p to 190p at its zenith, although it ended the year at 148p. What sent it spinning upwards? As with Polly Peck, the answer was a bid from Asil Nadir.

Cornell Dresses had always been a much smaller and weaker company than either Polly Peck or Wearwell. Set up by Mark and Samuel Cohen in Leyton in the East End of London in 1946, it specialised in cheap dresses for teenage girls and suits for women. In July 1964 it was floated on the Stock Exchange in a heavily oversubscribed issue. By the late 1960s, its profits were beginning to sag. Although it had been one of the earliest entrants into the teenage market, its fashion styles belonged to the 1950s rather than the 1960s. As the 1970s wore on, and its management grew older, Cornell's trading position worsened. Its turnover was under £1 million, and in the first half of 1980 it posted a pre-tax loss of £53,000.

Then, in the autumn, market interest in Cornell suddenly quickened. Around 4 September there was a whisper abroad on the London Stock Exchange that the company might be next in line for a Polly Peck-style take-over. 'A mystery Jersey company called Azania Investments is considering making an offer of 19p in cash,' wrote the *Evening News*. 'Speculators, scenting a revamping operation similar to the one at Polly Peck, chased the shares up 9p to 36p.'

A day later the mystery was resolved when Azania Investments (Jersey), hitherto largely unknown on the markets, declared that it had indeed bid 19p per share – well below the level the shares had reached on the market – and had persuaded Cornell's directors and members of their families to accept. As a result Azania would own nearly 57 per cent of Cornell's shares if it went ahead with its bid by November 29. The following weeks must have been distinctly uncomfortable for the Cohen family. Cornell's shares continued to rise on the market, touching 76p a week after the beginning of the bid speculation. The Cohens' commitment to 19p was irrevocable, however.

At this point Asil Nadir stepped forward and revealed that Azania Investments was his company. 'I personally will not be involved in Cornell at all,' he told reporters. By now the changes at Polly Peck and the building of its £1 million packaging operation at Famagusta were well under way. So why did Asil Nadir want to buy a new textiles operation? 'I do not think the ills of the textile industry will stay around for too long,' he said. Given the terminal state of much of the British textiles industry, this was an astonishing remark.

Businessmen around Nadir certainly did not favour the idea of a fresh take-over. 'Cornell was a problem,' recalls Peter Kleeman. 'Nobody really wanted to do [the] Cornell deal. Two companies [for Nadir] were enough. Three were too much.'

In the end, Azania Investments did not buy Cornell. The option was transferred to Polly Peck. By now Cornell's shares had risen to 142p. Nadir was buying for £570,000 a company whose market value had reached £3.2 million. Furious at what had happened, Cornell's brokers, Jacobson Townsley, approached the Takeover Panel to see whether Nadir's bid had broken any of its rules. They were told that it had not. There was also a preliminary Stock Exchange investigation to see if the bid had breached the rules under the Companies Act on insider dealing and its findings were forwarded to the Department of Trade.

By December Cornell chairman Samuel Cohen was recommending shareholders to take a sober view of the bid from Polly Peck. He warned them that Cornell's sales had been extremely disappointing in the second half of the year. This made the 19p bid offer a 'fair and reasonable offer', even though it would be foolish for shareholders to accept it since the market price for the share was so much higher.

Also in December 1980 Polly Peck announced its first set of results since the take-over. The share price had slackened somewhat during the autumn, perhaps because of the controversy which the Cornell bid had aroused. It now stood at 146p. Its actual trading performance in the twenty-three weeks to 31 August was recognised as not very important.

The company's entire future now hinged on the Famagusta packaging plant, which was originally intended to start production in September that year. Many investors must have remembered at this point that Polly Peck had not paid a dividend since 1975. Only a year earlier, Raymond Zelker had warned that it might be many years before the dividend was restored.

Nevertheless, Polly Peck was able to report a modest return to the black which was sufficient to pay shareholders a nominal dividend of 0.1p. There were other signs of improvement as well. Wearwell was said to be backing Polly Peck and enabling it to buy cloth for garments on better terms than it had been able to do in the previous few years. Turnover on the textiles business was now said to be running at more than 70 per cent above the previous year. 'It is comforting to see the year's best performing stock . . . creep its P & L account into the black,' wrote the results commentator in the *Financial Times*. By now Asil Nadir and Polly Peck were beginning to become familiar names. Polly Peck was the star performer on the London Stock Exchange, even if as yet buying the shares meant making an act of faith.

The project hit inevitable snags, however. One was that the floor of the shed in Famagusta had to be reinforced to bear the weight of the machinery. The 1980 citrus crop season came and went and the plant was not ready until February 1981. By March some of the fruit had been sold on the mainland Turkish market in a desperate last-minute drive to ensure that it at least found buyers somewhere. Three large orders came in, but the plant was still only working at half its planned capacity. In May a second case-making machine, costing £300,000, was installed, and throughout the summer workers toiled to get the plant ready for the autumn.

In January 1981, the bid for Cornell had finally gone through. Once it was complete, it became apparent that the company's future, like that of Polly Peck, might after all lie well outside its previous activities. But where was this to be?

In October 1981, Nadir revealed that Cornell was carrying out a feasibility study into the possibility of entering the Northern Cyprus poultry market. 'There is a strong demand for poultry in the Middle East,' the company said, 'which could in part be met by exports from Cyprus.' Some sort of shake-up was clearly needed. In 1981 sales dropped to £1.60 million, but the loss was cut to £35,000. In the first half of 1982 sales rose to £765,000, but losses climbed back upwards to £79,000, and for the second year in succession shareholders received no dividend.

While his name was becoming famous on the Stock Exchange, Asil Nadir and Ayşegül were living a distinctly unsettled home life. They had moved out of Bishop's Avenue without having found a permanent place to live, the Chelsea property having fallen through. They went from one rented home in Belgravia to another, unable to settle down, finally moving into a temporary home in Eaton Square. And there were beginning to be fresh arguments – and fierce ones – between them over other women.

But as the months passed after the Polly Peck flotation, the family enjoyed greater prosperity than ever before. Ayşegül found life in Belgravia society very much to her taste. There she could meet people easily, as she had never been able to do before, moving in the circles to which she felt her patrician Istanbul background entitled her. 'Once I was out of Bishop's Avenue, things suddenly went sky-high for me socially,' she recalls.

In May 1981 Asil Nadir returned to Cyprus after more than two decades away from the island. Why had he stayed away so long? In the 1960s, Ayşegül had wanted them to spend all their holidays in Istanbul whenever possible, and took no interest in the island where the Turkish minority was living behind barricades. And in the 1970s Asil seems to have been too busy.

This return was a business trip, and came a month after Michael Walters had written a widely noticed article about the port of Famagusta in the *Daily Mail*. Walters, a tough City journalist with a reputation for being able to spot weak or doubtful companies, later became convinced of Polly Peck's merits. But his initial scepticism alarmed investors, and Asil Nadir's intention in making the Cyprus trip was to reassure them. With him went a group of British bankers, and brokers including Geoffrey Bowman of Messel's and Nadir's old friend and leading Polly Peck investor Peter Kleeman.

The visitors noticed that wherever Asil Nadir went he was treated with great consideration and respect. Rauf Denktaş, the Turkish Cypriot president, was among those who welcomed him. A village *muhtar* (headman) gave a magnificent lunch in honour of the group at a village in the hills outside Kyrenia. When the group visited another landowner from whose vineyard a purchase of grapes was contemplated (the Turkish Cypriots, including the Nadir family, were still at this date trying to develop a viticulture and wine-making business to replace their traditional businesses which had collapsed with partition), Asil Nadir was treated with great deference. He was also an attentive and charming host and if the group had any doubts about his standing in his own country, these were dispelled by the end of the visit. They were also convinced of the existence of a great deal of untapped potential on the island. 'The land was good, the grapes were good. They were growing one crop of wheat; there should have been two. The orange groves were about 40 or 50 per cent as good as the Israeli ones. There was a lot of potential. Polly Peck was a company that had been losing money. It was going to make a million pounds, it would be a major turn-around,' Kleeman recalls.

The visit coincided with another upward move in Polly Peck's share price to a new peak of 385p, which seems to have been triggered by a detailed circular on the company's profits issued by Messel's. This predicted profits of over £10 million in 1981/82 as the fruit export business finally came on stream, and profits over £20 million in 1982/83. This was to be achieved by the establishment of a shipping line with two leased vessels, working between London and Limassol. For the first time it became publicly known that Polly Peck was planning to sell Cyprus fruit in the UK. In August 1981 Radar Reshad left government service and joined Polly Peck where he would remain until he resigned his directorship in January 1991.

In July 1981 Polly Peck announced its half-year results to 28 February. A loss of £43,989 a year earlier had been converted into a slender profit of £51,779. This, analysts and the company hastened to explain, was because the Famagusta cardboard box operation had not yet come on stream. Cornell Dresses made a loss and so contributed nothing. Polly Peck's turnover rose by half to £1.5 million, with the in-store boutiques and mail order and export business doing fairly well.

This turnover figure was smaller than the profits the company was forecasting for the year-end once the Famagusta packaging plant and fruit export business got under way. The company, backed by analysts, confidently predicted year-end profits of around £2 million after Polly Peck's financial year had been delayed from February to August in order to bring in the new operations.

A commentator in the *Financial Times* pointed out that this meant an average profit of £400,000 a month for the final five months of the year, compared to less than £5,000 a month profit in the first eleven months. How could such astonishing profits be achieved? The *Financial Times* commentator resorted to back-of-the-envelope arithmetic calculations of boxes, prices and sales, which were to become familiar over the next decade. 'If it can turn out 8 million boxes in the final period to August, the market believes the forecast is safe enough. The plant is capable of producing 35 million boxes a year. Cyprus alone uses 12 million to 15 million boxes and Polly Peck should be able to scoop the pool if imports are banned as expected. The hope is that mainland Turkey will be a willing importer.' Everything depended on the cardboard boxes that would flow from the new factory in Famagusta. The 1981 citrus export season would not get under way in Cyprus until two or three months after the August year-end.

Meanwhile, there was dissension inside the company board in London, which came to a head early in 1982 when Raymond and Sybil Zelker resigned from the board of Polly Peck. When they finally left in March, the Zelkers insisted that both sides reiterate the trade market agreement made in 1980 at the time of the takeover. According to this, the Zelkers claimed, if they left the group Asil Nadir would have to give up its corporate name and the Polly Peck brand-name on garments. By now the original East End textile business was a minute part of the group and the name issue might not have seemed very important, but after the Zelkers started to market garments on their own account under the Polly Peck brand-name, Asil Nadir took them to court in July 1982. His claim that they were infringing the group's copyright failed, and after the hearing the Zelkers were convinced that the trademark would return to their ownership on 11 September that year. Throughout the autumn two rival sets of products were on the market bearing the by now glittering name of Polly Peck. On 1 December 1982, the dispute came before the High Court, but the Zelkers had already given up producing from the Polly Peck workshop behind Oxford Street, apparently following a visit from Asil Nadir's Turkish Cypriot staff, who changed the locks, to bring it back under the control of the rest of the group. After that the Zelkers kept a low profile, as many of those who broke with Asil Nadir and Polly Peck would do.

On this as on many other occasions, Asil Nadir's attachment to the Polly Peck brand-name is in retrospect a little puzzling. He understood well enough that much of the UK textiles industry was a dying business, unable to fight off competition from Taiwan and other parts of the Third World, and indeed Turkey and Cyprus. Accepting a small cash offer from the Zelkers for the right to use the Polly Peck brand-name would have been an obvious option. But perhaps the Nadir family, who cared strongly about traditional Turkish Cypriot businesses like textiles and tourism, did not want to see the Zelkers continue with the name. Indeed, if it had been left to the rest of the family, the Nadir businesses would have probably continued to concentrate firmly on the established Turkish Cypriot specialities. But, by buying Polly Peck, Asil Nadir had shown that he wanted to take a radically new course entering businesses which were wholly new to Cypriots. The traditional involvements were largely left to the Nevzats, Asil's sister Bilge and brother-in-law Fehim, who ran Wearwell on the lines familiar to them.

Meanwhile, Asil Nadir received a rare reproof from Stoy Hayward, Polly Peck's auditors. Stoy drew attention to a note in the company's accounts outlining sales between Unipac, the Polly Peck cardboard box producer in Famagusta, and Nadir Holdings, a Cyprus company owned jointly by İrfan and Asil Nadir. The note pointed out that although Unipac had sold £2.16 million of corrugated boxes to Nadir Holdings, just over £2 million remained unpaid at the end of Polly Peck's financial year in August 1981.

Asil Nadir replied swiftly. Everything was really quite as it should be. The sale in question had been essentially a guarantee to local growers, who were worried that Unipac would start up too late to fulfil all its commitments, that they would get the boxes needed to pack their fruit. He hoped that by mid-summer 1982 Unipac would be producing 60 million boxes a year.

Asil Nadir believed that there was a much larger regional market for his cardboard boxes than had been generally realised. Some estimates now put potential total demand in Northern Cyprus and neighbouring countries at around 1 billion a year. This reflected, among other things, the perception that Turkey was being held back in its own exports drive by its inability to package its goods properly. So if Unipac could get even a relatively modest market share, it should be able to generate large profits.

In June 1982, first-half results of the Cyprus operations were announced. They had made profits of £3 million, up from £18,000 the previous year. Marketing of citrus fruit out of Cyprus was expected to contribute about 20 per cent of the group's total profits for the year. When the final results were announced on 24 November, pre-tax profits were £9.04 million. Everything did indeed look astonishingly healthy.

Asil Nadir chose this moment to announce that Polly Peck was planning something completely different: an electronics venture to build TV plants in Turkey and Egypt. Colour TV had come late to Turkey and regular colour transmission got under way only in 1982, but the market was extremely promising. Several Turkish industrial groups were assembling televisions for the highly protected local market under licence from world-famous Japanese and European companies.

This was a very different business from citrus exports, but Asil Nadir had long dreamed of going into a high-tech industry and was brimming with confidence. The strategy was simple: get into the protected local market and then see if it could be eventually used as a springboard for sales outside Turkey.

He selected Thorn–EMI as a joint venture partner, a slightly surprising choice since the British colour television industry had been almost wiped out by foreign competition. He decided, however, to launch a new brand-name, which was originally called 'Star' but later changed to Vestel.

At this point a new figure emerged, who for several years was to be perhaps the strongest personality in the group after Asil Nadir himself. This was Brian Handicott, then the general manager of Thorn–EMI's International Division, but soon to become Polly Peck's commercial director. Handicott was quietly spoken but tough and he had a clear vision of what could be achieved by the new venture in Turkey. Announcing the deal, he said, 'With most of the other [Thorn–EMI] licensees they are already manufacturing in the same area. In this case we are not only providing the technology, but also the know-how.'

The Turkish operation would be set up first, but a sister plant in Egypt would follow only a few months later. News of the deal did not scare investors, even though they might have feared news of another rights issue before too long. Fearing nothing, the share price shot up by £1.75 to £16.78. 'Phenomenal,' said the *Financial Times*, adding, 'and entirely in line with market expectations.'

Meanwhile, Cornell continued to mark time. The true destiny which Asil Nadir had planned for the company did not emerge until 8 September 1982 when plans were unveiled to revamp Cornell as a part-owner of a water-bottling plant in Niksar, a small castle town in the Pontic Mountains in north-central Anatolia, south of the Black Sea. (Niksar's water springs had been famous since the fifth century, when it had been known as the Roman city of Neocaesarea.) The project seems to have been selected from a list of possible investments for which the Turkish government was inviting foreign tenders. The Niksar project would be small, but it would attract Turkish government support because it involved an investment in a small town many hundreds of kilometres into the heartland of Anatolia.

Asil Nadir believed that spring water from an Islamic country could undercut Evian and Vichy in the Arab world. A further possibility was to bottle fruit juice for the Middle East – one of his ideas which was never realised at Niksar, though one day PPI would bottle fruit juice in Mersin. Cornell shareholders were asked to put up £2.76 million to build a bottling plant which would sell 43 million bottles of natural mineral water. Polly Peck would not take up most of its rights, so the burden fell squarely on the minority shareholders. Instead, Unipac would contribute cash of £3.24 million. Any further money needed would come from Cornell which was to sell its London factory for £200,000 and its stocks and manufacturing machinery to Polly Peck for £400,000.

Trading in the shares of Polly Peck and Cornell was suspended for nearly two weeks as from 27 August until the announcement was made. At this point Cornell – whose shares had not been traded on the Stock Exchange for a full five years – was hit by new legislation. It had to move down from a full quoting to the newly created unlisted securities market, a junior market for new shares which opened that year.

The deal with Polly Peck was approved by Cornell's shareholders at an extraordinary general meeting in October. But by 4 February the following year it had still not materialised. Asil Nadir explained that the deal was not important because it involved a very small amount of cash – a few hundred thousand pounds. The more important task was to merge Wearwell and Cornell with Polly Peck.

The idea of a merger between the three companies was first announced on 15 December 1982. N. M. Rothschild, the London merchant bankers, were called in by Nadir to handle the deal, with Singer and Friedlander acting for Wearwell and Arbuthnot Latham for Cornell. At that point, Asil Nadir owned 40.6 per cent of Polly Peck, 12.7 per cent of Wearwell, and 32.6 per cent of Cornell. The merger would create a group with a combined market capitalisation of £225 million: 'I have always maintained that it would be sensible to have the three under one management,' said Asil Nadir.

The market was not altogether convinced. On the morning of the merger announcement, Polly Peck's shares were trading at £26.50, but they slipped £1.50 on the news, apparently because of fears that Polly Peck would dilute its earnings power if it took the two weaker companies on board.

In fact the merger would not happen for another two years, for within a month Asil Nadir and his plans had been temporarily blown off course by a panic among stock market investors, and when Polly Peck's share price tumbled from £32 to £10 and Cornell's from 148p to 118p on 1 March 1983, plans for the merger were shelved.

The Niksar water-bottling plant was a surprising choice for Polly Peck. At its opening on 28 August 1984, company officials explained privately that it had been selected because it was a relatively small project with an investment cost of $5 million which the Turkish government wanted to see go through, and it was a fairly safe investment. Water in air-blown plastic bottles was new to Turkey, but as few Turks believed in drinking tap water and had always paid for spring water, it looked like a growth industry. And the quality of the Niksar water – which gushed straight out of a rock, within which, according to geologists, it had spent several decades filtering through the strata – was universally praised.

Though the water was initially marketed in bottles which carried labels printed in Arabic, showing an idealised picture of Niksar as a faraway town nestling in a lush green landscape, it was taken for granted that much of the water would soon be sold on the Turkish domestic market. There was talk of turning Cornell from a loss-maker into a company with profits of £15 million within three years.

Perhaps because of claims that the water-bottling plant did not in fact exist, Niksar was opened with lavish ostentation. Asil and Safiye flew there in their own plane. Journalists and analysts travelled from Istanbul and Ankara to Sivas in a jet chartered from Turkish Airways, with whisky flowing liberally from breakfast-time onwards. They then travelled on by bus to Niksar. Mrs Betül Mardin, doyenne of the Turkish public relations industry and the sister of the founder of Atlantic Records, presided over the ceremony.

Niksar was many hours' drive from any large centre and it was wholly unprepared for such a jamboree (the catering at the opening was carried out by hoteliers brought in from Samsun on the Black Sea coast). Determined to make the most of its brief moment of attention, Niksar addressed its visitors with unabashed bluntness. Banners hung across the streets addressed the Turkish Minister of State with unashamed bluntness: 'Give us a packing factory', 'We want a hospital and two new roads', and so on. Since it was less than a year since the general elections, and the government had already channelled one investment into the town, the municipality was chancing its luck.

In the yard by the factory, Asil Nadir and his companions waited for the speeches. Safiye Nadir had come with the party, as had one of Asil's sons. It was a slightly nervous debut, with the Nadir entourage uncertain about how they would be received in Turkey. Asil Nadir's speech at the opening provoked condescending remarks from some of his listeners: 'He speaks such nice Turkish for a Cypriot,' one said.

The visitors toured the plant, marvelling at the spectacle of the bottles being blown out of plastic by German equipment. In the early 1980s, the thin plastic bottles were something of a novelty, though not for long – the German manufacturer who had installed the machinery had another date near Afyon in western Turkey later the same week.

After the ceremony was over and the buses had departed, an Englishman, Norman Angling, was left in charge of the operation. He recruited and trained local workers for the plant and reported that, by and large, all went well. The operation was an interesting experiment in the establishment of industry in a traditional Third World agricultural community.

Niksar water gradually found its way on to the Turkish domestic market where it became the second largest-selling brand, regarded by Turkish consumers as better quality than many of its rivals. Analysts in London who put its profits at the end of the 1980s at around £5 million were probably wildly out – or so the figures of Niksar's larger Turkish competitors would suggest – but it was a genuine, if fairly modest, business success. By then, however, Polly Peck's name had taken on a new connotation among investors. Its blaze of glory as the star performer on the stock market had been followed by a disaster which investors would never forget.

6 · Free Fall

Polly Peck began 1983 as the undisputed ascendant star of the London stock market, with Asil Nadir as the market's darling. By common consent, the company was undoubtedly the most remarkable stock-market performer of modern times. It might have only a modest £11.6 million of assets, and turnover so far of just £21 million a year, but its market value was now over £200 million. The share price was still moving inexorably upwards with each piece of good news. Shares had started 1982 at 310p, and ended it at £25. When Polly Peck published its 1982 annual report on 13 January 1983, the shares leapt to £27.50.

'There is already talk of Polly Peck's shares doubling in 1983,' wrote the *Investor's Chronicle*. Small investors everywhere pricked up their ears, hopeful of easy winnings. Asil Nadir seemed to be well on the way to establishing himself as a latter-day Turkish Onassis, due largely, his admirers thought, to his superb efficiency and his unerring eye for business opportunities which older, jaded corporations, run not by entrepreneurs but by appointed managers, tended to be too timid to pursue.

The rapid growth of its market capitalisation had pulled Polly Peck ahead of many well-known British companies: Taylor Woodrow, Guinness, Phoenix Assurance and Babcock. By now the stock was no longer held mainly by risk-loving private investors. Institutional investors were said to control 84 per cent of the 60 per cent of the stock not owned by Asil Nadir.

But growth in the share price assumed that Polly Peck would find new markets and new lines of business to enable it to expand and generate even greater profits. The rewards to be extracted from fruit exports out of a small island like Cyprus were clearly finite. Here again, Asil Nadir did not disappoint his admirers. At the end of 1982, the market had been agog with the news that he was about to turn to a completely new line of business which had nothing to do with either textiles or the fruit trade. He was reliably believed to be contemplating opportunities through TV and video production and distribution in Turkey and Egypt. First-year sales of £75 million were being mentioned.

Projections of this sort reflected Polly Peck's existing pre-tax return on sales of 40 per cent plus. How was Polly Peck doing it? 'I sleep very soundly and I have excellent management,' was Asil Nadir's answer. Investors scratched their heads. Some were unconvinced and withdrew to the sidelines, confident that a day of reckoning would come sooner or later.

A few sceptics observed that in 1981 over half the £2 million profit had come from sales through Nadir Holdings, a private company owned by Asil and İrfan Nadir. The same sceptics detected a similar item in the notes to the 1982 accounts: sales of nearly £4 million to Wearwell, the original Nadir company. Challenged about the figures, Asil Nadir shrugged off his questioners. 'Profits from these deals were negligible. They are in excellent shape,' he told the *Daily Mail*. The explanation for the sales was simple. Nadir Holdings had acted as a guarantor for local farmers in Cyprus who were uncertain whether or not Unipac would be able to fulfil its initial orders.

His admirers were undeterred. They came up with plausible explanations for his extraordinary success. Polly Peck was tapping areas of neglected potential, particularly in the field of UK–Near Eastern Trade. Asil Nadir spoke confidently of putting UK production and marketing skills in vigorous young economies where consumers were hungry for a whole range of good taken for granted in the West. Turkey, now a newly industrialised country with a population of more than 50 million and an economy which in normal times grew by 6 or 7 per cent a year, was one such.

Then there were the advantages of avoiding taxation by operating in Northern Cyprus. This offset the costs of financing further growth, enabling Polly Peck to reduce its debt and the costs of debt. Finally, the enthusiasts argued, Polly Peck did everything itself, cutting out the middle man. There was some evidence for this. Unipac's packaging plant at Famagusta was agreed to be Nadir's most brilliant stroke of this kind so far. No wonder its costs were lower than those of its competitors elsewhere, and its profits higher.

The press reported that Nadir could land grapefruit and potatoes in London for £2.10 a case and sell them for over £5.50. A case of lemons would cost £1.90 when it arrived, and be sold for £3.50. Competitors in the fruit trade muttered bitterly that they themselves could not achieve results like this. Their margins were well below 20 per cent, perhaps around 10 per cent. Few fruit trade competitors voiced these views in public, however, and there was a ready answer to those who did: Asil Nadir's operations combined advantages such as tax immunity and low labour costs in Northern Cyprus, with better management. Besides, remarkable margins were not unknown elsewhere among UK companies.

As his prestige grew, some investors began to follow Nadir blindly. When he bought a stake in C. H. Bailey, a shoe repair group, so did his fans. When Türker Süleyman, another Turkish Cypriot businessman, became chairman of Mellins, another loss-making East End textiles company, its share price shot up from 15p to 43p in a fortnight, even though the new director was nothing to do with Asil Nadir.

Still, the steep ascent of the Polly Peck share price was sufficient in itself to awake some foreboding. What went up had to come down, sooner or later. 'There has never been a share price which has climbed like this and not come crashing down again. Never. The closest performer to Polly Peck was Poseidon, which started at 25p and peaked at £124 – and then crashed all the way back again,' wrote the *Sunday Telegraph* on 4 December 1982 in an article which was to seem uncannily prophetic only a few weeks later.

Just when things started to go wrong is difficult to establish. Polly Peck had always been surrounded by clouds of rumour in the City, and some of the speculation had always been unfavourable. A good deal of it could be instantly dismissed as prejudice. There were those – they included a fair number of anti-Semites and racists – who regarded the rag trade and the East End businessmen who made fortunes out of it with disdain. 'We only deal with Englishmen,' said one bank proudly when asked why it did not do business with Asil Nadir and Polly Peck. To such as these, Asil Nadir was simply a familiar kind of spiv.

Other critics opposed Nadir because he was a Turkish Cypriot, increasingly close to the governments of Northern Cyprus and mainland Turkey. In the City, there was at least one merchant banker whose Greek background was believed to have made him a sworn enemy of Nadir. More generally, there was a large number of Greeks, Greek Cypriots, and Philhellenes in the square mile who were loyal to the Greek cause. On the other hand, people with Turkish connections, even though Turkey is a much larger and more populous country, were hard to find.

Not all these London Greeks were hostile to Nadir, however. He had Greek friends and often employed mainland Greeks and even Greek Cypriots. Ted Petropoulos, a mainland Greek and a banker well-respected in London, was one of his principal friends and lieutenants for a year or two in the 1980s. It was Petropoulos who introduced Asil Nadir to Elizabeth Forsyth, the private banker who later headed South Audley Management, Asil Nadir's property and personal financial interests management company.

Another mainland Greek, Captain Constantine Koutrakos, headed Asil Nadir's shipping line all the way through until 1990. A London

Greek Cypriot, Yannis Tembriotis, worked with him in Polly Peck in the later 1980s, and Wearwell, less surprisingly, had three Greek Cypriots in its cutting-room.

None the less, it was obvious that many Greek Cypriots in the south of the island were dismayed by the spectacle of a Turkish Cypriot running a company which had become a Stock Exchange star. Greek Cypriots saw all too clearly that about 93 per cent of the orange groves which Polly Peck cultivated had been owned by Greek Cypriots before the 1974 invasion and partition of the island. The Greeks incessantly monitored developments across the UN Green Line which divided Cyprus in two. There was little that they could do, however. Although they had persuaded the rest of the world not to give diplomatic or political recognition to the Turkish Cypriot government (thereby making a negotiated settlement on Cyprus very difficult to achieve except on Greek Cypriot terms), they had not been able to prevent the Turkish Cypriots from trading. That did not mean that they were content to sit back and watch the situation: the battle of words continued in the USA and Britain. Any journalist or broadcaster who uttered a word in defence of the Turkish Cypriot point of view, could be sure of a barrage of angry letters to his editor. The pressure had a considerable impact on events. Northern Cyprus failed to shake off its isolation, and any mention in the press was invariably accompanied by an emphatic repetition that it was self-proclaimed and unrecognised. Indeed, the newspapers even bent the laws of English spelling to ram home this point, spelling 'northern' with a lower case 'n', thus implicitly reducing it from a *de facto* but unrecognised small country with its own people and government to a mere tract of land.

One point which confused many outsiders was that although at this stage the Turkish Cypriots claimed to be a state in their own right, they did not as yet claim to have declared their independence from the Republic of Cyprus set up in 1960. The rather cumbersome name of the 'Turkish Federated State of Cyprus' proclaimed that the Turkish Cypriot government was merely the state government of the Turkish part of a future federal republic in Cyprus. This *de facto* status conferred various rights on it and allowed Turkish Cypriots, including Asil Nadir, the ability to trade through their own agencies and ports.

City opinion was often bemused by the political aspects of the Cyprus dispute, but it appreciated that there was little likelihood of renewed hostilities between Greeks and Turks on the island and that Asil Nadir enjoyed a close relationship with the Turkish Cypriots, which among other things allowed him immunity from taxation for his operations in the Famagusta free zone.

nything upset this arrangement? A few paragraphs in a news
e *Financial Times* published on 24 January 1983 mentioned in
at the Turkish Cypriot Ministry of Finance was trying to levy
Unipac. It looked as if some officials were uneasy about
Unipac's tax exemption. The Turkish Cypriot Ministry apparently maintained that the government (of which it was itself a part) did not have
the power to grant tax holidays to investors.

This story was not in itself Greek Cypriot propaganda. It had been
written by Metin Münir, the *Financial Times* Ankara correspondent, a
Turkish Cypriot who later that year joined Polly Peck as a consultant
and later still became editor of *Güneş*, the Istanbul quality daily newspaper which Asil Nadir owned at the end of the 1980s. The thrust of
Münir's article was that the Nadir family were rapidly increasing their
investment in the island, and that it was the Turkish Cypriot operations
which had contributed to the phenomenal increase in the share prices
of Polly Peck, Wearwell and Cornell.

Furthermore, the danger of losing the tax exemption was not very
great. The politicians clearly favoured it. Münir ended his story by
revealing that the Turkish Cypriot government was tabling a new bill in
the National Assembly which would grant tax exemptions for eight years
to all activities in the zone.

At first this news aroused little interest. Asil Nadir's attention was
concentrated on the merger of his three companies under a £300 million
holding company, announced the previous December. Three merchant
banks, Rothschilds, Singer and Friedlander, and Arbuthnot-Latham,
were working on the plan which was to be unveiled at Polly Peck's
annual general meeting on 9 February – the first to be held in newly
built headquarters in Commercial Road. Asil Nadir, smiling radiantly
at his audience as always, and bubbling with optimism, did not formally
announce the merger but told shareholders that it was a very considerable operation which was going ahead smoothly. He was also asked
whether some experienced City figures could be brought in as non-
executive directors to strengthen the board. Yes, he said, the Polly Peck
board would be strengthened around the time of the merger with the
other companies, but there would be no purely cosmetic appointments.

This was evidently not quite the news that investors had been hoping
for. That day the share price slipped 75p, falling to £34.25. The market
often eddies in the opposite direction to expectations. For Polly Peck,
however, the change was to prove serious. Many investors felt the shares
had travelled up as far as they could possibly be expected to do. They
were increasingly in the mood to take their profits and run.

One reason for this was gossip, always a factor in the life of Polly

Peck after 1980. Rumours of a rift between Asil Nadir and Rothschilds were circulating in the City. Earlier in the month the bank had persuaded Asil Nadir not to go on BBC television to discuss the dispute between the Greek and Turkish Cypriots. Nadir strenuously denied these rumours. 'The path of any entrepreneur is usually strewn with the corpses of his detractors. The merger will succeed,' he said a day after the Polly Peck AGM. Other speculation was more optimistic. It linked Polly Peck to a possible pharmaceutical venture with a large company like Glaxo or a motor industry deal with Nissan.

But the market was still nervous. Now came suggestions of a rift with the Turkish Cypriot authorities, and claims that the Ministry of Finance in the north of the island was about to sue Unipac for non-payment of TL137 million of taxes. According to some versions, a tax bill of TL185 million (£619,000) had in fact arrived, even though the company's accounts stated clearly that it had no tax liability in Northern Cyprus. Why had Polly Peck not informed the shareholders of this? In a jittery market, it made little difference that Asil Nadir was easily able to refute these claims and that the Commercial Attaché at the Turkish Cypriot Representative Office in London confirmed that Famagusta was to remain a free zone.

Then, on 24 February 1983, the Greek Cypriots moved in earnest and the share price of Polly Peck fell heavily for the first time. The Cyprus government declared that it was seriously considering including Polly Peck in a suit it was making against the Turks at the European Commission on Human Rights and that it might ask the British government to investigate 'certain activities of Polly Peck'. It said it was also considering civil proceedings against Polly Peck and Wearwell in the UK courts. It claimed that the by now famous shed on the Famagusta water-front which housed the Unipac plant had been Government Store No. 20 before the 1974 invasion and that the Cyprus government was its legal owner. There was even a whiff of espionage: part of the Greek Cypriot case rested on photographs of Polly Peck's operations in the north of the island which had somehow been smuggled across the UN Green Line.

Many of these actions had been going on for years and were a sort of rearguard attempt by the Greek Cypriots to reverse the consequences of the 1974 invasion in the courts wherever possible. With the accession of Greece into the European Community, mainstream European attitudes towards Cyprus shifted steadily away from the neutrality which had prevailed in the 1970s towards a position which was basically much closer to that of the Greeks, leaving the Turkish Cypriots isolated and unrecognised.

How far could Polly Peck be enmeshed in this dispute? The Greek Cypriots thought that changes in UK legislation on trespass, introduced in 1982, could be used to enforce their rights. They also argued that it was now clear that Turkish Cypriot fruit exports must include some fruit grown in orchards owned by Greek Cypriots in 1974.

The Greek Cypriots told David Tonge of the *Financial Times* that they believed that whether or not Polly Peck had no foreseeable tax liabilities in Northern Cyprus, this could not alter its obligation to give shareholders adequate material for the appreciation of the group's affairs. They also made one sortie against Nadir which took them well beyond the somewhat technical legal disputes arising from the partition of Cyprus and into the commercial arena. How much of the substantial item on the Wearwell balance sheet referring to 'debts' related to possibly shaky business in Libya? Greek Cypriot officials told journalists that they wanted to know why a subsidiary of Wearwell, called Sunzest (later to become known as the brand-name of Polly Peck citrus fruits from Cyprus), was bringing citrus into the UK. What was a dress company like Wearwell doing selling paper to a packaging company like Unipac and then buying fruit back from it? Above all, they argued, there should be a much fuller disclosure of profits and turnover attributable to each sector of Polly Peck's principal business and a statement showing the impact of the devaluation of the Turkish lira (TL) on the group's debts and assets.

Many of these questions were indeed awkward ones, and they touched raw nerves. The market was always uneasy over the lack of detailed information in the accounts of Polly Peck and Wearwell about the performance of their subsidiaries. Right down to the final set of accounts in 1990 these always gave only indirect details of the profitability of the subsidiaries, showing the turnover and profit for each type of activity – textiles, food and electronics – and the same information for each of the geographical areas in which the group operated. It was thus possible to ascertain that in 1989 Polly Peck had made profits of over £100 million in Turkey and Cyprus, but there was no way – other than through informed guesswork – of knowing how this was made up and how much each subsidiary was making.

The devaluation of the TL was another point which investors tended to overlook. The Wearwell 1983 accounts, prepared by Stoy Hayward, had only three lines on the impact of exchange-rate variations on the balance sheet. Overseas currencies would be translated into sterling at the rate in force on the balance-sheet date at the year-end, except for fixed assets such as buildings and machinery which would be translated at their historical values. Any differences on translation and costs as well as any arising from the conversion of foreign currencies would be treated as normal trading transactions.

The dry language of accountancy perhaps fails to convey how important exchange-rate risks were for Asil Nadir's Turkish Cypriot operations. Not only was the TL, the currency in use in Northern Cyprus as well as the Turkish mainland, not fully convertible until 1990, it was also an extremely weak one, and the purchasing power of sums in TL held for any length of time could normally be expected to drain away.

By the early 1980s, when Asil Nadir and Polly Peck came on the scene, there was no longer any great difficulty in remitting profits on investments in Turkey and Cyprus. But Turkey's economy had been plagued by very high inflation since the 1960s. In 1980, inflation in Turkey was more than 100 per cent. By the mid-1980s, after several years of drastic and painful economic reform, things were a bit healthier. Inflation ran at 24 per cent in 1982 and 39 per cent in 1983 – though these figures were to prove among the best performances of the decade for the Turkish economy.

In the 1970s, the Turkish government had relied on a fixed exchange rate and made only occasional devaluations of the TL. But from May 1981 onwards, the TL was adjusted on a daily basis and the government generally allowed it to move down even faster than Turkey's inflation rate required in order to help Turkish exporters. So any assets in TL held by companies such as Polly Peck or Wearwell had to grow exceptionally fast if they were not to shrink in dollar or sterling terms. It was a problem all foreign investors in Turkey knew well: once the investment was made, it was very hard work ensuring that it retained its original value in the currency of the foreign parent. Leaving deposits to earn interest was not a practical solution, since interest rates, though they looked very high by international standards, actually lagged behind inflation a good deal of the time. In practice, companies, even foreign banks investing in Turkey, found that it was often impossible to avoid heavy losses on their TL deposits.

The root cause of the problem for Polly Peck was extremely simple, but few observers outside the company ever grasped its working. For Polly Peck's accounts, a sale in TL was entered as revenue on the books the day the invoice was sent out. If on that day the pound sterling was worth TL2,000, and the invoice was for TL2 million, this would be entered on the books as turnover of £1,000 for the group. Because of Turkey's very high interest rates there was a constant liquidity squeeze, and buyers rarely paid up without delays running to at least three or even six months. So by the time that Polly Peck actually got paid, the exchange rate had usually fallen substantially. There might now be

TL3,000 to the pound sterling, and the payment was currently worth only £650, even though according to the books, it was £1,000.

So how did Polly Peck handle its losses on the depreciation of TL? Around the time that the company was heading for administration in the autumn of 1990, it emerged that these losses had been charged, not to its published pre-tax profits, but to its reserves. This was absolutely legal and correct procedure, and was recorded in the notes to the accounts, having been blessed by the auditors. Few people seem to have realised that if TL and other foreign-exchange losses were deducted from its profits, Polly Peck's star would have burned much less brightly.

The Greek Cypriots did not press this particular point for long. In early 1983, as at all other points of the Polly Peck story, they were primarily concerned about their claims to ownership of property and land in the north of the island. But many of them also saw the campaign against Nadir as part of a 'Long Struggle' begun by President Makarios to push the Turks out of Northern Cyprus and regain everything Greek Cypriots had lost in the 1974 War. Just how far the Greeks were prepared to go was shown by reports that the mainland Greek government had approached Thorn–EMI to persuade it to drop its tie-up with Polly Peck. The approach was described in the press as 'unofficial diplomatic representations'.

The High Commission and the Cyprus government had timed their moves shrewdly. Alarmed by the thought of trouble, and fearful that the share price had now become a bubble which was about to burst, Polly Peck's shareholders took fright. As with many furores, it was often difficult to tell what was going on. The Cyprus High Commissioner visited the Foreign Office to tell them of his government's objections to Polly Peck. It was revealed that a leading firm of London solicitors had been instructed to begin proceedings against the company under Section 30 of the Civil Jurisdiction and Judgement Act of 1982 which under certain conditions extended the powers of UK courts to property owned overseas. 'Polly Peck has become a shuttlecock in a political fight between Greek and Turk,' said the *Observer*. 'It is an organised smear and propaganda campaign directed against Mr Nadir,' said Fikri Tansel, the Turkish Cypriot Commercial Attaché in London.

One very damaging aspect of the situation for Asil Nadir was that conflicting signals appeared to be coming out of Northern Cyprus. There was never any doubt that Asil Nadir had the support of the Turkish Cypriot president, Rauf Denktaş. But Denktaş was not an executive head of state. Some factions of Turkish Cypriot officialdom appears to have been hostile to Nadir. Fikri Tansel backed Nadir strongly, but other Turkish Cypriot officials questioned about the affair either said they knew nothing about it or declined to comment in terms reminiscent of the polite but unmistakable coded denials beloved of British civil servants.

These were quickly picked up by the market. It had been assumed until now that Asil Nadir had the almost automatic support of the Turkish Cypriot authorities. But if this was not the case, then his investments in Northern Cyprus would look a great deal more precarious than anyone had supposed. Particularly puzzling was the attitude of the Turkish Cypriot cabinet. On the morning of Friday 25 February 1983, it met to consider the tax exemption. Anxious journalists and shareholders called Nicosia to see whether this had been confirmed. It had not. 'The decision is still being considered and we expect news on Monday,' a spokesman said. 'Personally I would think that we would support Mr Nadir who is a very important businessman, but of course this is a policy matter and I cannot say what the decision will be.' It looked very much as though the Turkish Cypriot government was split on the issue. The problem appeared to be that the date by which the tax exemption could be legally granted had come and gone, and retrospective legislation might be needed. Yet again, the Stock Exchange pressed Polly Peck to make a statement.

Just what reasons lay behind this somewhat self-conscious slowness by Turkish Cypriot legislators has never been fully clarified. Local jealousies and rivalries may have played a part. Turks and Turkish Cypriots often accuse their compatriots of holding each other back rather than showing solidarity. There were already people in Cyprus who regarded the Nadirs as upstarts and a possible threat. Simple administrative sluggishness and a failure to realise the urgency of the situation in London may also have been factors.

In Nicosia there were reports of angry confrontations between mainland officers and local politicians, stories of ministers and parliamentary deputies being roused from their beds to vote the necessary orders through. The paperwork was finally completed and rushed to London. On Monday 28 February, the Turkish Cypriot cabinet belatedly revealed that it had indeed confirmed the tax exemption. The news came too late. The instant that the London Stock Exchange opened for the week's trading Polly Peck's shares went into free fall in a general rush to sell.

The share price crashed downwards on the market, falling from its pinnacle of £34 to touch £16 for a while before other buyers emerged who took it back up to £23.50.

In twenty frantic minutes that Monday, almost £49 million was wiped off the stock-market value of Polly Peck. The company requested and obtained the suspension of its shares. By then the price had dropped

again, to £17, £6.50 down in less than an hour of market chaos. Wearwell
and Cornell, waiting in the wings for the merger with Polly Peck, now
spiralled down with their larger sister company. Cornell fell 30p to 118p
on 1 March and Wearwell dropped 9p to 61p, having touched 50p at
one point.

The Quotations Panel of the Stock Exchange, in an unusual move,
asked Polly Peck to make an explanatory statement to all its shareholders
about what had happened. Polly Peck finally confirmed that it had got
a tax exemption, but it was to run for six years, ten months from 1978
– the date at which the Nadir family had first begun trading in the free
port at Famagusta – and not for eight years as Polly Peck had expected.
Outside the company, however, there were those who believed that the
concession was not retrospective at all and that it would run only from
the date when it had been awarded the previous week. Either way, the
announcement was embarrassing, for it conflicted with the statement
published in the annual accounts.

Polly Peck would probably not have weathered this crisis had it not
been supported throughout by its brokers, L. Messel, one of the largest
and strongest stockbroking firms in London. Messel's trust was
unwavering, and when it stood by its profits forecast for the company,
of £25 million for 1982/83 and £42.5 million for the following year,
many doubters were reassured.

The merger with Cornell and Wearwell was the first casualty of the
share-price crash. There was no chance now of going through with it.
'The postponement of the three-way merger is first blood to the Republic of Cyprus, the Greek Cypriot government,' wrote the *Daily Telegraph*
on 1 March.

Many UK investors had also been hurt, as well as some companies
which had nothing to do with Asil Nadir or Polly Peck. The investors
who suffered were the adventurers on the fringes who specialised in
'dealing on account' – buying shares and hoping to generate a sufficient
profit on dealings in the fortnight before payment fell due to clear the
amount due. Polly Peck was the brightest of a bunch of shares beloved
by speculators – investors who cannot or will not put cash down at the
outset of a deal to pay for the shares they are buying. The shares they
went for promised rapid profits' growth and their performance depended
heavily on tips, word of mouth and market rumour, and bullish forecasts
from stockbrokers' analysts.

When Polly Peck's shares started to plummet, this triggered off a fall
in the share price of other stocks from which investors had been hopeful
of a quick return. Many small investors on the edge of the market found
themselves in serious trouble. They had borrowed to buy Polly Peck

shares and other miracle stocks. The only way they could now cover
their borrowing was to sell shares from other companies, whose share
price consequently sank along with that of Polly Peck. Mellins, Bio-
isolates, G. M. Firth, London and Liverpool, James Wilkes – there was
a long list of casualties around Polly Peck. Some of them fell proportion-
ately much further than Asil Nadir's company. London and Liverpool,
for example, fell from 534p to 152p during February and March.

After March 1983, things were never quite the same again at Polly Peck.
Some parts of the market never forgot or forgave the share-price crash.
But the company survived. On 9 March the government announced that
it did not intend to investigate Polly Peck's activities in Cyprus. The
hearing of Cyprus's complaint at the European Commission on Human
Rights was postponed until the autumn. The crash was over.

A fortnight later, by the middle of March 1983, Polly Peck's share
price was back at £22 and for a while it began to look as if the whole thing
had been a temporary upset. On 14 March Thorn–EMI announced that
it had concluded a first-stage agreement with Polly Peck to build a plant
at Gebze, near Istanbul. But instead of perking up at the news, the share
price fell by 50p.

Although Asil Nadir was still a millionaire on paper, he was now
pressed for cash on many fronts. At home, he promised Ayşegül that they
would survive this crisis as they had survived the years of near-disaster at
Wearwell. His optimism was undiminished. But his friends could see
that he was deeply distressed by what had happened.

The Greek attack was not yet finished. On 18 March, the Greek
Cypriot attorney-general approved a thirty-five-page dossier on Polly
Peck which was handed by the High Commission to the British government. It alleged that Polly Peck and Wearwell had both breached regulations on the information to be given to shareholders. An even thicker
dossier was handed by the Greek Cypriots to the Department of Trade
the following Monday.

Asil Nadir tried to shrug off these allegations, but a few weeks later
his opponents returned with yet another devastating blow which would
have ruined many companies. An exclusive story by Michael Gillard in
the *Observer* of 24 April revealed that many disturbing new questions
had been raised about the company as a result of investigations by
Gillard in Turkey and Cyprus. The article cast doubt on almost every
aspect of Asil Nadir's business. Much of what Gillard wrote would not
have caused a stir had Turkey and its business world been better known
in the UK.

The *Observer* showed that the crucial operations in Northern Cyprus

– which contributed most to Polly Peck's profits – were not audited primarily by the group auditors but by a three-partner firm of local accountants, Erdal and Co. Shareholders had never been specifically informed of this fact or told of the subsidiaries audited by Erdal with detail of their turnover and profits.

Yet although Gillard's article itself quickly became part of the Polly Peck folklore, his discovery about the auditors sank without trace. The auditing role of Erdal and Co., which in fact was part of Horvath and Horvath, the US group to which Stoy Hayward also belonged, either went unnoticed or was forgotten by all other papers until the autumn of 1990, and it seems also to have been overlooked by Polly Peck watchers and enthusiasts on the Stock Exchange. Some would say after the company had been placed in administration that they would have taken a very different view of it, if only they had been aware that Stoy Hayward did not directly carry out the auditing of the Eastern Mediterranean subsidiaries. In fact these anxieties may be misplaced.

Hüseyin Erdal and his brother are both chartered accountants with UK qualifications. They operate from small premises in a Nicosia street. Erdal and Co. is nevertheless the largest firm of accountants in Turkish Cyprus – a country with a population of 180,000, it should be remembered. Mr Erdal is a quiet man who likes to keep a low profile. He appears not to be in the habit of returning calls from journalists and seems never to have given an interview to the Western press.

Challenged about Erdal's role, in 1983 and again in 1991, Stoy Hayward insisted that they fully checked the Erdal audits as required by the Institute of Chartered Accountants and felt that they were satisfactory.

Gillard also thought he detected another oddity in Polly Peck's accounts in its unusually high debts and pre-payments – a phenomenon it shared with Wearwell. 'These totalled no less than 50 per cent of turnover, and at £10.6 million comfortably exceeded profits,' he wrote. 'Who are the debtors? And what, if any, provisions are made to cover non-payment?'

Before the Stock Exchange opened, on the morning of 25 April, the day after the *Observer* article appeared, the City was surprised to find a strong statement from Nadir landing on investors' desks. It challenged some of Gillard's alleged facts – about the number of packing stations in Cyprus, for example. Asil Nadir said that there was no question of giving away information to competitors, but anyone wondering about Polly Peck's superior profitability should consider the virtues of an integrated operation and the benefits of buying fruit from buyers (and thus being able to select only the best). As for Niksar, there had never been any suggestion of annual sales of £150–200 million. The £3.6 million profits forecast for Cornell were based on anticipated production of 64.5 million litres.

As for Erdal and Co., the statement went on, 'Stoy Hayward have confirmed to Polly Peck that they did not in the circumstances consider it appropriate specifically to indicate in their reports that Unipac's accounts were not directly audited by them.' Asil Nadir added that Polly Peck and its auditors were satisfied that adequate provision had been made in the accounts and that the level of debtors was reasonable in the particular circumstances of the company's business.

It was an uncharacteristically forceful public statement – but it was not sufficient to prevent another £4 being knocked off the Polly Peck share price during the day's trading on the Stock Exchange, though it eventually closed at £18, down 150p on the day. In the following Sunday's *Observer* Michael Gillard conceded that Asil Nadir's statement had managed to spark at least a temporary rally in Polly Peck shares. The shares had closed the week at £15.50.

Gillard was pressing for an interview with Asil Nadir, something he had not succeeded in obtaining for his first piece. But on Friday evening, Gillard told his readers, Asil Nadir had refused an on-the-record interview, although he agreed to give written answers to questions. A total of eighteen of these was then despatched. No answer was received, but Nadir consented to meet the *Observer* at 10 a.m. the following Friday.

Alas, *Observer* readers were not after all given the opportunity to read about an encounter which promised to do for City journalism what *High Noon* had done for the movies. The following Thursday Asil Nadir informed the paper through Nicholson, Graham and Jones, his lawyers, that he had cancelled because the *Observer* had reaffirmed its claims in another article the previous Sunday. Instead, the paper got a batch of written answers and a libel writ. A court battle began which lasted several years with both sides claiming a victory of sorts. Polly Peck and its supporters felt sure of vindication. Gillard's coverage continued, but his articles grew shorter and, as the court case progressed, he ceased writing about Polly Peck in the *Observer*.

However, a series of attacks continued in *Private Eye*. Though unsigned, the articles were assumed inside Polly Peck to be the work of Gillard. One point that they emphasised was the difficulty of reconciling the published export figures in fruit and fresh vegetables for Turkey and Northern Cyprus with Polly Peck's own figures. But since the Turkish figures were known to be inexact, and economic information about Northern Cyprus was regarded as a virtual military secret by the Turkish Cypriot authorities, the world at large was not convinced.

Polly Peck's half-year results for the period between August and

March were published in May. They looked pretty encouraging. Turn-over had more than doubled to £18.16 million from £7.7 million a year earlier. Pre-tax profits were up by 164 per cent to £8.07 million, and – though Polly Peck was not a generous company where its dividend was concerned – the interim dividend went up by 42 per cent to 9p. There was also a board change to announce. Richard Strong was joining Polly Peck as a non-executive director. He was of course already a director of Wearwell.

All the subsidiaries were said to be performing satisfactorily and for the first time, Polly Peck declared that it might be going into the pharma-ceutical business in the Middle East. Rumours that it intended to do this had been circulating for many months and the declaration can have come as little surprise to shareholders, though in the event Polly Peck never became seriously involved in the industry.

Was this reassurance enough? Not for many people. The division between believers and sceptics had become unbridgeable. 'Disgraceful', said the Lex column in the *Financial Times*. The writer felt that investors should have been told much more about how Polly Peck made its profits. He felt that the company had missed an opportunity to reduce the speculative atmosphere surrounding its shares. Just how did Polly Peck achieve a profit margin of 44 per cent? When Lex thunders, institutional investors grow nervous. There was another £1 drop in the share price. What the more sceptical investors could not understand was why, if the Cyprus cardboard box and fruit business was so profitable, the cus-tomers did not revolt to force prices down, or rivals move in to take their share by undercutting the company.

Six days after the interim results, Messel's upgraded its 1983 profit forecasts from £42.5 million for the year to £50 million, even allowing for very modest first-year output by the television and video operations. Asil Nadir could begin to breathe easily once more. In July, he angrily denounced a fresh spate of rumours that the Stock Exchange was investigating dealings in Polly Peck's shares. 'There have been no sus-picious dealings in the shares,' he said. The rumours followed a vituper-ative report in one of the Sunday papers of a lunch given on 14 July by City stockbrokers Williams de Broë in honour of Asil Nadir and Mark Ellis, a young lawyer who was joining Polly Peck from Arbuthnot Latham. In fact the real reason for the lunch was simply that Ellis had a university friend in the firm who wanted to introduce him and Asil Nadir to his colleagues.

Meanwhile, out in Turkey, Brian Handicott and Mehmet Şakir, one of Asil Nadir's first Turkish business associates who came not from Cyprus

but from the Turkish mainland, were setting up the electronic operations. Asil Nadir also persuaded Gordon Triggs, the former general
manager of the Sony Bridgend colour TV plant, to join as consumer
electronic products project manager. Handicott was one of the toughest
and shrewdest of Nadir's lieutenants, and largely responsible for laying
the foundations for the group's success in the electronics industry in
Turkey in the second half of the decade. But as the months went by,
he found Nadir increasingly difficult to work with and the relationship
between the two men was sometimes stormy.

Meanwhile, Asil Nadir was thinking about other opportunities. An
obvious growth area was in deals with the military who wanted to set up
their own defence electronics industries. Turkey had been ruled by its
generals for the previous three years and they believed passionately in
building up the country's arms industry. The country's Western allies,
led by the USA and Britain, tended to view this as a remarkable business
opportunity. The generals pushed through several projects, the most
ambitious of which was a $4.5 billion deal to 'co-manufacture' 160 F-16
fighter jets – the most expensive industrial investment ever undertaken
by Turkey.

At this stage of his career, Asil Nadir moved with the fashion. During
the summer of 1983 he sounded out Racal Electronics about a possible
joint venture making defence communications equipment in Turkey,
but the idea never came to anything. Undeterred, he began to explore
other possibilities. The main one was a possible joint venture with the
Turkish military, bringing in Daihatsu of Japan. The natural partner in
Turkey would be OYAK, an industrial conglomerate owned by the
Armed Forces Pension Fund. Talks were conducted through Şeref
Durugönül, a retired senior civil servant who had become Polly Peck's
representative in Ankara and kept Asil Nadir informed of changes in
the Turkish capital. Asil Nadir was expected to contribute finance, technology and an agreement with Daihatsu, with OYAK remaining a substantial minority partner. This was to leave a certain legacy of
bureaucratic suspicion towards Asil Nadir in Ankara.

The deal was still-born, probably because Polly Peck at this stage did
not have the muscle to push such a large venture through. When it
finally became apparent that it had got nowhere, the pashas in Ankara
were distinctly irate. 'It is all very well to make promises which you hope
will keep people happy when you are dealing with little businessmen in
Cyprus and Turkey or some party political shyster. But if you do that
with Turkey's pashas, I'm afraid there is a price to pay,' says one
businessman. 'I think that has got a lot to do with the way he was disliked
by MIT [the Turkish secret service] and some other parts of the Turkish

establishment. The only big contact he has ever had in Turkey is Özal.'

In Turkey this episode grew in the telling. Newspapers and magazines would write darkly about military hostility towards Nadir: the country's secret service was even whispered to have investigated him and to have turned its thumbs down. The truth was more prosaic.

Meanwhile Asil Nadir was beginning to forge an alliance which would be far more important for his future. His acquaintance with Turgut Özal dates from this period. By the end of the 1980s, Özal was Turkey's head of state and generally recognised as the man who had done most to change the country in the half century since the death of Kemal Atatürk. But all this as yet lay largely in the future. Early in 1983, Özal was in the wilderness, watching the impending return of Turkey to a military-sponsored version of democracy. He had been deputy prime minister in the military government after September 1980, largely – so it is generally believed in Turkey – as a result of behind-the-scenes pushing from the USA. In July 1982, he had quit the government along with the finance minister of the day after the sudden collapse of Turkey's largest savings company had wiped out the savings of many middle-class families. Now he was waiting to see whether he could set up his own political party when military rule came to an end.

In the spring of 1983, Özal had boldly decided to go ahead and launch his Motherland Party, even though it was clear that the military would exclude most genuine political parties from the forthcoming elections and had set up two tame parties, one to serve as government and the other as a loyal opposition.

He began to seek diplomatic approval, particularly that of the USA, to set up a new party – as a counterbalance to the reluctance of the generals. During a stop-off in London on one of Turgut Özal's visits to the USA, he met up with Asil Nadir at a diplomatic cocktail party. It was the beginning of a friendship which would continue until the autumn of 1990.

As the spring turned into summer, Polly Peck's fortunes began to recover on the market. The share price climbed back above £20 and then went on to £25.35. There was renewed talk of a merger between Polly Peck, Wearwell and Cornell. It was announced that the entire first year's production of Niksar water had been sold in advance and that the original profit forecast had probably been too low. There was a seven-year deal with Albert Abela Corporation of Saudi Arabia, to supply food produce from Turkey and Northern Cyprus.

The 1983 crash coincided with a general recovery in the market as the British economy moved out of the depression of the early Thatcher years. Perhaps because the rest of the market was swinging into a boom, it was not such a difficult time to restore confidence in a stock.

Odd goings-on among some other small stocks did not help build up Polly Peck's credibility, however. Although they had nothing to do with Polly Peck, the City press tended to view them as the company's peer group. Several of them did not have auspicious histories.

In August, dealings in Harold Ingram, a very small textile company, jumped from 165p to 328p in a day's trading and then were suspended at 300p. The price had shot up when the chairman and his wife sold 52.6 per cent to Wasskon Establishment, a private Liechtenstein company, owned by Mehmet Tanju Tecimer, the brother of Ayşegül Nadir, and Yalçin Akçay. A lemming-like excitement still seemed to grip investors when they heard that Turkish businessmen were buying a shell company. In this case a Polly Peck-style miracle did not follow. Ingram's next result was a slightly reduced pre-tax loss of £33,000.

Then there was Bellair Cosmetics. It was a loss-making hair lacquer company. Wasskon bought a 76.2 per cent stake in it in early 1983 and the share price moved up from 20p to £13.38. In January 1984 it was ordered to stop trading until it could explain its prospects.

The story of Mellins was not much happier. This textile company had become a cult stock among some investors when Türker Süleyman, another Turkish Cypriot businessman, became chairman. As it became apparent that the company was still a loss-maker, its shares tumbled from 240p to 52p. But this was still a long way above the 5p at which the shares had traded earlier, despite an interim loss of £166,000 announced in November 1983. Mellins' story came to an abrupt end in March 1984 when it went into receivership.

In fact none of these little companies had much in common with Polly Peck. Only Asil Nadir seemed to have the magic touch which could turn a loss-maker into a vastly profitable international concern.

At the year-end, Polly Peck's pre-tax profits were £24.68 million, only fractionally below Messel's forecast of £25 million for the year. It was a superb showing which seemed to give the lie to the company's enemies. 'We are not out to match or even beat that forecast,' Asil Nadir said, 'but we are pleased with the company's performance.' The stock market was less pleased. Instead of reacting favourably, the share price dipped by £2, and then rose again slightly to close at £24.12, down £1.50 on the day. 'I do not concern myself with the share price. It is of no interest to us what the market thinks. We are concerned with the company,' Asil Nadir said defiantly. In fact all those who knew him were aware that he found it difficult to keep his eyes away from the share price and constantly grumbled that the company was undervalued by the market.

Why the unfavourable response? The reason seemed to be that although the figures were brilliant, there was virtually nothing to explain how they had been achieved. There were just seven lines in the preliminary profit and loss account for 1983 published on 2 December 1983: mere snippets of information when the market was hungry for detail. Investors complained that they were still not getting enough information, and distrust hung in the air. 'The credibility gap remains – only the numbers get bigger', as the *Investor's Chronicle* put it on 16 December. But the writer went on to conclude: 'Nadir has established the makings of a major industrial base.'

Not all investors were hesitant, nor was Asil Nadir only able to appeal successfully to small investors rather than the institutions. Legal and General, one of the largest British insurance groups, now held a 5.1 per cent stake in the company which it had been quietly building up over the previous year. Peter Simon, Legal and General's investment manager, said that he had researched Polly Peck fairly heavily and had a considerable degree of confidence in its future. News of the stake helped build the share price back up to £30.50 – not so far from where it had been in February before the crash. Legal and General was followed by another large life assurance group, Friends Provident, which by early 1984 also held over 5 per cent of Polly Peck.

But the recovery in the share price did not last. The market could interpret any piece of relevant news as a danger signal and take fright. On one occasion it leaked out that Shell, the international oil company, was contemplating a water plant in Turkey. This was seen as possibly dangerous competition for the Cornell project at Niksar. Down went the share price. Shell eventually decided not to go ahead with the project.

The greatest blow to confidence in Polly Peck that autumn ironically came from a close ally of Nadir, Rauf Denktaş, who on 14 November 1983 finally declared the Turkish state in Cyprus to be independent from the rest of the island. Denktaş had wanted to make this move for many years, but it was only from the spring of 1983 onwards that his speeches began to indicate unmistakably that he was actually about to do it.

Ever since partition, the Turkish-controlled sector of Cyprus had been run as a separate state, with its own officials, government and external relations. But the Turkish Cypriots continued to pay lip-service to the idea that Cyprus was still one country: their state, proclaimed in February 1975, was simply one part of a federation that would eventually be established when there was a settlement. After eight years of isolation, Denktaş hoped that a declaration of full independence would bring recognition from perhaps half a dozen Islamic countries, as well as Turkey. That in turn would mean that perhaps some day the rest of the world would follow.

The move came as a shock to the outside world, though it did nothing to alter the *de facto* situation on the island. A new constitution, a new flag and a national anthem were hastily prepared for the new state: the seventeenth Turkish state in history, as Turkish nationalists proudly noted. 'That only means we've managed to get through sixteen so far,' quipped an Istanbul cynic.

This development was particularly infuriating for Greek Cypriots since it meant that Turkish Cypriots no longer paid even lip-service to the idea that Cyprus was one country. Denktaş had been contemplating UDI for nine years. Why did he finally move in November 1983?

One reason seems to have been the general elections in Turkey and Denktaş's awareness that there was going to be some sort of transition to a civilian government before long, which might be more willing to compromise over Cyprus. Another factor was almost certainly the furore over Polly Peck created by the Greek Cypriots the previous spring. To Denktaş and his followers the moves were simply further proof that the Greeks would always take up any chance that presented itself to strike another blow against the Turkish Cypriots and their economy.

Asil Nadir's enemies in the press warned that the Turkish Cypriot UDI could possibly mean UN sanctions against the north of the island, possibly backed by Britain. This would obviously have had serious consequences for Polly Peck. None of this materialised, however, and most Turkish Cypriots felt that on balance they benefited from the change. But could their independence be maintained? The Turkish Cypriot economy was totally reliant on help from mainland Turkey with the annual subsidy continuing. A Turkish Cypriot Onassis, if such a figure could be imagined, might be able to change the financial prospects of the new state.

Throughout 1983, however, Asil Nadir tended to play down the importance of Cyprus in the group's operations. He told journalists that the role of Cyprus would diminish sharply once the new Turkish operations got under way. As for the political troubles in Cyprus, they were 'very overblown'. In this judgement, events were to prove him right.

Just before Christmas 1983, Asil Nadir raised £5 million by placing about 3 per cent of the group's shares with an unnamed Middle Eastern associate. Nadir explained that this would not only enable the group to go

ahead with its development plans for 1984 and beyond without holding a
rights issue, it would also 'cement relationships' with the unidentified
associate. He said that he still planned to merge Wearwell and Cornell
into Polly Peck as soon as possible. This now meant some time early in
1984.

Polly Peck's shares, then trading at around £27, more or less exactly
where they had been at the beginning of 1983, were also to be split,
with each 5p unit being broken up into new units of 0.5p in a 'ten-for-
one' split. Asil Nadir believed that this would make them more appealing
to small shareholders.

At the same time, Polly Peck bade farewell to the East End rag trade.
The group's textile interests in London – the remnants of the older
Polly Peck fashion company which the Zelkers had founded – were
closed down. Despite new management, it had continued running at a
loss. In the twelve months to September 1983 it lost £935,000, and had
incurred similar losses in the previous year. About 170 jobs would go.

These announcements coincided with the publication of the
1982/83 accounts, which were generally agreed to be much fuller and
more informative than their predecessors. There was talk of Asil Nadir
seeking a possible listing for Polly Peck on the New York Stock
Exchange, the first of many such reports over the years. A New York
listing would have meant submitting to US Stock Exchange regulations,
which were more rigorous than those of the London Exchange. It was
a sign of considerable self-confidence that this step was ever contemplated.

So ended one of the most extraordinary years in the history of any
British company. All the efforts of Asil Nadir's critics and enemies
seemed to have achieved very little, though Nadir himself was understandably left with a near-paranoid attitude where Greek Cypriots and
Polly Peck were concerned.

Greek Cypriot newspapers and the media continued to lambast Asil
Nadir and his companies, but there was a change in Greek Cypriot
tactics. A special parliamentary committee was set up to monitor Nadir's
activities, and from now on there were few subsequent public attacks
on him in the UK by Greek Cypriot officials. When asked about him,
Greek Cypriot officials generally confined their criticisms to allegations
that he was using property which continued to belong to Greek Cypriot
owners.

As for Polly Peck, much of its original speculative following in the
market had fallen away for ever. But in the course of 1983 it had become
a truly international conglomerate for the first time, and its profits looked

set to move above the £100 million mark in a year or two. Asil Nadir had arrived as an international tycoon, and the intense faith in him felt by his admirers among investors and analysts was undimmed.

Despite everything, the story of the company still seemed, as one onlooker put it, to be a case of vertical take-off.

7 · The Grand Agenda

A year after the crash of 1983, Asil Nadir's mood as he surveyed his growing empire from his increasingly grand penthouse office at the Polly Peck headquarters in Commercial Road was once again buoyant. A former colleague from those years remembers him travelling across Europe, irrepressibly optimistic and bubbling with ideas about possible deals that could be struck with almost everyone he met, sometimes to the unconcealed disapproval of his advisers who felt they were being left with the awkward job of tidying up after him.

It was not that Asil Nadir or the market had forgotten the crash, but the memory had not deterred him from pressing ahead with a much grander agenda than he had openly contemplated hitherto. He was embarking on plans to turn Polly Peck into a global corporation. A temporary setback on the Stock Exchange seemed insignificant by comparison with what he hoped to achieve in the near future.

Investors were sharply divided between those who believed in Asil Nadir and Polly Peck as strongly as ever – and saw them as the victims of malicious rumours – and those who had now decided that the market did not trust the shares and they should not be touched with a bargepole. In early 1984, the Nadir supporters on the market believed, on the basis of the word coming out of Commercial Road, that Asil Nadir was now setting his sights on the ultimate ambition of becoming a 'world-wide industrialist', an entrepreneur whose business was based on more than one or two slightly unfamiliar markets in the Eastern Mediterranean.

At every stage of his career Asil Nadir always looked for new ideas, at times to the consternation of his advisers. While the rest of his family and many of his Cypriot business associates favoured sticking to the knitting, Nadir enjoyed the challenge of new markets and new lines of business. How could Polly Peck be turned into a multinational corporation with a truly global set of operations? What would be the next projects which would form the stepping-stone between his Turkish and Cypriot operations and the global destiny which now seemed to be awaiting him? How would these projects be financed?

Market rumours abounded. There would be major industrial development in Egypt – Asil Nadir was known to have been discussing packaging and marketing the country's fruit crop with government officials. There was the mooted deal with Daihatsu which would give him exclusive marketing rights in Turkey and some other Middle Eastern countries, and he might also manufacture some Daihatsu cars under licence.

While these rumours circulated, 1984 began with several bits of good news for Asil Nadir as well as a faint whiff of scandal. Messel's, his brokers, once more revised their profits forecast in an upward direction. Profits in the current year were expected to be £60 million, not £50 million. Encouraged by this prospect, investors returned to the stock and the share price moved up £1.25 to £28.38.

There was also extremely encouraging news from Turkey. The previous November, general elections had been held. The generals allowed only three parties to run, and the voters therefore rushed to support the only choice which was not explicitly backed by the military. As a result, Turgut Özal and his Motherland Party found themselves in power, with 45 per cent of the votes and 211 seats out of 400 in the Grand National Assembly. Özal was now going to be allowed to carry out his free-market reforms as the head of a democratically (relatively speaking) elected government rather than just as the appointee of a military junta.

This was an almost miraculous stroke of good fortune for Polly Peck and Asil Nadir. Polly Peck's operations in Turkey were already well under way. Apart from the colour TV venture, there were also plans to set up fruit and vegetable operations in Adana and Mersin, in the country's bread basket, the fertile Cukurova plain on the southern coast.

Özal was to prove much more friendly to Asil Nadir than Turkey's generals had been. As the glitter wore away from Özal's election triumph, it became clear that even if he had a majority in parliament, he had few allies in the country as a whole. Even the older generation of Turkish industrialists did not like him much, though they paid lip-service to the slogans of free enterprise and trade liberalisation, since they had grown up in a protectionist environment. Some industrialists had openly backed other parties against Özal and the Motherland Party in the elections. Most were privately very uneasy when Özal moved to liberalise foreign trade almost as soon as he took office. Tinned pine-apple, Danish blue cheese, foreign cigarettes, Duracell batteries, smoked salmon and even French champagne started to appear in grocers' shops in large cities. They carried a stiff surcharge, but to Turkish consumers this was not very important when compared with the cost of travelling abroad to buy these things.

Özal's ministers made it clear that the barriers to imports – which had dominated the Turkish economy over the previous sixty years –

were going to be dismantled in stages. Foreign investors and inter-national traders could look forward to a period of unprecedented oppor-tunity in Turkey. And few foreign investors knew as much about Turkey as Asil Nadir and Polly Peck: most large corporations would watch the country warily for the next few years. It was a situation in which Asil Nadir could make a disproportionate impact by investing in the country early on.

His first investment of 1984 lay closer to home. In mid-January he decided to purchase a 25 per cent stake in Strong and Fisher, the Northampton tanning and leather company owned by his old friend and ally Richard Strong. Asil Nadir had been discussing the deal since the autumn, when he had proposed a price of 70p a share. News of his purchase sent Strong and Fisher shares soaring from 27p to a peak of 275p. Now rumours sped around the market of a tie-up between the two companies. Was Polly Peck about to go into meat-canning in Turkey? Would Strong and Fisher build a tannery and abattoir there?

Perhaps there was a simpler explanation. Richard Strong had remained very close to Asil Nadir, as a board member of Wearwell, ever since he had bailed out the company nine years before, thus saving Nadir from financial collapse. Now Asil Nadir was demonstrating his commitment to Strong and Fisher, which in the first half of the pre-vious year had slipped into the red, though it recovered in the second half.

In retrospect, some of the ventures that Asil Nadir was considering at this time look unrealistic. However, entry into the motor industry was one of his most cherished dreams: it was indeed a fairly standard ambition for a Turkish entrepreneur in the 1970s and early 1980s. The Turkish motor industry was still largely at the fledgling stage and there might be room for a late entrant.

On 17 March, Polly Peck announced that it had exchanged letters of intent with Daihatsu Motors and that feasibility studies on plans to make Daihatsu cars in Turkey were in hand. Polly Peck would then become the sole licensor of the brand in Turkey and perhaps be able to sell the cars in some neighbouring countries as well. That left quite a lot of questions unanswered. The main one was how such a grandiose deal could be financed. Again the sceptics shook their heads. The *Sunday Telegraph*, for example, warned its readers against becoming share-holders in Polly Peck. 'There are far too many stock market "spivs" in it for my liking,' wrote Alex Murray on 18 March.

On Daihatsu at least he was right. The Turkish military built up Polly Peck's hopes of the deal, but it was well beyond the company's capacity at that stage of its history. This was why the preliminary talks fell through, leaving a further legacy of distrust among the top brass of the Turkish military.

In his *Sunday Telegraph* article Alex Murray also warned that when the merger of Polly Peck, Wearwell and Cornell did finally happen, it would almost certainly include some sort of cash-raising operation, even if it was not a conventional rights issue. Investors did not have much longer to wait to see whether this would turn out to be true. On 18 May, Asil Nadir announced the takeover of Wearwell, nearly eighteen months after it had originally been placed on the agenda. The merger with Cornell was left for later.

There was not a hint of a rights issue. Polly Peck would offer fifty-three new Polly Peck shares for every 100 Wearwell shares, issuing just under £3 million of redeemable preference shares for the purpose. The market was uneasy. Though there was no cash call, the move did mean some dilution of the rights of existing shareholders in the company.

As always, when things moved at Polly Peck, they moved suddenly. Asil Nadir had rung up Richard Strong, then visiting Christchurch in New Zealand, at three in the morning to tell him of the merger plans. For a while telephone calls and telex messages flew between London and Christchurch.

'I was well aware that Wearwell had the assets and Polly Peck had the profits,' says Richard Strong, who moved on to the Polly Peck board as a result of the merger. 'The attraction of merging Polly Peck with Wearwell was that it gave Polly Peck UK assets, hard assets and UK profits and dividends. It was a tremendous attraction to Polly Peck shareholders.'

Polly Peck's price dropped slightly, falling by 24p to 289p (the equivalent of £28.90 before the share split) and continued to fall for much of the summer. Asil Nadir and his advisers had anticipated this. To proclaim the strength of the two companies now being united, the announcement was timed to coincide with their half-year results. Polly Peck had made profits of £18.6 million, up from £8.07 million a year earlier, while Wearwell reported a more modest £2.73 million, up from £2.47 million. Yet again, Polly's profits were soaring apparently effortlessly towards the stratosphere.

The strong showing by Polly Peck raised some eyebrows. How had it been achieved? The Niksar water plant had not yet begun production, though it was due to be opened very soon. The Turkish consumer electronics plant was even further away from being ready. So the fruit export business in Cyprus had apparently grown even faster than anyone had expected.

By mid-June the shares were down to 223p. This time there was no headlong fall but a depressingly steady decline: by 20 July they were down to 187p. What was causing investors to take fright? Part of the problem was that the new investments in Turkey were turning out to be slower to build than analysts had anticipated. As a result, profits forecasts of the previous year were scaled down by some stockbrokers, though Messel's stuck to their prediction of £60 million for the year.

The absorption into Polly Peck of Cornell and Inter-City Investments, a loss-making clothing wholesaler, was announced in July, with an offer of twenty-one Polly Peck shares for each twenty shares in Cornell and one Polly Peck share for every five Inter-City. Both offers valued the shares slightly below their price the days they were announced. Cornell by now consisted only of the Niksar water-bottling plant.

To build up confidence among institutional investors, Asil Nadir organised two trips of fund managers to the Turkish plants at the end of August and early September. These trips helped push up the share price again – in the last two days of August it rose to 235p from 205p. Meanwhile, Asil Nadir's critics had found new ammunition. A mysterious private document was circulating in the City, alleging that the price Polly Peck was paying for some of its smaller acquisitions in the Near East was well over the odds. Why, the document asked, pay £650,000 for a business with a turnover of only £65,000 in 1983? Yet Nadir had apparently done just this when buying a pharmaceutical plant in Cyprus. Then there were two small cold-storage units, in Adana and Izmir. They had been purchased for £4.9 million, but the document said that they were worth only £2 million. Exactly who wrote this document, and why a need was felt to circulate research of this sort anonymously is not clear. Although thought by Asil Nadir's critics to be true, it did not contain new evidence to back up its claims.

When Polly Peck announced its 1984 profits, they were £50.4 million, up from £29.9 million a year earlier, but well below the £60 million which Messel's had forecast. Turnover was up to £137 million from £84 million. Though the Turkish TV and video plant was now in operation, no benefit from it was yet feeding through into the accounts. The Cornell merger was now said to be likely to wait until the following year, perhaps until the summer. The old Polly Peck group had contributed only £44.5 million, again below expectations. On the stock market, the share price went down again, falling by 12p to 227p. The shares once again looked very cheap.

'Polly Peck's era of soaring profits growth appears to be coming to an end,' wrote the *Investor's Chronicle*. 'I certainly do not find the figures disappointing. If all the plans had been completed by the year-end, the analysts might not have been wrong in their assumptions,' Asil Nadir told the press.

He must, however, have been bitterly disappointed by the sagging share price. Before the February 1983 crash, Polly Peck had enjoyed some of the highest price/earning (p/e) ratios – the best measure of the market's appetite for a share – ever known. The ratio had once or twice even strayed into three digits and had often stood at over 30. Now it was only 4, even though a whole range of investments was due to come on stream in 1985, which should guarantee a strong profits performance in the year ahead. But even that seemed to be in some doubt. Though some analysts continued to predict pre-tax profits of £100 million in the following year, Messel's made a strikingly cautious forecast of £80 million. But as events were to show a year later, it was not cautious enough.

It was not the only reverse Nadir experienced at this time. In Turkey, a country with a large population but an economy smaller than the balance sheets of the larger British banks and building societies, he was rapidly becoming well known as a leading Turkish industrialist. Newspapers and magazines began to take an interest in his life – for example, there were snide Turkish press reports that he was taking a stronger than usual interest in his sister-in-law, Ceylan, a claim hotly denied by her family.

Turkey's financial system was still rudimentary by international standards and most industrialists owned their own banks. In fact Asil Nadir already did so on Cyprus where he had founded the Kıbrıs Endustri Bankası – Industry Bank of Cyprus. But that was a minute institution by comparison even with the banks of Istanbul. The moment seemed to have arrived when a purchase of a bank in Turkey's financial capital would be appropriate. Asil Nadir set his sights on the Ottoman Bank, a 115-branch institution, with its headquarters in an elegant nineteenth-century building in the Galata district of Istanbul.

As always, Asil Nadir wanted the best. The Ottoman Bank had a pedigree and would have been an extremely classy acquisition. It had once been the central bank of the Ottoman Empire and its shares are quoted on the London and Paris Stock Exchanges. One legacy of its proud past is that it also enjoys a distinctly advantageous legal status in Turkey where it is viewed as a local bank by the Turkish government, despite its foreign shareholders, and so is immune from the restrictions imposed on foreign banks.

The timing looked favourable, too. Ottoman Bank, like most other large commercial banks in Istanbul, had just been through a difficult period in the wake of the economic changes of 1980. Paribas, the French banking group which was its main shareholder, was about to send in new management to shake it up. Through Rothschilds, Asil Nadir approached Sir John Colville, chairman of the London management committee of the bank. 'We are not in the least interested,' came the disdainful reply.

It was to be another four years until Asil Nadir bought a bank in Turkey, and then it was to be a far smaller bank than the Ottoman. One question surrounding the episode is how he would have been able to pay for the purchase, which would have cost at least £30 million. This would almost certainly have meant a further Polly Peck cash call on shareholders at a time when the market would not have responded favourably, and one which would have crowded out the group's existing plans for development. But Asil Nadir could hardly have contemplated buying the bank privately at this price.

Early in 1985, Polly Peck's attention was diverted yet again to the political situation in Cyprus. For a brief moment it looked almost as if intercommunal talks on Cyprus might actually achieve a breakthrough under prodding from the UN and the Americans. In the event, the discussions broke down almost immediately. The two sides were still as far apart as ever. Investors were left wondering what impact a settlement would have had on Polly Peck. It was a question that the Greek Cypriots were ready to answer. The Greek Cypriot High Commissioner said he believed that Polly Peck's extraordinary profits simply reflected its exclusive rights in Northern Cyprus, for example to sell cardboard boxes. 'Things will not be the same if a Federal Republic of Cyprus comes into being. Such favours will not continue,' the ambassador warned.

On 31 January 1985, Asil Nadir took the market by surprise when he announced that he was asking shareholders to put up £42 million in a rights issue. Polly Peck had not gone to its shareholders for cash since the original 1980 cash call to set up Unipac's Famagusta operations. Indeed, after the events of the spring of 1983 Polly Peck was in no position to even think of doing so, though it had raised a little cash by private sales of newly issued shares. Now confidence seemed to have returned.

The money was needed, Asil Nadir said, to fund expansions and improvement in Turkey and Cyprus. Some of the money would go to Meyna, intended to become a giant fruit and vegetable company based in Mersin. It would get a third cardboard box factory, fruit and vegetable packing houses, and an apple tray factory. Two fruit juice factories would also be built, one in Turkey and the other in Cyprus. Unipac would get its distribution and capacity increased. These projects accounted for £30 million of the £42 million – fruit and vegetable operations always contributed the lion's share of Polly Peck's profits. By the end of the 1980s, Meyna's operations in Mersin and Adana would show up in the group accounts as one of its main sources of profit.

Then another £8 million would have to be spent on developing Vestel's video and TV plant at Manisa, which was to be tripled in size, and a further £7 million would go on expanding the range of TVs by the end of 1986.

In some respects this latest rights issue was not quite like its predecessors, which had offered investors who took their rights up, ordinary shares with a relatively pedestrian yield. Since investors needed some sort of additional incentive, the company devised a sweetener. The money would be raised through an issue of 9 per cent convertible loan stock on the basis of £9 for every 220 shares. This was a yield over four times that available on the ordinary shares. The issue was underwritten by N. M. Rothschild, and Asil Nadir himself would be entitled to take up £12.2 million worth of shares in the offer – in fact he undertook to take up at least £6 million.

Soon afterwards a joint venture with Strong and Fisher was announced – not a meat-canning or abattoir operation in Turkey, as had often been predicted in the previous year, but a 300-room hotel in Antalya in southern Turkey. Strong and Fisher would invest about £250,000, rising later to £1.5 million, which would give them a 25 per cent stake in the project. Although this was Nadir's first large-scale entry into the leisure industry outside Cyprus, tourism appealed to him for several reasons. It generated foreign currency and tourism investments were strongly supported by the Turkish government.

Early in May, another party of forty institutional investors and stockbrokers were flown out to Turkey to look at the operations there. A place on the tour cost £400, but they were eagerly taken up by investors wanting an insight into the mystery of Asil Nadir's success. In fact the tour was heavily oversubscribed and some latecomers had to be politely turned away.

Just before the party left for its whirlwind trip to the Eastern Mediterranean, it was given a few sharp questions to ask its hosts. *Private Eye*, in its regular onslaughts against Polly Peck and Asil Nadir in its City column, posed a list of questions for them to answer. One concerned who bought all the cardboard boxes and paid such high prices for them. Where did all the 100 million surplus cardboard boxes from Unipac go, the author wondered? The article, published on 19 April 1985, ended with a quotation from Carlyle: 'The Unspeakable Turk should be immediately struck out of the question.' These and similar remarks gave some Turkish readers the impression that the articles were the products of the Greek propaganda machine.

If the fund managers read *Private Eye* before their journey, they cannot have taken much notice. They were genuinely impressed with what they saw. Mark Ellis, Polly Peck's joint managing director, said that the aim had been to give people an open and free look at the company's activities. 'We wanted to let them wander around and see what they thought,' he said.

The tour took the fund managers to Manisa, near Izmir, where the Vestel plant was formally opened on a windy May morning by Prime Minister Özal. Several of his ministers sat beside him and Asil Nadir in a ponderous East European-style ceremony of the kind beloved by Turkish officialdom. The speeches were long and extremely solemn and, of course, unintelligible to the foreign visitors. It was one of those minor and usually unnoticed culture clashes which occurred from time to time in Polly Peck. 'In Britain a prime minister would at least make one or two jokes in the course of an opening speech to lighten things up a little for his listeners,' groaned one stockbroker a little wearily. But Özal's basic point – that the Vestel plant reflected the dynamism and potential of the Turkish economy now that it was being opened up to competition and market forces – was clearly sound.

Afterwards, the analysts and bankers wandered around the electronics plant, which was still being enlarged, but Polly Peck said that it was to be the third largest in Europe and had cost £30 million to build. It had a cheap, well-organised work-force, which did not belong to any union. Manisa had been selected because it offered an excellent industrial park. The fund managers walked up and down the assembly line, some of them admitting to each other that they did not know exactly what a TV and video plant would look like. But their instincts told them that Vestel was a sound business. 'If you have any doubts, go and look at an English TV factory for comparison,' said the Polly Peck officials. They were right. Vestel was to prove a sound and rapidly growing business, displacing longer-established companies in the battle for market share in Turkey.

The party also visited Cyprus to inspect Unipac and its packaging plant, and the citrus packaging plants at Güzelyurt. Some visitors were surprised to find that these were not working flat out, but were reminded that they had come to Güzelyurt after the end of the fruit season when activity was not to be expected.

In Adana they visited Çukonam, a £20 million packing and cold store development, which was part of Meyna, the fruit and vegetable operation on mainland Turkey. Niksar and the water-bottling plant would have added an extra two days to the journey and so were left out.

'They are doing extremely well in Northern Cyprus, though the expansion there won't be as dramatic as in Turkey where the opportunities are immense,' one broker told the *Financial Times* when he got back. Others thought that they had discovered the secret of Polly Peck's extraordinary profits. Turks lived in a hyperinflationary environment where the cost of borrowing was astronomical – up to 5 per cent a month. It was a market where you had to make huge margins to survive. Polly Peck was funding from the UK at much lower rates, bringing in foreign technology and know-how, but unlike other foreign investors it was a Turkish company which was fully at home in the country. So that, the enthusiasts said, explained the profits. As for worries about the weakness of the TL, costs were in the weak currency but earnings came largely from export earnings in harder currencies.

The optimistic view prevailed. On 2 May 1984, the analysts' first day back in England after the trip, there was heavy ordering of Polly Peck shares. Over £23 million was added to the company's value on the Stock Exchange as the shares went up by 25p. There were reports that a European bank was trying to buy several million of the company's shares on the Exchange. The trip had cost Polly Peck several thousand pounds – although the company denied suggestions that the bill had run into tens of thousands – but it seemed to have established that there were real businesses in Turkey and Cyprus which were worth reckoning with, and so demonstrated clearly that Polly Peck was not a 'spiv' stock.

All that remained for the market was to wait for the Polly Peck half-year results, due out two and a half weeks later.

When May arrived, the interim profit figures were duly published, and once more they seemed dazzling at first sight. Polly Peck notched up another 32 per cent advance in its profits for the half-year. Turnover was up 41 per cent to £82.23 million from £56 million a year earlier, while profits moved smartly from £21.36 million to £28.16 million. For the first time, the Turkish electronics and the Niksar water-bottling plants contributed to profits. The profit figure also included £1.2 million from the sale of Ferguson colour TVs and video recorders under the Vestel brand-name and £1.1 million from bottled water.

For most companies, this would have been a splendid result. But Polly Peck's performance was measured against the extraordinary expectations created by its mystique. Peter Jones at Messel's, the analyst who was closest to Polly Peck, had been forecasting pre-tax profits of not £28 million but over £30 million, perhaps £33 million.

Nevertheless the effect of this slightly subdued performance was, perversely, rather reassuring. Fund managers had recently visited Turkey and seen the group's plants for themselves. So suspicions that investors were being asked to take too much on trust were less acute than they had been six months earlier. In any case, the dividend went up by 50 per cent to 1.5p, a significant gesture since Polly Peck had a reputation for being somewhat tight-fisted where the dividend was concerned. But if believers were impressed, the market as a whole was not. The price failed to move up and the p/e ratio remained doggedly stuck at 4.

Clearly, many investors still did not entirely trust the evidence before their eyes. The poor rating of the shares brought other thoughts to mind. When a company underperformed to that extent, predators would usually start sniffing around for a possible bid. But that was one danger Asil Nadir did not have to fear. Whatever the secret of Polly Peck's profitability, everyone agreed that only Asil Nadir could unlock it.

In April 1985, Richard Strong left the Polly Peck board. Strong and Fisher was going through a bumpy period and he wanted to spend more time on its affairs. He did not feel that his departure would be taken amiss in the City. 'The business was growing and I knew very well that unless one kept in very close touch with Asil, one would have no idea of what was going on. I didn't have the time to do that. The cash-flow problems were rearing their heads. And I felt that having given him my views on cash flows and management structure it was time to move on,' he says.

Asil Nadir took the news calmly. In place of Strong, he appointed two new non-executive directors, Neil Mills, former chairman of Sedgewick, the insurance group, and Larry Tindale, deputy chairman of 3i, the venture capital organisation. Slightly to Strong's surprise, there was no meeting between himself and his successors.

On 3 June, Asil Nadir returned to the work of unifying Cornell and Inter-City Investments, the textile wholesaler, in a £31 million merger. It would, he said, be a tidying-up operation. The terms were very similar to those which had been announced the previous summer: investors would get twenty-one new Polly Peck shares for every twenty Cornell shares and one Polly Peck share for every five of Inter-City. There would be 6.8 million new shares issued by Polly Peck, worth around £18.47 million on the closing price on 3 June. The Cornell deal had not been completed when originally planned, apparently because its shareholders had been encouraged not to sell by a rising price and the bright prospects for the Niksar water-bottling plant.

Asil Nadir had offered a price slightly below the current trading price and it had not been enough. The latest offer to Cornell was 282p a share – about 8p less than the market was expecting. One surprise in the terms was the high value placed on Inter-City. Though it made half-year profits of only £23,000, the offer gave it a value of £15 million, only slightly below the £16.3 million for Cornell and its famous water-bottling plant.

In August came more acquisitions. Polly Peck was now trying to build up a fruit business on the Turkish mainland, which seemed a logical next step for the group. Turkey has a long Mediterranean coastline and its potential far outstripped that of Northern Cyprus, but its fruit had been singularly under-exploited as far as the Western European export markets were concerned. Despite Turkey's huge agricultural wealth, successive governments and almost all investors looked down on agriculture and farming, preferring to invest in industry, if possible heavy industry. Three fruit and vegetable packaging plants in Turkey were bought for £12.2 million, to be paid for in Polly Peck shares.

The month marked a much more important moment in Asil Nadir's personal life. On 9 August 1985, he and Ayşegül remarried at Marylebone Registry office, thirteen years after their divorce. It was her birthday.

The previous year, their life together in Eaton Square had finally come to an end. He had moved out and gone to live in a bachelor flat near Green Park. For nearly a year, he did not see Ayşegül and contacts between them had dwindled to a few telephone calls. And then, when neither side perhaps expected it, the marriage had suddenly been rekindled.

'We got remarried because the children wanted it very much,' recalls Ayşegül. On 16 June 1985, Birol, their elder son, had celebrated his twenty-first birthday. Asil Nadir asked him what he would like as a birthday present. 'I would like dinner with my parents together, and my brother, the four of us together again as a family,' Birol said. Asil Nadir agreed, and decided to invite Ayşegül to one of her favourite restaurants, just outside Cannes on the road to Saint Tropez. The family dinner was a success and the ice melted once more. Within a week or two, the Nadirs were beginning to think of remarrying. The new marriage was also fated to end in divorce – a year later Asil Nadir's affections would be chiefly dominated by Joanna MacKay, a new girlfriend – but it was made in hopes. When these were finally dashed and it became clear that although Ayşegül and Asil could not live entirely without each other, enjoying regular meetings, they could not live together either, both sides registered their quiet disappointment. Ayşegül denies reports – fairly widespread among the couple's friends – that the remarriage was simply intended to settle any doubts about the status of Serhan, their second son. She points out that under English law, he was legitimate anyhow, while in Turkey, the Nadirs have never been formally divorced.

By the time of the remarriage more than two years had gone by since Polly Peck's share price had crashed. During that period the group had diversified into electronics and demonstrated to a visiting group of share managers that its new enterprises did exist. Despite that, the share price languished throughout the summer of 1985. When the autumn came, it was actually 50p lower than it had been in the spring. Why could the company not shake off a distrustful feeling among investors that it was still convalescing after the disaster of 1983?

On 15 November trouble struck once again from a familiar quarter: there was a renewed outbreak of panic among Polly Peck investors in London. Viewed from a distance, this might have seemed yet another instance of the market's apparently irrational tendency to overreact. Throughout 1985, there had been signs suggesting that although the Turkish electronics business was expanding rapidly, it was going to grow more slowly than had been originally planned and the company would have difficulty meeting the £82 million pre-tax profits for the year which Messel's was forecasting. However, Peter Jones stuck by his estimates throughout the summer and autumn. When he too decided in a research note that £82 million was unattainable, about two weeks before the company published its annual results, there was another fit of panic-selling among investors. In a few hours the share plunged by 52p to 173p. There was nothing in Jones's statement to suggest that Polly Peck was in difficulties. The reason for his downgraded forecast was that currency movements, in particular the weakness of the dollar, had eaten into the company's earning power. Mark Ellis elaborated: 'We hedge currency risks but we have not got it absolutely right. We are now dealing in twenty currencies and there are risks. We are not talking about losses, although our margins have been eroded by currency movements,' he said.

News of Peter Jones's visit to Polly Peck on Thursday 14 November 1985 quickly reached the Messel's salesmen, and throughout the later part of the day and all through Friday morning, Messel's sold the share. It was not a disaster on the scale of 1983, but it was still a significant setback which left a number of the group's admirers looking rather foolish. None more so perhaps than Prudential, the largest UK life assurance group, which launched a new unit trust the morning after the mini-crash with the slogan, 'If only I'd bought Polly Peck.'

Once again, the Stock Exchange Quotations Panel was unhappy about what it saw when it looked at the market in Polly Peck shares. David Lloyd, Messel's senior partner, was called in and asked about sales of the stock by his firm on the Friday morning following Peter Jones's discussions with Mark Ellis. At least one other broker had sold substantial lines of the stock that morning, but other securities houses were enraged at what had happened. They felt that price-sensitive information had been made available to a competitor on a privileged basis. Messel's firmly rejected any suggestion of impropriety. Others asked how it was that the company had still been agreeing well into the year that its profits would be around £80 million, even though it had presumably realised by then what the effect of the exchange rate movements would be.

Commentators remarked that £62 million for a company which had £50.6 million in pre-tax profits the year before hardly looked like a disaster, especially as the future outlook was undiminished. Even in a booming market, these figures ought to have been viewed as a superlative performance. But the shares remained ludicrously cheap. 'People just don't believe the figures,' one analyst said in the *Sunday Times*.

A few days later, the company was buffeted on another front when it lost a round in the two-year-old legal battle with the *Observer* over Michael Gillard's April 1983 broadside and two subsequent articles. Polly Peck contended that the *Observer*'s defence should be limited only to those parts of the articles which had triggered the libel suit. The *Observer* wanted its defence to range much more widely and to include other facts mentioned in the article. This would have meant that Polly Peck would have to make internal documents available to resolve questions about its profitability and the reliability of its accounts. This the company was reluctant to do.

Two weeks later, on 2 December 1985, Polly Peck unveiled its final results – and they turned out to be slightly worse than Messel's had predicted. Pre-tax profits for 1984/85 were £61.1 million, up only £10 million from the previous year, even though turnover was up by 50 per cent to £205.5 million. What had happened? Mark Ellis, deputising for Asil Nadir who often preferred to stay in the background on such occasions, pointed to a 44 per cent depreciation in the value of the Turkish lira against sterling in the second half of the year.

There had also been an unexpected £4 million in extra costs on the Vestel operation in Turkey, and – a significant change – interest charges including the new loan stock had gone up from £1.66 million the previous year to £5.48 million. Agriculture and food – the fruit business – had made profits of £53 million, but even this had been squeezed by increased competition in a changing market.

In the acrimonious discussion of Polly Peck's profits and their dependence on exchange-rate movements, no one seems to have looked very closely at the accounting problems involved to which Michael Gillard had referred in the *Observer* in April 1983, and the policy of charging exchange-rate losses to the reserves rather than the profit and loss account.

Around the same time, *Private Eye* picked up another apparent contradiction. An article in the *Financial Times*, written by its Ankara correspondent who had just visited Cyprus, quoted Turkish Cypriot official statistics as showing that the total exports of Turkish Cyprus in 1984 had been $38 million or £26 million, of which £14 million had been exports to the UK. But Polly Peck's Near Eastern operations had made pre-tax profits of £45.45 million on sales of £109 million, of which the lion's share could hardly have come from anywhere except Northern Cyprus. There seemed, the writer said, to be some discrepancy.

Meanwhile, Polly Peck decided to snip the lines that tied it to forecasts from Messel's. The rest of the world assumed that Peter Jones and Geoffrey Bowman enjoyed a popularity at Polly Peck which was not always the case. There were moments of rage, and sometimes of dark suspicion, towards the analysts, which never became public. No long-term relationship with Asil Nadir could ever be without its moments of exasperation and jeopardy. Yet some of the annoyance was misdirected.

At the beginning the company had been served very well by its close relationship with the analysts, and Messel's had been a staunch ally at the bleakest moments in Polly Peck's fortunes. Without Messel's loyalty early in 1983, it is hard to believe that Polly Peck could have weathered the first major disaster in its history and been able to go on finding the funds to expand its operations. Now Mark Ellis said that the company would no longer comment on analysts' forecasts, and the City would have to draw its own conclusions. He hoped that the company would be able to outperform the forecasters' guesses anyhow.

Polly Peck's subsidiaries were mostly based in a country which had no sophisticated banking or financial services industry and where balance sheets were not as yet taken very seriously. Without bankers and analysts to guide them, investors could do little more than stare at the auditors' report and accounts for Polly Peck and wonder what each coming half-year would bring. Those reports were, of course, notoriously uninformative in the eyes of ordinary mortals. The course the company was taking meant that investors would attach even more importance to the only thing that leapt out of the accounts: the pre-tax profit figure.

How long could a series of near-miraculous results be maintained? The most difficult phase in Polly Peck's history since the 1980 take-over was about to begin.

8 · The Long Haul Back

One disaster can be forgotten. Two serious mishaps within three years stick in the memory, particularly of those who have money to lose. After the events of November–December 1985, the following two years were a sombre period for Polly Peck on the London stock market; during this time almost all the glitter in Asil Nadir's life came from his operations outside the UK and he began envisaging a future away from London.

Although 1986 was to prove a year containing no sudden shocks for Polly Peck, the shadow of a share price which signalled market distrust hung over all the company's activities, and this persisted into 1987. 1986 was a gloomy year, too, in Asil Nadir's personal life: it saw the death of his father and the final breakdown of his marriage with Ayşegül. He was well into middle age now and, one by one, the chapters of his early life were closing, although he was not by any stretch of the imagination a lonely man: he was courted by friends and admirers in Britain and Turkey and enjoyed the affections of a succession of girlfriends. The warmth and affection of these relationships were important to him, and they were more than short-lived affairs. Yet they overlapped and he seemed unable to commit himself to any single woman sufficiently to contemplate a second marriage. Some extra tension was created in his life by the fact that most, though not all, of his girlfriends were English and came from the English side of his life, yet his business life was increasingly drawn towards Turkey.

Asil Nadir had continued to invest heavily in Turkey after 1983, where, within a year or two, he moved from total obscurity to become a national figure. Newspapers and magazines in Istanbul quickly began taking an interest in his and Ayşegül's personal lives. *Nokta*, the country's leading weekly (which Asil Nadir was later to buy) compared the Nadir family to the Ewings of Dallas. Though there are strict laws against subversion and against insulting officials in Turkey, libel law is far weaker than in Britain. When Asil Nadir, stung by a scurrilous article in a paper which he was later to buy, consulted Turkey's top lawyer, he was told that newspapers were not actually under any obligation to report the truth.

It seems to have been at about this point that Asil Nadir began to think in terms of becoming a press baron himself. There was a long-standing unspoken agreement that newspaper proprietors do not set their reporters loose on each other. Meanwhile, he concentrated on fruit, water-bottling and electronics. Much of his work in Turkey at this time was a natural progression from Polly Peck's Cypriot fruit business. At Adana, Mersin and elsewhere along the southern coast, Polly Peck's plans to build up a vast fruit and vegetable packaging organisation were going ahead. Asil Nadir would fly into Mersin to instruct his managers to hire the latest machinery or to seek out and buy ailing plants along the Mediterranean coast. There were plenty of them on the market, for in the late 1970s and early 1980s many hopefuls had entered the fruit production business, only to go under when they failed to keep up with the interest payments on their Turkish bank loans.

Asil Nadir filled his recruits with a vision of a Turkish fruit industry which had pushed its way ahead of Israel and Spain to first place in the Mediterranean. 'I thought that this was the man that I and the whole of Turkey had been waiting for. He filled us all with extraordinary enthusiasm and we thought that we were on the brink of great things,' one of his Turkish former managers recalls.

Ken Sweet, a veteran British fruit specialist in Polly Peck who had worked with Asil and İrfan Nadir since the late 1970s and taught them the basics of the citrus business, was sent out to supervise the new operations which, it was hoped, would eventually far surpass the citrus operations in Cyprus and one day make Turkey into a giant in the fruit export business. But for the time being at least, these investments ate up cash from head office, for nothing was done cheaply, even when local managers specifically suggested that it should be.

A share price of 200p now seemed to be hard for Polly Peck to attain. On many days Asil Nadir's mood alternated between mournfulness and resentment as he gazed at the screens in his office which showed the price of the company's shares on the Stock Exchange.

It was not, of course, simply a matter of pride. The low share price limited Asil Nadir's ability to raise cash and to buy or develop new businesses. Banks were cautious about lending. Shareholders would obviously not take kindly to cash calls from a company whose shares were under-performing. Another route to expansion was to buy companies by giving their owners shares. A low share price meant that they would have to be given far more shares (and eventually more cash when dividends were paid) than would have been necessary if Polly Peck's share price had marched in line with its profitability.

The second collapse of Polly Peck's share price at the end of 1985 put paid to any lingering hopes that the market would shake off its reservations about the company. The *Investor's Chronicle* bluntly pointed out that its historic p/e ratio of 4 meant 'that the stock market places the company firmly in the leper category'. Asil Nadir's exasperation grew during the summer when, instead of rising, the shares slid downwards, dropping from 200p to 130p over a few weeks, although they recovered later. What lay behind the fall? The interim results published at the start of June were simply rather dull. They showed pre-tax profits up by one-sixth to £26.8 million with sales again up by one-third to £79 million.

Investors stuck to their once-bitten, twice-shy attitude. Two crashes were enough for most fund managers, though as always there was a loyal minority. Friends Provident, the life assurance company, for example, maintained a 5 per cent stake in Polly Peck.

The failure of Polly Peck shares to find popularity with investors might not have mattered that much if Asil Nadir had been content to let his group grow more slowly. A strong minority – which included many distinguished names – believed in the company and saw Asil Nadir as a man likely to be remembered as one of the great entrepreneurs of the late twentieth century. But even quite modest development of the group's existing business required finance. Leaving aside Nadir's ambitions in Turkey and in the electronics business, there were still fundamental aspects of Polly Peck's fruit business which needed developing. The fruit exporting business was becoming increasingly a year-round operation as shoppers in Western European supermarkets grew accustomed to the idea that fruit was no longer a seasonal pleasure. Polly Peck had only limited links with the Southern hemisphere where most exotic fruit is grown. Moreover, even though Asil Nadir and Mark Ellis always stressed the need to market the best-quality fruit which could command the highest prices, Polly Peck lacked a good brand-name to which shoppers in supermarkets could respond. And it needed a distribution operation.

Suppose Asil Nadir and his finance director Anil Doshi wanted to increase the company's profits from the UK and European fruit business by adding a distribution operation to Polly Peck's packing and import businesses. They could only do this by buying an existing distribution network. That was only possible with cash. If Nadir borrowed from the banks to do this, the share price would probably drop. If he went to the shareholders for cash in a rights issue, the same thing would happen.

In the City some people looked at the company and concluded that the only way out for Asil Nadir and Polly Peck was to do what any other company with a weak share price would probably have done: join forces with another company. But no predators came forward, though the names of Geest and Albert Fisher would sometimes be mentioned, and Polly Peck received – and rejected – one private take-over approach late in 1986.

The taunts of the press and the hostility of some parts of the City had taken their toll too. In a certain mood, Asil Nadir still loved the limelight as much as he had done in his days as a student pop musician. But since 1983 he had become more reclusive. He fell back on an inner circle of friends he could trust and in particular on Turks and Turkish Cypriots as the number of his operations in Turkey began to develop and he established himself there as a national figure. Many of this inner circle were not old friends, however. They were people who had met him first in the two or three years after the Polly Peck take-over, but he was able to relate to them more quickly than he was able to do with most Englishmen: it was a question of shared attitudes and experiences.

Members of his Turkish and Turkish Cypriot coterie, most of them fairly rootless people who were less than a generation away from traditional Near Eastern life, were rewarded with great generosity. Anglo-Saxons might have seen this as an attempt to buy friendship, but in Eastern Mediterranean eyes the generosity was simply the gesture of a chief to his followers.

Generosity invites betrayal, however. As time passed, Asil Nadir would find that not all his new friends were loyal. Some took more than they were given. When business expectations were disappointed, the friendships tended to break down. (It was a different story with the women in Asil Nadir's life. Obviously they were attracted by his wealth, but his love affairs and friendships tended to be long-lasting.)

There may have been a higher cost than Asil Nadir realised for allowing what personal life he had to be dominated by a Turkish and Turkish Cypriot entourage. For few of his Turkish friends were real businessmen (unlike his English friends or indeed his Greek friends such as Ted Petropoulos or Sir Reo Stakis). They encouraged him to growing extravagance and conspicuous consumption, especially in his Istanbul and Cypriot operations. Ordinary business values, the thrift and caution of his parents and sisters, were forgotten as Asil Nadir chased a constantly receding dream of ultimate opulence.

At the same time the suspicion that British society – or at least the British financial establishment – was tinged with deep Turkophobia began to grow in him, fanned by the jokes in *Private Eye*, for example the constant references to 'Turkish delight'. 'He knows he will never be accepted in England,' his friends were now saying. Anil Doshi, who suffered even more from racialist taunts, blamed the City's distrust of his chairman upon them.

Ironically, however, it was questionable whether Asil Nadir would be fully accepted in Turkey either. It had turned out to be fairly easy to make a grand splash in the Turkish media, ever hungry for stories. Ayşegül had returned to the city of her birth where she sponsored social events and became a patroness of arts events and exhibitions. The vast hall of the Nadirs' fine Ottoman wooden mansion on the Bosporus, the Saadullah Paşa Yalısı at Çengelköy, was painstakingly restored to look exactly as it had done 200 years earlier. But it was not clear that the Turkish business world would applaud Asil Nadir any more than the British did. The older holding groups in Turkey feared Asil Nadir as a competitor whose company was growing with terrifying speed and who enjoyed the friendship of Turgut Özal, with whom they were engaged in an uneasy relationship. Turkish bankers did very little business with Asil Nadir and Polly Peck: the company was financed in hard currency from outside the country.

The press disliked Asil Nadir precisely because he was an ally of Özal, a figure who was heartily detested among some sections of Turkish public opinion, but nowhere more than among journalists. The left-wing nationalists, a wide cross-section of the educated middle class, did not regard Asil Nadir and his investments as Turkish at all, but merely as the latest tentacle of British capitalism and imperialism.

And there were other reasons for hesitation. A leading Ankara banker summed them up: 'This is a small and tightly knit business world. There are about forty of us who really count and all forty of us know at any moment of the day what each of the others of us is up to. But none of us knows anything about Nadir or what he is doing. We don't even understand how he makes the profits on his fruit business. Plenty of others have tried to do the same thing and failed. He is a mystery to us. You could say he is outside the club.'

Perhaps it was this sense of isolation on all sides which often made Asil Nadir touchy about criticism from within the company, though he welcomed suggestions. If anyone asked why Polly Peck was mistrusted or what reason lay behind the market's lack of enthusiasm for the company, there were serious consequences for them if Asil Nadir got to hear of it. One Polly Peck employee found himself out on his ear for suggesting to a business contact that the market might think better of the company if it changed from Stoy Hayward to a larger firm of auditors.

Throughout 1986 and 1987, the question of funding continued to hang over the group, dominating the minds of Asil Nadir and Anil Doshi. There were sometimes nasty moments when the cash flow ran low just before some large payment on salaries or the dividend loomed.

But these things are part of the inner life of many companies, and Polly Peck was able to keep its difficulties to itself. More worrying were signs that the group's legendary profit growth was slowing down quite rapidly.

Pre-tax profits rose by only 15 per cent to £70.4 million in the year to August 1986, though turnover rose 33 per cent to £273.7 million. Earnings per share crept forward to 56.6p, only 7 per cent above the previous year. So once again Polly Peck had to be generous with its dividend, putting it up by 28 per cent. However, its experience was not as exceptional as it feared. The City's mood had changed once again and expectations were lower than they had been a year earlier. In 1985, a 22 per cent growth in profits triggered panic shares sales. In 1986 15 per cent profits growth was saluted merely for being on target.

During the spring of 1986, Asil Nadir and his family had other things on their mind, however. İrfan had spent most of the previous three years with Safiye back on Cyprus. He was now sixty-eight years old, and until autumn 1985 he had enjoyed very good health throughout his life, despite a continuing slight chest problem – this had prompted the family's move out of London to Romford when they first arrived in England, and was also why İrfan had retired to Cyprus when he began to feel his age. When he grew seriously ill in the autumn, the doctors diagnosed a gallstone and in December he had an operation in London. It was not a success and for the next few months he lay on his sickbed at his home near Kyrenia below the Five Finger Mountains, growing steadily weaker. The problem with his gall-bladder had been cancer and secondary cancers were now spreading throughout his body.

In London, on hearing the news that his father's illness was incurable, Asil Nadir wept in the presence of his colleagues. For the first time in his life, optimism and cheerfulness deserted him. Grief temporarily blotted out everything else.

İrfan realised that death might be approaching. Even then he still seemed full of life to the family, with plans and projects for things he still wanted to do.

On 1 April, he woke at 5.30 a.m. Dawn had not broken and he did not know whether it was morning or evening. He asked for the curtains to be drawn and watched the sun rising behind the Five Finger Mountains. Asil came up and spoke to him for some time, and then İrfan's consciousness began to wander slightly. 'Asil has got a lot of things to do,' İrfan said in Turkish, as if unaware that his son was standing beside him, and then he died.

The lynchpin of the family was gone, and in the opinion of some of his friends, the one restraining influence in Asil Nadir's life had also been removed. His father had consistently advised him against taking unnecessary risks or attempting more than he could be reasonably certain of achieving. Father and son had been attached to each other in a very close relationship, but over the years there had also been plenty of disagreements between them. There had been times when they did not see eye to eye on the way the business was run and on people they knew. The difference between them can partly be explained in terms of their backgrounds. İrfan was an old-style Cypriot trader who spent much of his life on Cyprus. Asil Nadir had spent only the first eighteen years of his life there. He was a European businessman who had a better education than his father and had spent his twenties and thirties living on the fringes of the City of London. Although İrfan liked to maintain a patriarchal exterior, in practice he had listened to Asil Nadir's views very seriously from an early age, perhaps recognising that his son possessed knowledge and experience which he did not.

There was a further difference between father and son. İrfan had dabbled in many kinds of business in his life. Asil would be equally willing to go into unfamiliar businesses and industries. But he had a streak of tenacity and indomitability which was entirely his own. Once he was decided on a course of action, or wanted something strongly, he could not be deflected from it by normal means. A few reverses along the way would not depress him: he would convince himself and those around him that the setbacks would be only temporary. And if he encountered a problem, then he would conclude that somewhere there must be a pragmatic solution to it which should be invoked.

But now Asil Nadir was facing what he regarded as a board-room revolt, aimed at drastically cutting back his powers within Polly Peck, which had got under way during the weeks of his father's illness. This coincided with a confrontation on the board between himself and commercial director Brian Handicott, which had been coming to a head for more than a year. Now Handicott, exasperated by what he believed were mistaken strategies and management methods, attempted to rally the other members of the board.

Handicott's tough stance and constant criticisms and considerable support, for he was regarded as an effective administrator who fought more than the rest of the board when trying to shape up his two areas of responsibility, electronics and personnel. Several other directors seem to have regarded Handicott as indispensable to the company's future. He was the man who was turning a small business into a multinational corporation. Perhaps it was this sense of his importance to the company that encouraged Handicott to confront Asil Nadir head-on, producing a chart which showed a possible new hierarchical structure for Polly

Peck which would have made it more like other large companies, but, of course, diminished the direct personal power of the chairman and chief executive. For a while it even looked as if the revolt might get somewhere, though it would presumably have had an alarming effect on the company's share price. Investors regarded Asil Nadir with awe and tended to believe that it was his magically superior entrepreneurial abilities that they were putting their money into. 'Everyone wanted to meet Asil Nadir and not Polly Peck,' recalls one director.

Despite this, some of Asil Nadir's closest friends on the board went along for a time with plans to impose the new order on him. They included Mark Ellis, Anil Doshi, and Radar Reshad. 'They saw themselves not as defectors but as genuinely very loyal friends,' says an accountant who was close to the company at the time. But their united front melted away rapidly when Asil Nadir returned to London from his father's deathbed in Cyprus. He was of course not just chairman and chief executive, but also the main shareholder in the company, owning a quarter of its shares. Even if he had not possessed a far more powerful personality than any of his critics on the board, there would have been little chance of proceeding with any course of action to which he was seriously opposed.

Handicott threw his last bolt. He approached the non-executive directors about possible improprieties – though word of it never leaked inside the company – and his suggestions were investigated and rejected. With Asil Nadir exonerated and firmly back in the saddle, Handicott was left with little option but to resign from the board to pursue his own business interests in the South of England.

Although Handicott's original role had in any case diminished somewhat as Thorn–EMI's part in the Vestel joint venture began to fade, the rest of the board was none the less stunned by his departure: somehow they had not expected him to leave and his going meant that those who had backed him even partially against Asil Nadir, were now left to confront the chief executive on their own. There was also a sense that had he succeeded in holding his own against Asil Nadir, the company might have been taken in a completely different direction. Equally, Asil Nadir felt that some of his longest-standing allies and friends on the board had not stood by him to the extent that he was entitled to expect. Bitter feelings had been aroused on both sides and it took a long time for them to blow over. In fact the Handicott affair was never forgotten inside the company, partially at least because of the fissures which it temporarily opened up in the relationship between Asil Nadir and several of the directors who were otherwise always closest to him over the years. Why had they turned on him? It was a crucial question, but one to which there was no easy answer.

What was surprising, given the swarms of rumours which always surrounded Polly Peck, was that word of the row did not leak out into the City, when there had been a vague expectation around this time that Asil Nadir might step down as chairman of Polly Peck. The press made nothing of Handicott's departure, largely no doubt because he remained completely silent about his time at the company. Even *Private Eye*, which did mention in passing that Handicott had gone, was apparently unaware of what had happened.

Around this time – October 1986 – Polly Peck's head office moved to the West End of London and a new life in Berkeley Square. The Commercial Road premises belonged to a smaller East End business, and Asil Nadir and Polly Peck had outgrown them. For the next few years Berkeley Square and West End fashion were to become almost synonymous with Polly Peck. It is one of the many ironies of the company's history that the idea for this change, which would establish Polly Peck in its rightful place among the most glittering international companies, seems to have come from a Greek, Ted Petropoulos.

The site obtained at 42 Berkeley Square was rich in associations for Asil Nadir. Annabel's, London's top night club, was only a few doors away, while just across the road at 41 Berkeley Square was Citibank, his private bankers, where Asil Nadir's account executive was Elizabeth Forsyth, introduced to him by Ted Petropoulos. The Citibank doorman who used to greet Elizabeth Forsyth as she came in and out of the building soon found himself watching her new career as Asil Nadir's in-house personal manager and banker. He also noted approvingly that the inmates of number 42 kept very long hours. Asil Nadir was as likely to come to the office on a Saturday as on any other day of the week. He was even there on Sundays, when every other company door was shut.

Gülderen Tekvar, the wife of Armağan Tekvar, Asil Nadir's company architect, took on the work of furnishing the new offices which were to be even more sumptuous than Nadir's penthouse in Commercial Road. Ayşegül, though she was once more living with Asil following their remarriage, took no part in this work. Relations between her and Gülderen were not warm.

In all, more than £7 million would be spent over three years on furnishing the office with the finest antiques from West End dealers. When they were assembled and blended together, and the fittings edged with gesso, a gilded plasterwork, 42 Berkeley Square became a palace which dukes and princes would have envied. Admiring the paintings and prints on the walls, how many visitors realised that they were sitting on George III chairs each worth thousands of pounds? Or that the chairman was addressing them from a Queen Anne walnut wing arm-chair which had cost more than £15,000? Or that the wooden Regency wine-coolers holding pots of flowers cost more than £3,000 each?

In the chairman's office stood two globes, made in the late eighteenth century by J. and W. Carey. One was a conventional terrestrial globe, which showed the known world as it was in 1799, with New Zealand and other recently discovered countries proudly displayed. Its com-panion was a celestial globe, from which astrologers were supposed to be able to read the future. And across Asil Nadir's desk crawled an assembly of little golden tortoises: the office toys of a self-proclaimed billionaire and, as such, his one palpable lapse into ostentation.

When the time came for the collection to come under the auctioneer's hammer, it would seem an almost scandalous mixture of splendour and extravagance. Before Polly Peck crashed, however, visitors to 42 Berke-ley Square had their eyes firmly fixed on Asil Nadir and his business activities. The furnishings were merely a delightful and soothing super-opulent backdrop against which he did his work.

When the new offices were ready, the next question was who would move with Asil Nadir from the East End and who would be left behind? Berkeley Square was much more of a public showcase than Commercial Road had ever been. Everyone wanted to move there, but several long-standing figures in the company did not, much to their chagrin. Those members of the board who had not stood by Asil Nadir the previous spring now got their come-uppance. Mark Ellis, Anil Doshi and Radar Reshad were not invited to join the select group in Berkeley Square, although Reshad did move his office there in April 1990, shortly before the collapse. Those who were left behind felt as if they were stuck in the East End past which the company was now quitting. They were also, of course, losing the opportunity of daily informal contact with the chairman.

Upstairs at head office were the directors and other senior officials. Aisling Daly, a tall, elegant and warm-hearted Dublin girl, became Asil Nadir's secretary, succeeding Jean Thomas, who had worked for him for more than a decade before he became famous. Jean Thomas's depar-ture was another breach with the past and to some people it seemed a sad one. Ivor Shapiro, nicknamed 'Ivor the Driver', was now the main survivor from the earliest days of Asil Nadir's career. But he was soon replaced by a Turkish Cypriot and did not return to work for Asil Nadir until after the collapse of Polly Peck.

Asil Nadir himself was low-spirited for months after the move, but the source of his depression was his father's death rather than the abortive revolt inside the company. He was once more on difficult terms with Ayşegül, as well. There were rows over the children and since he did not see them, particularly Serhan his younger son, now aged ten, as often as he wished, he found the emotional warfare inside the family insidious.

He began to make new friendships. He had been introduced to Joanna MacKay, a tall blonde who had worked in the textiles business with Joe Harris, and after a while she moved into his flat in the mews beside 42 Berkeley Square. Joanna was a home-maker and knew how to receive the constant stream of visitors to the house who came partly as friends, partly on business. She is remembered as a calm and relaxed hostess. Her sense of humour at a time when Asil was often depressed clinched the friendship between them – she would sometimes persuade him that he had far too many clothes – though he did not often appear with her in public. Later they moved to another flat in Mount Street and then to Aldford Street, where Safiye Nadir owned a house. These were expensive residences, but they were all somehow temporary. Asil Nadir seemed destined never to have a permanent home of his own, while his sisters and his mother had comfortable, though unpretentious family houses with adjoining gardens in a London suburb.

In Turkey Brian Handicott was replaced by Tahsin Karan, a cool, efficient businessman with a naval background who had come from a rival electronics group. Karan was a shrewd professional manager, accessible when needed, and basically determined to build up Vestel as a strong business.

The final spin-off from the Handicott affair was the resignation of Anil Doshi as finance director to pursue his own business interests. Doshi had been a close associate of both İrfan and Asil Nadir, but it was felt that the market did not like him, though those who worked with Doshi generally warmed to him. It was again said that an element of racialism was involved, that the City wanted a man with a paler skin. Afterwards Asil Nadir would say that he respected Anil Doshi more than some of the others around him, because Doshi alone had been man enough to resign in the wake of the board-room skirmishes against him, and in fact Doshi would eventually return as a consultant and advisor.

In Doshi's place came an entirely new face, that of David Fawcus, aged fifty-two, head-hunted by Coopers & Lybrand and Tyzacks from Guinness Overseas. With his public school background, David Fawcus was something of an establishment figure, a reassuring presence on the board for shareholders who were not sure what to make of Turkish Cypriot businessmen like Asil Nadir and Radar Reshad or whiz-kids like Mark Ellis. Throughout his time at Polly Peck, however, David Fawcus remained a rather isolated figure. He did not hit it off with most of the Polly Peck old guard, and the presence of Anil Doshi in the wings made him uneasy. None the less Fawcus was destined to stay with Polly Peck all the way through until January 1991, two months after the company had been placed in administration.

With the new finance director in place, the recent upsets within the company were speedily put to one side. In the autumn of 1986, Asil Nadir and the board decided that the moment had come for a major acquisition – this time to be in the UK. In December Polly Peck bought Russell Hobbs, a well-known British electric utensils and coffee-maker manufacturer, and Tower Household Products from TI Group for £12 million.

Russell Hobbs looked like a brand-name ripe for development. Most British families had a kettle or toaster made by the company, but in 1985 it had made only £1 million in pre-tax profits on sales of £40 million and it exported only a meagre 15 per cent of sales. Could the brand-name be put on goods manufactured in Turkey? Perhaps the Turks could be introduced to the automatic electric kettle, a device which English families seemed unable to do without but which for some reason had never found favour even among tea or instant coffee drinkers in other countries.

The market quite liked the deal. The price looked right: Polly Peck's accounts showed that it held £18 million in cash at the end of the last financial year, so the outlay of £12 million on Russell Hobbs Tower was well within its range. Polly Peck's shares climbed up 2p from a dismal 180p.

Nor was this the only venture into new territory announced by Polly Peck that year. Across the world, much bolder plans were being hatched. Asil Nadir's sights were concentrated on the Hong Kong stock market, where he believed Polly Peck could obtain a listing within a year or two, and in 1986 he moved into South-East Asia in a joint venture with Macao businessman Stanley Ho. For shareholders the first information that Polly Peck was about to make an acquisition in the Far East came on 20 October, when news broke of the purchase of Impact Textiles, a Hong Kong garment trading company. It was a small acquisition: Polly Peck spent HK$61.5 million (£5.5 million) to buy the company which had made profits of HK$13.4 million.

Impact bought clothes and shoes made in South-East Asia and sold them to European chain stores and mail order houses. At the same time,

Polly Peck let it be known that it also wanted to buy out the remaining 50 per cent of the shares of Shui Hing, the textiles group it had bought into the previous year, and this it subsequently did.

This seemed to some a slightly strange choice of activity for Polly Peck, because the textile industry was one line of business in which Turkey seemed to be most successful. By the mid-1980s, Turkey had supplanted Far Eastern suppliers, including Hong Kong, as the main textile supplier of the European Community. Moreover, because Turkey was only a day or two from Europe by truck, its role as textile producer seemed set to grow steadily. Surely it was in Turkey rather than the Far East that Polly Peck should be investing? But Asil Nadir was strongly drawn to business opportunities in the Far East, which he regarded as an area of obvious growth potential: 'Japanese have a lot in common with Turks,' he was fond of saying. In this he shared the views of Turgut Özal, the Turkish prime minister, who also admired the Japanese for their ability to combine business dynamism with a modern but non-European culture.

In late March 1987 Barry Buttifant, a British businessman in Hong Kong, was invited to head Polly Peck's Hong Kong operations after a meeting with Asil Nadir in the Regent Hotel. Buttifant, who took over on 1 July the same year, was summoned to London to help decide whether the group's Far Eastern operations should concentrate on fruit, textiles or consumer electronics. When he walked into the group's offices, he was impressed by the frenetic activity he encountered. A team from Bear Sterns of New York was in town, discussing ways in which there could be a Polly Peck flotation on the New York Stock Exchange.

Buttifant knew the fruit business well and at first he seems to have seen Polly Peck's destiny in the Far East in terms of fruit exports. But on returning from London to Hong Kong, he decided that the way forward lay in consumer electronics, and Polly Peck should buy up an existing company. It was not until the following May, however, that Asil Nadir finally bought a company which gave him the Hong Kong Stock Exchange listing he was seeking. On 25 May 1987 he purchased Rainbow Orient Corporation from Sir Ron Brierley, the New Zealand entrepreneur. Orient was an investment company and its assets consisted entirely of cash. Polly Peck paid £36 million for a 96.6 per cent stake in it, which included £445,000 of goodwill. The plan was to place 25 per cent of its equity on the Hong Kong Stock Exchange by the end of the summer. Shui Hing and Impact were to be grouped with Orient in a new entity: Polly Peck Far East. However, the idea did not work out as had been hoped. In August the following year – 1988 – Polly Peck announced that it was going to buy out the minority shareholders in Rainbow Orient.

One strong motive for building up a presence in Hong Kong was that Shui Hing and Impact could act as the core for a possible Polly Peck flotation in the colony in a year or two. But Hong Kong investors did not want to invest in textiles, and textiles no longer had much of a place in the group: they tied up quite a lot of cash, and eventually Asil Nadir became eager to sell off the textiles businesses. So the Hong Kong public company owned by the group was disposed of.

In October 1987, led by Buttifant, Polly Peck made its next acquisition in the Far East. This time, however, it looked not to the textiles industry but to electronics. Capetronics was a Taiwan-based high-quality electronic research and development company which also made consumer electronics, audio equipment and computer monitors, selling them to well-known brand-names in Japan, Europe and the USA who then sold the goods under their own label. Norbert Wirsching, Capetronics' general manager, was a German-American entrepreneur living in the Far East. He had spent much of 1987 looking for a new partner in Capetronic who would buy out his existing partner and put in new cash. Wirsching had never heard of Polly Peck or Asil Nadir, but he agreed to fly to London.

Still not sure of what sort of company he was dealing with, he told Polly Peck that he would see Asil Nadir only on Saturday morning. To his surprise the appointment was made without demur. He was even more surprised when he observed the decor of 42 Berkeley Square as he waited for twenty minutes in the office with David Fawcus and Stevan Breeze, one of Polly Peck's top electronics specialists (and formerly managing director of Tefal UK) who was later promoted to the board.

Eventually Asil Nadir arrived. Again Wirsching could not believe his eyes. It was not an auspicious first meeting, for Wirsching was put off by Asil Nadir's smart appearance – he felt disinclined to deal with a man who looked more like a fashion model than a conventional company chairman. Years afterward he would tease Asil Nadir by telling him that at first sight he had judged him to be just a playboy. After some polite discussion, Wirsching arranged a further meeting but told his US lawyer who had flown in specially from New York not to bother to attend.

However, Wirsching's scepticism melted unexpectedly at the next meeting a week later when he realised that Asil Nadir, alone of the people he was negotiating with, had clearly read and mastered a due diligence report on Capetronics commissioned from Coopers & Lybrand. Sensing that Wirsching was still uneasy, Asil Nadir said after a further half hour that he would call his Turkish electronics people to London to meet him.

The following day, Tahsin Karan, the general manager of Vestel, arrived in London. It was Sunday, but Asil Nadir spent the day working with Wirsching, as if this was an entirely normal way for a chairman of a public company to pass the weekend. Lawyers were brought in after all, and at the end of the day, Asil Nadir and Wirsching shook hands and made a deal.

In fact that was not quite the end of the story. Other difficulties erupted along the way and the deal was not formally closed until just two days before the Stock Exchange crash on 19 October 1987 – Black Monday. The purchase, one of its biggest acquisitions, cost the group a total of US$35.4 million (£20 million), nearly three times the amount which Lee Ming Tee, Capetronics' previous owner, had paid for it not long before. But the Taiwan operation did prove a steady source of profits for the group and a strong rapport developed between Wirsching and Asil Nadir, leading eventually to an invitation to Wirsching to join the board. He accepted, but only on condition that he had nothing to do with Russell Hobbs, the loss-making kitchen appliances company, which he considered the group should never have bought.

Within Polly Peck, the Far Eastern electronics group was pitted against its Turkish counterpart, in line with Asil Nadir's habit of encouraging those working for him to compete against each other. Wirsching became a rival for Tahsin Karan and Vestel and the relationship between the two men was not always easy, though Wirsching did his best to steer clear of Vestel.

Asil Nadir's first visit to Hong Kong was memorable for a slightly uncanny coincidence and also as one of the few occasions on which he lost his cool. He had been in Taipei, visiting Capetronics, and was due to fly back to Turkey via Hong Kong in his private jet. He was the last of the Polly Peck group to leave, the others having flown out on a scheduled flight, after saying their farewells to him at the closely guarded Taipei International Airport.

Late that evening, phones began ringing wildly in Hong Kong. It was Asil Nadir, still in Taipei and sounding uncharacteristically distraught. The plane had engine problems and he was furious with his pilot, David Dale. Hong Kong suggested that he should come instead by a commercial flight which connected with the next day's British Airways flight to London.

Then Asil Nadir revealed the real reason why he was so upset. He had lost a gold ring set with a single diamond given to him by his father, which he treasured and regarded as a sort of private talisman. Could maximum effort be made by staff in Hong Kong and Taipei to find it? He asked Nil Adula, head of his PR operation in Istanbul, who was in Hong Kong that day and about to catch the next flight to London, to do what she could.

So the next day Asil Nadir caught a Cathay Pacific flight to Hong Kong. Always a nervous flier, he cannot have been looking forward to the famously abrupt descent which jet planes make when coming into Hong Kong. On the approach, however, the second engine of the plane cut out, and the flight was diverted, without explanation, to China. Meanwhile Polly Peck officials waited for hours on the runway in Hong Kong, persuading British Airways to delay its flight so that Nadir and other passengers on the diverted flight would be able to carry on to London. After several hours, they were able to escort Asil Nadir, safely landed in Hong Kong, but not in the best of spirits and with only his briefcase for luggage, to the British Airways flight where Nil Adula was waiting for him.

An hour later the phone rang again. Asil Nadir, now even more shaken and unhappy, was once more back in Hong Kong. Soon after take-off, the British Airways plane's second engine had also cut out and it had been forced to return. This time Asil Nadir did not attempt to carry on to London, but booked into the Marco Polo suite of the Peninsula Hotel for a few days. Two emergencies in the air on the same day, both involving the second engine of the plane he was flying, looked like a malign coincidence. Had his good luck disappeared with his father's ring? If so, his talisman was quickly restored. In Taipei, the missing ring was unexpectedly found in the pocket of his car and sent across by courier to Hong Kong. After that Asil Nadir's usual sunny optimism returned and he was able to make the journey home in his own plane.

Asil Nadir's eye had also lighted on a totally new industry: tourism and the hotel business. Many small and medium-sized businesses in Turkey were rushing to get hotels constructed in Istanbul and along the Mediterranean and Aegean coasts. The tourism business had little to do with electronics or fresh fruit, of course, but a holding group in London, able to tap finance and good management, ought to have a significant advantage over local entrepreneurs. Once built, the hotels would generate earnings in hard currency for the group. In Northern Cyprus they would also have far-reaching effects on the local economy.

Not everyone on the board was eager to see Polly Peck diversifying in this way, but Asil Nadir had made his mind up. For over a year, there had been talk of the company building a 300-bed luxury hotel on the Mediterranean coast, originally through a joint venture with Strong and

Fisher. Nadir was determined to press ahead with the deal, even after Strong and Fisher withdrew in March 1986. He began to explore the possibility of a management licensing agreement with the Sheraton Group for the project.

The Antalya Sheraton Voyager, as it later became known, was one of the projects dearest to Asil Nadir's heart. It was built just above the best beach in Antalya, with dramatic views of the peaks of the Lycian mountains 20 miles away across the bay. Several other businessmen had plans afoot to build five-star hotels in or around the town, which was regarded as the main resort of the Turkish Riviera, so Asil Nadir wanted to ensure that his hotel would outshine all the others. Antalya was also increasingly used by the Turkish government and some private sector bodies for conferences. By including conference facilities, the hotel would also be able to steal a march on others which could only cater for regular tourists.

On 25 May 1987, it was announced that Cementation International, a subsidiary of Trafalgar House, would be construction manager for the hotel. A mouth-watering prospectus outlined the main details of the project. It would stand eight storeys high in three wings, with a vast atrium. Below would be its own private beach, to which residents would travel in a cable car. Every room would be larger than normal and enjoy a panoramic view, and in addition to the usual range of restaurants, conference rooms and shops there would be extensive sport and leisure facilities, including a golf course and an international casino. Armağan Tekvar, Polly Peck's group architect, declared proudly: 'This hotel will be the first in a series of international leisure developments which Polly Peck is planning.'

With Strong and Fisher out of the project, Asil Nadir decided that the entire hotel could be financed from the company's cash flow. It would take twenty-seven months to build and be ready in the autumn of 1989. In practice things turned out very differently. The hotel did get built and opened (although two immediate drawbacks proved to be its lack of direct access to the beach and the fact that it had no golf course), but it took a year longer than scheduled. It was not until early September 1990 that Asil Nadir and scores of hand-picked guests flew out to Antalya to celebrate the opening. It was a fleeting moment of qualified triumph at a time when storm clouds were unmistakably gathering over the company.

In August, Nadir announced a new project in Cyprus. The Zephirus Hotel near Kyrenia had been almost complete when the Turkish invasion took place in 1974. It had been bought by an Arab finance group which hoped to turn it into an Islamic University college, part of

a broader Saudi effort to reclaim Turkey from the secular and Euro-
peanising orbit on which it had been launched by Atatürk. The Turkish
Cypriots decided to turn down the project – an Islamic college next
door to their main tourist resort might have unfortunate repercussions
one day.

Nadir then stepped in to negotiate a five-year deal on the hotel with
an option for another twenty years. The whole project would cost about
$1 million, with half of it paid up front. Rumours circulated on the
island that he could not go ahead with the deal because he was strapped
for cash – but eventually the deal was clinched. The Hotel Zephirus
was to become the Jasmine Court, the finest hotel in Northern Cyprus
and Nadir's main base on the island during the autumn and winter of
1990, from where he would try to grapple with the growing problems
of his empire before his final return to England.

At the annual general meeting on 16 January 1987, Asil Nadir admitted
to shareholders that there was an image problem with Polly Peck. 'We
have tried to address some of the criticisms and question marks in
people's minds. Today the problem of the company is just perception,'
he said. After the meeting, he told reporters, 'I think the company has
got to be re-examined. You can't keep looking at it as a one-product
company. It has become very diverse.'

The cash problem was still there. The year began with the news
that Restro Investments, the private company in Jersey which held Asil
Nadir's shares in Polly Peck, had raised £272,250 through a series of
share sales and purchases. According to a statement issued, it had sold
775,000 shares at an average price of 170.2p and then bought back
600,000 with an average price of 174.4p. Asil Nadir was left with 27.6
per cent of the total.

In April 1987, the company raised £20.3 million by a placing of new
shares – the largest amount it was able to issue without going to the
existing shareholders with a rights issue. The London arm of Drexel
Burnham Lambert, the famous US junk bond specialist of the 1980s'
boom years, was chosen for the placing of a large part of the new shares.
In April Polly Peck made arrangements for US investors to buy its
shares by arranging for dealing in its American Depository Receipts.
The move was welcomed in London, and the shares moved up to
234p.

After being spurned by the City, would Asil Nadir really be able to
market Polly Peck's shares in the USA, where the obligation to disclose
detailed information about the company was greater than in Britain?
There were precedents. Mark Ellis began to hold regular meetings with

US investors. Americans were now said to make up about one-fifth of the Polly Peck shareholders – double the level in early 1986.

In May there was a pleasant surprise for Asil Nadir as he watched the share price on his screen. Polly Peck announced a fairly strong set of half-year results with pre-tax profits at £36.8 million, up from £31.2 million, and the dividend jumped by 40 per cent from 1.25p to 1.75p. The market responded warmly, with the share price going up to 297p. Allowing for the dilution effect created by the issuing of additional shares over the years, this was just above the £36 peak which the share had touched in the spring of 1983 on the eve of the first crash.

Reports that Vestel was among a group of Turkish TV producers threatened by the Turkish Radio and TV Standards Board with proceedings for making sub-standard radio and TV equipment led to another flutter of excitement. But it was short-lived. The Turkish Ministry of Trade and Industry stepped in to ensure that there was no threat to production.

It was not only the Turkish market which might have been affected. In June Asil Nadir and Bush, one of the UK's oldest and most famous TV brand-names, announced a deal to market around 50,000 Turkish-made Polly Peck TV sets in Britain under the Bush labels. The sets had already received British Standards safety approval. It began to look as if Turkey was indeed turning out to be a new Taiwan or Singapore on Europe's doorstep.

Attracted by this exciting prospect, Polly Peck now began to recruit a new generation of managers with the skills needed by an international conglomerate. Perhaps some of the gloom which had overshadowed the company in 1986 reflected the fact that its management was over-burdened and overstretched. In the following few months, the upper echelons of Polly Peck were completely restructured as new talent was recruited from industry and the City.

Asil Nadir also brought in a manager for his private financial affairs and family property around this time. Elizabeth Forsyth, his account manager at Citibank, who had the Scots virtues of preciseness, neatness and a flair for organisation, was invited to take on this role. She travelled out to Cyprus with Asil Nadir and his sister Bilge and spent a holiday on the island, quickly becoming a staunch supporter of the Turk Cypriots – even though she had relatives who lived in Greece. With her, Asil Nadir seems to have had the jokey, easy-going and unclouded friendship which he found easier to sustain with women than with men. Bonds of trust quickly developed on both sides. Mrs Forsyth's loyalty to Asil Nadir remained absolute, even after Polly Peck had gone into administration.

Her arrival on the scene at 42 Berkeley Square, however, was –

typically – unannounced. One morning Aisling Daly found herself showing Mrs Forsyth, whom she had not previously met, into the chairman's
office.

'Excuse me, what are you doing here?' she asked.

'I'm going to be Mr Nadir's personal assistant,' replied Mrs Forsyth
proudly.

Since this was Aisling Daly's job title, the news came as something
of a shock. Was it possible, Aisling reflected to herself, that she had
been sacked and not told of it? Such things sometimes happened at
Polly Peck. But when she enquired, she discovered that Mrs Forsyth
had not in fact joined the company but was to head South Audley
Management, a private company which would run Asil Nadir's property
interests and private finances and act as the London liaison for his
growing personal business empire in Turkey and Cyprus.

The new arrivals at the top of Polly Peck brought a financial and
managerial sophistication which the company had not previously possessed. That helped reassure shareholders and the City.

Any executive who joined Polly Peck stepped into a new and sometimes baffling world. Few of them had visited Turkey or knew much
about Turkey or Cyprus, and indeed Asil Nadir would stress to them
that this was not expected of them. But inside the company, they would
work alongside Turkish colleagues and they would find themselves
frequently encountering Asil Nadir's Turkish staff, in particular his
bodyguards, Hasan and Niyazi.

But it was also a stimulating and exciting world. New opportunities
in the market, ideas about possible ventures seemed to flow from every
conversation. Asil Nadir was fascinating, charming and deeply sensitive
to the feelings of whoever he was talking to. And by now he could point
to a thriving electronics empire and several other promising acquisitions.
There seemed to be less to say about the businesses which went back
further. The textiles business was clearly in decline, while his fruit
ventures in Turkey and Cyprus were cash-cows which were best left to
their existing managers.

The next step was to raise additional finance. With the share price
now around 350p, doors began to open once more. On 26 August, Polly
Peck published details of its first long-term financing. It was raising
Swiss Fr.75 million in five-year bonds guaranteed at 6 per cent a year
until 1992 through Warburg Soditic, the Swiss offshoot of the City
merchant bank. The deal had been designed for Nadir by Tim Wood,
his new head of Treasury and possibly his brightest recruit by far, who
had joined Polly Peck from Capel Cure Myers earlier that year, along
with David Stoddart a little later, another talented corporate finance

specialist. Both these men understood how to tap the markets for borrowing, and for the first time, Polly Peck had sophisticated financial engineers on board.

The bonds would enable Polly Peck to go ahead with Asil Nadir's plans for acquisitions. All but one of the consortium of twenty-six banks – led by Warburg Soditic in handling the deal – Lloyds Bank – were from outside the UK, and there was a preponderance of Japanese and Swiss banks. It seemed a clear signal to London that Polly Peck was approaching the point when unfavourable attitudes in the City might no longer matter to it.

Less than two weeks later came another landmark announcement. Polly Peck was to have a group managing director for the first time. Anthony Reading joined the group in September 1987 as its first ever general manager. He had been one of several candidates considered for the job by the head-hunters and seems not to have been the original candidate selected for the job.

Reading's background was impressive. He had worked as chief executive for manufacturing and engineering at BTR, one of the tightest-run operations in London, and it was assumed that he was being brought in to lick Polly Peck into shape. In many ways, both Reading and David Fawcus had been appointed precisely in order to make Polly Peck work as a large corporation. But their task was not going to be easy. The intention was that Asil Nadir would hand over the day-to-day management of the group and concentrate on strategy in his role as chairman. Mark Ellis, who had been joint general manager with Asil Nadir, would continue to handle the company's external relations and administration. The shareholders liked the news and the share travelled up to a new high of 372p. 'The changes were quite good news for a company which had been run by a Turkish Cypriot and an Indian. Now you had an Old Brightonian and an Old Malvernian in their place. Just what the City wanted and understood,' says one stockbroker.

However, Reading and Fawcus did not step into a vacuum when they arrived at Polly Peck. They had to contend with the Polly Peck old guard among the directors and the senior executives. Anil Doshi was still very much in evidence and he combined a very quick mind with an intimate knowledge of the company's business which no outsider could hope to rival. Understandably enough, there were some personal jealousies and resentments.

There was also a more fundamental problem. While Tony Reading and David Fawcus were used to doing things in the way that they are usually done in large multinational corporations, the existing executive directors had worked for years in a different business culture: that of the small East End company with short lines of communication and very few institutional and financial controls in place.

Tony Reading stayed with the company as group general manager for two years, during which it succeeded in shedding its doubtful image on the market. But unlike Mark Ellis, who had rapidly become a trusted lieutenant after his appointment in 1983 and remained with the company until the end, and David Fawcus, who stayed with Polly Peck until several months after it had been placed in administration, Reading did not settle easily into his new job. Tempers were quickly lost. 'Within a few weeks, there was a virtual state of civil war in the company, between the old guard and the new,' recalls one Polly Peck executive from those years.

One reason seemed to be tensions between Reading and Tim Wood. The two men found themselves constantly at loggerheads over both small and large issues. And relations between Wood and David Fawcus were if anything even less cordial. Whatever the reasons, by the end of the year Tim Wood's position as treasurer had become untenable. Reading and Fawcus issued Nadir with an ultimatum: 'Either he goes or we do.'

Asil Nadir did not want to part with Wood, whose negotiating ability with the City had been proven in the Warburg Soditic bonds deal. He decided to place the issue on ice by transferring Wood away from Polly Peck to his personal property and management company, South Audley Management, which operated on the other side of Berkeley Square, at no. 24. Elizabeth Forsyth was a little disconcerted to discover Tim Wood on her door-step without advance warning. She rang Asil Nadir. 'He's a good man, find something for him to do,' Asil Nadir told her.

Inside South Audley Management, Wood was set to work on a series of feasibility studies on tourism projects in Spain and other countries. It involved a great deal of detail and a fair amount of travel which kept him away from London much of the time. It was hard work. Some mornings, Wood – an early riser who likes to be at his desk by 6 a.m. if possible – would get up at four to drive to the office. Sometimes in the evenings his wife Marian, realising he was still immersed in his work, would arrange for food to be sent round to him. 'He was a good worker and he completed his reports on time,' says Elizabeth Forsyth.

Below the surface, however, lurked some strong personal undercurrents. Marian Wood belonged to the minority of women who did not find Asil Nadir charming. She mistrusted him from the outset and relations took a sharp downward turn when she organised a reception at the Woods' home at which Asil Nadir was to have been the guest of honour. As quite often happened, he accepted the invitation but did not turn up. The Woods were infuriated and embarrassed. It was not the only occasion in Asil Nadir's life where a broken engagement damaged an important relationship. In the final weeks before Polly Peck's collapse in 1990, he would find himself dependent on the good will of a Turkish minister he had once stood up for lunch.

There was also the question of whether Tim Wood should eventually become a director of Polly Peck. He had secured a promise in writing that this would soon be offered to him. Wood was clearly at least as able as some of those already on the board and he was playing a momentous part in the life of the group by setting up a host of new financing arrangements. But any decision on that would have to await his return to Polly Peck from South Audley Management.

When December 1987 arrived, Polly Peck was still convalescing from the stock-market crash which had wiped around 100p from its share price. But it looked outwardly more resilient than many companies. Able to show a 22 per cent rise in profits to £86.2 million, Asil Nadir described the results as a record. Most of this – 84 per cent – still came from the fruit and vegetable industry, but Vestel, the Turkish electronics business, now contributed a profit of £9.2 million, double what it had achieved in the previous year, and it was able to point to an import order from the UK for 80,000 TV sets to be sold under the Bush brand-name.

Not all the news was good, though. One item was a glaring exception to the legendary run of successes. Russell Hobbs had slipped into the red soon after the take-over, and the Polly Peck management genius had evidently not begun to work, for it was still operating at a loss. This was something of an embarrassment, for Russell Hobbs was one of the group's new UK businesses where performance could be easily understood by investors.

On the other hand, with Vestel's rapid expansion, Polly Peck said it now planned to make microwave ovens in Turkey in partnership with Gold Star of South Korea. It had already become the market leader in the colour TV and video market in Turkey – a remarkable achievement – although, as it turned out, microwave ovens were slow to catch on with the Turks. Still, Tony Reading proudly answered that he expected the bulk of profits to come from electronics within a few years. Hardly anyone now remembered the disasters of the past few years – or the excessive profit forecasts which had preceded them. Had these proved correct, Polly Peck's profits would already have passed £100 million. But the company did now seem to be proving itself on all fronts.

A few days after the results were posted, the senior management was strengthened again. Stevan Breeze joined the board to run the consumer electronics division. Nicola Pearse, a corporate finance manager, became company secretary.

In Turkey, there had been a general election – the first free general election in a decade, representing a real hurdle for Turgut Özal and the Motherland Party. It was hardly less important for Polly Peck and Asil Nadir, who by now had firmly identified himself with the Motherland Party.

In 1983, the generals had banned all the pre-coup political parties from running, and though quite a few politicians outside Turkey seemed prepared to overlook this, ordinary Turkish people never forgot it. By 1987 Turgut Özal's popularity was clearly waning and, even allowing for the fact that his years in office had been a period of stability and relative prosperity for most people, his future prospects looked questionable.

Özal, however, had shrewdness and extraordinary good luck on his side. In the autumn of 1987, he held a snap general election. His share of the votes did indeed diminish, but he still remained well ahead of the other parties. More remarkably, with only 35 per cent of the votes cast, a quirk of the Turkish electoral system gave Özal two-thirds of the seats in parliament. Polly Peck could look forward to another four or five years during which the free market revolution in Turkey would carry on and business opportunities would abound.

By now Asil Nadir knew several members of President Özal's inner circle, including his son Ahmet Özal, a businessman who had worked for American Express, and Bülent Şemiler, a US-educated banker still in his early thirties. Özal was using Şemiler, ranked as one of his many official advisers, to reform the weaker state banks. Şemiler had acquired mainland Turkish nationality, but he was Cypriot-born and cared passionately about his birthplace. He and Asil Nadir became close friends and allies.

Early in the New Year of 1988, however, it was not politics but pizzas which were the talking-point at 42 Berkeley Square. Polly Peck unexpectedly took yet another totally new direction and entered the fast food business. On 14 January the company signed a ten-year agreement with Pepsico to operate an exclusive franchise for Pizza Hut in Turkey – Tony Reading explained that young Turks liked international theme food restaurants just as much as their counterparts in London or Tokyo.

The Pizza Hut chain in Turkey would form the first part of a new leisure division of the Polly Peck group, along with the Antalya Sheraton. At the end of the month, Geoffrey Tucker, from Celebrated Country Hotels, was appointed first chief executive of the leisure division. At the end of April David Marks, a Sheraton hotels sales manager, was made operations and development manager of the Pizza Hut Turkish operation.

One or two eyebrows were raised in the City at the Pizza Hut deal. Young Turks might have the same tastes as young Japanese or Americans, but did they have the same purchasing power? What was the size of the local market and how much profit could it be expected to generate? Wasn't moving into the fast food business in Turkey a step away from international trading activities which earned hard currencies?

Two or three years earlier, the move would have been greeted with real alarm. By January 1988, however, Polly Peck's image had settled down and the shares rose 6p on the day, to close at 314p. The *Investor's Chronicle*, which usually looked with a well-disposed eye at Asil Nadir and Polly Peck, surmised that Polly Peck might be a kind of Eastern Mediterranean Lonrho. Did it not specialise in classic counter cyclical businesses – cheap food and clobber, cardboard boxes and the like? If one thought of it in those terms, the case for Polly Peck became stronger. But this was not quite how Asil Nadir, with his passion for only the top quality in everything, viewed his company.

Polly Peck's rising level of borrowing was now also attracting some attention. The arrival of Tim Wood in the company's treasury meant that for the first time the group borrowing had risen sharply in 1987, from 51 to 74 per cent. In February 1988 the company went to the markets again, with Credit Suisse–First Boston arranging a £75 million syndicated loan in which seventeen other banks took part. In April DM100 million was raised in five-year bonds by Dans and Co., a German bank. In September there was another bond issue through S. G. Warburg Soditic, this time for Swiss Fr.125 million at a slightly more favourable rate to the company. Again, European, Japanese and US banks flocked into the syndication, though the familiar English bank names were missing. But this was still a relatively expensive form of borrowing. When would the moment arrive when Polly Peck felt strong enough to do what it had done throughout its early years and turn to its shareholders for more cash?

Soon after came more acquisitions, which looked modest but sensible. Polly Peck bought a Valencia citrus-packing complex for Pta150 million and announced that it was setting up a new French distribution company for fresh produce in Marseille. These moves were easy to understand: the company was setting up the fruit distribution operation which it had long lacked. Later in the year, Polly Peck bought fresh fruit and vegetables companies in the USA and The Netherlands, spending £6.7 million to buy Prevor Marketing and paying £9.4 million for Jas van den Brink of Holland. Later still, a West Coast company in the USA, Mendelson-Zeller of Fresno, was added.

Ian Walton was brought in from Hunter Products to become managing director of Sunzest UK, the marketing arm of the group's fruit operations. He was to work alongside Siggy Fees, the marketing manager, who had been running Sunzest and who had masterminded the group's biggest coup so far – entry into the East European market and a deal with Czechoslovakia under which Polly Peck supplied a quarter of that country's citrus consumption. Curiously enough, this deal, which was celebrated inside the group as one of its greatest triumphs, was not much heard of elsewhere. Perhaps the rest of the world would have found it modest by comparison with some of the other things that Polly Peck was doing.

Polly Peck was selling the best fruit to the best international markets and so obtaining much larger profits than its competitors. The trouble was that because Polly Peck was a wholesale supplier it was difficult for the rest of the world to recognise its fruit or to be sure just how much of the market it had in the UK or other North European markets.

On 24 May the half-year results for 1988 were announced. As always, turnover raced ahead of profit growth, rising by 83 per cent to £314.8 million, while pre-tax profits grew by 30 per cent to £48.1 million. Shareholders now had to contend with a very complex pattern of global operations, with businesses stretching from London and Rotterdam to Hong Kong and Taiwan. Electronics were now contributing £9.5 million – just under a fifth of profits. Russell Hobbs had moved back into the black.

Investors were encouraged. A re-rating of the shares had got under way several months earlier, but this latest set of results gave a further boost. Fears that Polly Peck was too reliant on the possibly risky and certainly little understood Turkish market began to lessen as the company claimed to be becoming steadily less dependent on any one product area or country. The share price jumped sharply upward again. The management brought in over the previous year appeared to be delivering the goods. Though the shares still underperformed – the company's profits and size would have suggested a share price of around 360p or 370p, the p/e ratio was now at a somewhat more respectable 7 and there seemed every reason to hope for more.

Throughout his career, Asil Nadir had always bought small companies in (more or less) friendly purchases. Sometimes he bought shell companies, as Polly Peck itself had been in 1980, to serve as investment or finance vehicles. More recently he had been purchasing small distribution and packaging companies in Western Europe, the USA, the Far

East and Turkey. But at the end of June 1988, it looked as if Polly Peck was bracing itself to make a hostile take-over bid. The apparent target was Borthwicks, a food manufacturer and trader which was going through a difficult period.

Within a few weeks, Asil Nadir had built up a stake of 4.65 per cent. Borthwicks was at a point when it was obviously vulnerable to predators. It had lost £2.1 million in September 1987 on sales of £282 million and had accumulated tax losses of £10 million. The latter was a distinctly attractive feature, for it meant that some of the loss could be offset against future corporation tax if its profits were to rise suddenly in the future. But if there was a predator tracking Borthwicks, it was not Asil Nadir. The rumoured bid plans seem to have existed only in the minds of market reporters.

Soon afterwards Asil Nadir did make an acquisition, albeit a much smaller one than Borthwicks. Polly Peck bought Joseph Le Shark, a small East End textile marketing company, for £3.3 million. The move was a curious throwback to Nadir's earliest times at Polly Peck. Joseph Le Shark was run by Joseph Kemal, a Turkish Cypriot businessman. The chance of a relatively well-known brand-name – popular with work-men – attracted Asil Nadir, but the company did not seem to fit very neatly into the electronics, food and leisure group which PPI had now become. When the group went into administration, Joseph Le Shark was one of the first subsidiaries to be sold off.

In two and a half years, Polly Peck's fortunes had turned around. Asil Nadir, now well into the second half of his forties, was one of the wealthiest and most famous men in two countries. There had been some heavy personal costs to this achievement. His marriage had broken down not once but twice, and nothing permanent had taken its place. A succession of girlfriends from several countries and cultures was not the same thing as a stable Turkish family home. Joanna MacKay came closer than anyone since Ayşegül to becoming his wife. She ran his household and received his guests, but they never married.

Nadir's life-style was now an incessant race to keep up with the flow of demands being made on his time, but he showed no signs of wanting to rest or of losing his zest for new businesses. He even began to dream a little of going into politics. After all, there was no obvious candidate to take the place of President Denktaş when he retired. The day of the Turkish Cypriot Onassis seemed to have arrived.

9 · Upheavals and Acquisitions

In London, the news from Polly Peck was good, as far as the market could discern it, and Asil Nadir was beginning to take his place in the pantheon of lonely but unassailable British entrepreneurs alongside 'Tiny' Rowland, Lord Hanson, Alan Sugar and Rupert Murdoch. There was just one strange thing about Polly Peck in 1988: for the second time in its history, it was changing its year-end from August to December. So audited final figures for its performances were not published until April 1989 and then the figures were for a one-off sixteen-month year which was not easy to compare with its predecessor. Nevertheless all appeared to be well. The group's profits continued to grow steadily in 1988. There seemed to be no political upsets in the Eastern Mediterranean waiting to ambush the company.

That at least was the public image of the company. From inside its headquarters at 42 Berkeley Square, things looked rather more complex. Throughout the year, two problems overshadowed Polly Peck. One was the very high level of its debt – much higher than outsiders tended to realise – and regular shortages of cash. The other was the permanent state of siege warfare between the newcomers and some of the old guard.

None the less, by the second half of 1988, Polly Peck's fortunes had recovered sufficiently – and its image was strong enough – for Asil Nadir to take a step which he had not been able to contemplate for several years. On 21 October, he once more asked his shareholders for cash, a sign that he no longer felt that they would take fright at such a move. It was by far the largest rights issue in his career to date. Polly Peck sought £133 million in a one-for-four issue, priced at 255p, well below the 317p opening price of the day on which they were issued to make the new shares attractive to investors.

The move was to a considerable extent the work of corporate financier Tim Wood. One of his former colleagues recalls: 'Tim had been pressing for Polly Peck to beef up its financial strength throughout the year. Indeed, he was quite worried about what would happen if it did not take some step of this sort.'

Asil Nadir and Anil Doshi had long realised that the unwillingness of investors to buy Polly Peck shares after the 1985 crash had left Nadir with little option but to turn to the banks, if the company was to grow. By borrowing small amounts widely, almost always from banks outside the UK, the necessary funding had been found. By early 1988, however, the extent of the group's borrowing was causing serious alarm inside the company. How had it been allowed to rise so high? Could the company survive indefinitely on such a high gearing without a fresh injection of equity capital to balance the bank borrowing? Where had the borrowing, estimated at £376 million at this date, come from anyhow?

Several factors seem to have been at work. One was Meyna, the ambitious fruit and vegetable export operation which Asil Nadir had been trying to build up in Turkey for over four years. It had come on stream much more slowly than hoped, while the investment consumed capital. So did Vestel, the other Turkish operation. To the company's corporate finance department, the Turkish subsidiaries seemed to be eating cash rather than producing a strong investment performance.

The rights issue would take off some of the pressure, and although it took the City by surprise, there was little sense of shock or alarm. The ground had been carefully prepared. Conscious of past criticism on occasions when he had not taken up his rights, Asil Nadir said that this time he would take up half his rights as a shareholder at a cost of £15.6 million, a move which would lower his stake in the group to 22.1 per cent.

Among the other changes which had been introduced in the company in the previous year was the hiring of a public relations consultant. Anthony Bennett came from Barclays Bank where he had been a public relations officer. His appointment – the first of its kind in the history of the company – was a further sign that Polly Peck was now a professionally managed corporation.

Like other large groups, Polly Peck also now had its own corporate video. In 1988, David Frost was retained as its presenter. It began with the famous toothsome Frost smile: 'Welcome to the world of Polly Peck – and I do mean world.' Tony Reading and Mark Ellis then guided Frost through the group's business.

At the meetings with analysts and the press to launch the rights issue, Tony Reading explained that the company was looking for acquisitions in Europe and America. What sort of take-over targets did Asil Nadir have in mind? The market recalled the 5 per cent stake in Borthwicks, the food group which Asil Nadir had supposedly been stalking since the summer. Its shares moved up 1p on the news. Polly Peck's shares dropped, but only by a very modest 7p to 310p, suggesting that the shareholders were no longer nervous about the company. Analysts in the City stockbroking firms quickly decided that the danger to Borthwicks was not too great. A glance at Polly Peck's balance sheet and in particular at its multiple of 6 indicated that it was in no state to launch a large hostile takeover. Perhaps there had never been any real interest by Nadir himself in launching a bid and the City press had misjudged his intentions.

Whatever, the rights issue had the desirable effect of bringing Polly Peck's gearing – the ratio of its debt to its equity capital – down sharply. It dropped from a perilous-looking 135 per cent, which it had reached in September 1988, to 60 per cent. Asil Nadir's admirers had always assumed throughout the miracle growth years of the early 1980s that one of the main secrets of his success was that he avoided debt and the high costs that came with it. When the debt figures were announced along with the news of the rights issue, several analysts admitted that they were taken aback by the extent of borrowing. Sixty per cent gearing was still a high figure, but much less alarming. 'If the expense has been funded by debt until now, that is only because the equity market has been reluctant to do the job,' was how the *Financial Times*'s Lex column put it.

By now Polly Peck's market capitalisation – the total value of its shares on the market – stood at £760 million, almost a 100-fold increase since 1980 and the take-over from the Zelkers. When its figures for the twelve months to September 1988 (a second set of interims since the new year-end was not until December) were published six weeks after the rights issue on 15 December, Polly Peck's pre-tax profits advanced satisfyingly into three figures for the first time, reaching £107.3 million compared to £86.23 million the previous year. As always, turnover shot up even faster, rising from £380.85 million to £705.42 million.

The increased turnover was said to come partly from the businesses which Polly Peck had bought during the year. Not all the City observers were satisfied. Even under its new management, Polly Peck was still very coy about giving clues as to how its profits were made, and there was no indication of what contribution to profits the newly acquired businesses had made.

Profit margins were said to have narrowed slightly, but Capetronics contributed £9.3 million – nearly half the price which Polly Peck had paid for it. Russell Hobbs, on the other hand, had made a loss. Whatever management changes Polly Peck had attempted there had clearly not yet worked.

A block of thirty-nine holiday apartments had opened in Northern Cyprus and the company said that the Antalya Sheraton Voyager, now described as a 407-bedroom hotel, would be operational before the end of 1989. 'Polly is turning into a well-balanced international agricultural group, sacrificing a certain amount of margin growth for the cushion of a wide spread of sources of product,' commented the *Investor's Chronicle* approvingly.

On this satisfying note, Asil Nadir departed to Jamaica for a Christmas holiday with Joanna MacKay. Perhaps he felt able to relax after successfully negotiating a difficult year. He did not usually take Christmas holidays at all. At 42 Berkeley Square the holiday was interpreted by some as a sign of his growing closeness with Joanna; by others as an indication that, now in his later forties, he was beginning to realise that he needed to adopt a slower pace and take more time for relaxation.

The next move came early in the New Year when Polly Peck bought Fruco Fructenhandels, a leading German fruit importer and distributor, for £14.8 million. This looked like just the sort of deal the market had been expecting Asil Nadir to make in the wake of the rights issue but it was not done with much cash. The German owners accepted shares for 90 per cent of the price, but agreed not to sell them until March 1990 at the earliest.

There was a clear logic to buying Fruco. Polly Peck was assembling its European fruit distribution operation piece by piece, though it was by no means the only food and fruit company to be doing so. The food industry knew that it was likely to be among the first to feel the effects of the single European market after 1992.

Albert Fisher, a rival company, had already become the largest fruit handler in The Netherlands, holding a third of the Rotterdam fruit pier. It had made five acquisitions in that country – regarded as the hub of Europe's fruit and vegetable business – where Polly Peck had only made one, Jas van den Brink. Tony Reading explained that Polly Peck's plans for expansion on the Continent had less to do with the coming European single market and the erosion of trade barriers than with its desire to cut costs by carrying out all stages of the fruit business itself.

When Polly Peck's accounts for 1988, which as mentioned earlier had been a sixteen-month year as a result of the change in the year-end, were published on 12 April 1989, turnover was just below the billion pound mark at £967.1 million and pre-tax profits were £144.1 million. The results were slightly ahead of the forecasts made the previous autumn at the time of the rights issue. Asil Nadir said that the group was now one of the top three European distributors of fresh produce and one of the largest TV manufacturers in Europe. It was now setting its sights on pharmaceuticals and cosmetics. The share price faltered slightly, but some City opinion was benign. 'Buy and tuck away,' advised the Tempus column in *The Times*.

Others seized on a curious feature of the accounts. The source and application of funds table showed Polly Peck's working capital had shrunk by £98.9 million, when normally it would have grown. 'The shares may drift again unless the company shows it is not relapsing into its earlier mysticism,' said the *Investor's Chronicle*. Where had the £98.9 million of working capital gone? 'Other variances', said the accounts. This was taken to mean the weakness of the TL.

Tony Reading and David Fawcus were well advanced in their work to set up the sort of management structure and financial controls which existed in most large corporations. It was no easy task, because the siege warfare between them and some of the old guard among the company's senior managers had never ceased and their opponents invariably had much better lines of communication to the chairman's office. But the two men considered that their mandate from Asil Nadir was quite explicit. They had told him they wanted Polly Peck to have all the internal management structures and financial controls that its competitors did.

David Fawcus had brought in Vi Jansen to put financial controls in place throughout Polly Peck. When the chairman was told of these plans, he murmured his approval. He was in fact generally receptive to criticism from his top executives, though the fact that he agreed to something by no means necessarily meant that it would actually happen.

In May 1989, rumours of a board-room row within Polly Peck once more began to seep out into the City. Asil Nadir was said to be now at loggerheads with the two senior directors he had brought in nearly two years earlier. The row boiled over in an explosion of ill-feeling during the 1989 Windsor Horse Trials, in which Polly Peck was a sponsor – the occasion was the sort of flamboyant gathering which Asil Nadir always loved. While Fawcus and Reading were away from the office, Asil Nadir quietly ordered five dismissals from the company. The most significant of these involved Vi Jansen, the corporate financial controller. On the face of it, she was one of the people the new-style Polly Peck International could least afford to lose. She was David Fawcus's main lieutenant and her dismissal sent tremors through the organisation. Why had she gone? Some said that she had talked too much and become involved in the maelstrom of personal rivalries at the top of the company. Others thought the reason was obviously that her tight managerial style was too much for a buccaneering chief executive, not used to corporate restraints and disciplines.

News of the firings reached Tony Reading towards the end of the morning at Windsor. Realising that he had been totally outmanoeuvred by the chairman and that he had reached the end of his career at Polly Peck, he left abruptly to return to the head office for a showdown.

Fawcus himself had suffered an even sharper humiliation. Not only had Vi Jansen gone, making it impossible for him to continue with the work they had embarked on together, but his secretary was also removed without him even being advised of the fact. He threatened to resign.

On 13 June Tony Reading made his resignation, delivered in a stinging letter on 1 June, public. The press was aware of some of the dismissals, and the fact that there had been a major row, but Reading still acted with remarkable decorum, and seems to have remained totally discreet at all times. He said that he was going because his responsibilities were to be divided between several people. 'My job is being diluted,' he said, and would go no further.

His statement was taken to mean that Polly Peck was about to introduce a tier of regional general managers in its offices across the world – Istanbul, Hong Kong and New York. It sounded like a fairly plausible excuse, yet it was not what investors wanted to hear. They had been hoping that Reading and Fawcus would turn Polly Peck into an organisation which the rest of the world could make sense of. The official version of the row was that Asil Nadir, feeling that he was not getting a full flow of information and worried about the prospect of the company growing middle-aged and slow, had decided to install six regional managers to ensure that decisions were taken rapidly and on the spot.

Inside 42 Berkeley Square, many of the executives hired in the previous two years were wondering whether they too should resign. There had been a steady stream of quiet departures over the last year or two. Was it sensible to stay?

David Fawcus, the finance director, decided to stay on. He must have known that his decision would be crucial for the future of the company. Without him, Asil Nadir would have been very isolated. 'We have grown to be a £100 million-profit-a-year company in eight years. Things have to change,' he said. Although relations between the two men did not get any easier, Fawcus's decision to stay was a major coup for Asil Nadir. Had Fawcus gone, much of the credibility which had been built up in the company since 1986 would have been destroyed, leaving the way open to another run on Polly Peck's share price.

Tony Reading moved on to become managing director of Pepe, a jeans manufacturer, and then the divisional manager of a large PLC. 'I am attracted by the prospect of a quality company which is going places,' he told the *Daily Telegraph*, adding loyally, 'I enjoyed my two years at Polly Peck and I still have some shares in the company.'

Now Asil Nadir arranged a further injection of executive talent from ıside, recruited as usual through head-hunters who were told that ıly the best-quality personnel would do: a three-man business support group was set up under Mark Ellis, consisting of Dominick Henry, the former general manager of BP's operations in Turkey; Donald McNaughton, who had worked in Unilever, Thorn–EMI, and Grand Metropolitan; and David Tanner, who was leaving the Beecham Group after thirteen years. 42 Berkeley Square did not appear to be sinking back into the isolated state it had been in before Tony Reading arrived.

All the same, discussion of the new network of regional managers did give cause for thought. Even some of Polly Peck's fans had long wondered where the management of the company was. Take the Istanbul office: it was directing on the spot operations such as Meyna, Vestel and Niksar, which already contributed much of the group's profits and whose role was expected to rise steadily in the months and years ahead. How did Polly Peck's management work in Istanbul? It was a question that management consultants and journalists would sometimes ask each other. Was there a visible chief lieutenant co-ordinating all the operations and reporting directly to Asil Nadir – or were things run from London down the telephone lines? Could a company work that way and remain super-efficient?

The answer was that in the early days many decisions were indeed taken over the telephone or simply waited for Asil Nadir's next visit to Istanbul. In London, executives at headquarters often felt they knew little or nothing about the activities of many of the subsidiaries or even how much money they made. All lines of communication ran through Asil Nadir. But as some individual subsidiaries took root, strong chief executives emerged. Vestel achieved a great deal of autonomy under Tahsin Karan. The same was true to a degree of the Meyna fruit and vegetable trading company, headed by Fahrettin Otluoğlu. Later still, Fahri Görgülü, a retired provincial governor and former head of the Turkish police force, became a virtual vice-regent for Asil Nadir in Turkey in his publishing and private business empire. Görgülü was also important inside Polly Peck as the chairman of Meyna. On the other side of the world, the same applied to the Far Eastern electronic subsidiaries where Norbert Wirsching played the leading role.

But much of this management pattern had sprung up without planning. Broadly speaking, it was now becoming possible to separate the business into two: the autonomous corporations run by strong managers and those that depended on a constant flow of ideas and orders from Asil Nadir himself.

In either case, which way was the group travelling? It was already known to those working in Berkeley Square that Asil Nadir was hoping to take it private again. He thought increasingly of shifting the group's headquarters to Geneva – conveniently midway between London and Istanbul – and living most of the year there. As a non-resident, he would still be able to visit London for two working days most weeks. He would also be able to tap equity capital in other markets: Switzerland, New York and perhaps Tokyo. The deal would probably have to be financed by some disposals to finance the rest, but Asil Nadir could probably live with that.

Word of this idea had leaked out to the City where stockbrokers began to joke that this time around, Nadir might not be unhappy at a falling share price, indeed it would be an essential condition of a management buy-out. But why should he want a buy-out anyway? 'Because London hates him and has not recognised his achievements. He wants to turn his back on it,' responded his admirers. They pointed out that the shares – now at 279p – were selling on six times prospective earnings for 1989. 'That is absurdly low,' wrote Michael Walters in the *Daily Mail* on 1 July 1989. 'No wonder Mr Nadir grows impatient.' He added, 'Old worries about unstable Middle Eastern economies and currencies no longer hold good . . . The Nadir way works – and keeps on working.' Walters thought that if there was a management buy-out, a price of 400p would be generous. He pointed out that the buy-out could be triggered any day if Nadir bought enough stock to take him to the 29.9 per cent at which he would be legally obliged to make an offer to buy the rest of the company.

In any case, a buy-out of a group with a market value of more than £700 million would be an enormous undertaking. All the other shareholders would have to be bought out, and at the same time Polly Peck would also have to refinance all its borrowing. Asil Nadir was eager for the buy-out to go through as soon as possible, but when those around him, particularly Tim Wood, pointed out how much extra cash he would need to refinance the company's existing debt burden, he agreed that there was no option but to wait. The ideal setting for a buy-out would be one in which the share price was low or stagnant, but when one or more of the larger subsidiaries was in shape to be sold off.

The break with Tony Reading did not affect Asil Nadir's main declared plan for that summer: getting Polly Peck's shares listed on the Swiss Stock Exchanges in Basle, Geneva, and Zurich. For years he had wanted the company's shares to be traded outside the UK. Banks in Europe and North America were more favourable to him. His expectation was that shareholders in these countries would be more enthusiastic about Polly Peck than British investors.

In 1987, he had been able to take the first step in that direction by allowing company paper to be traded in the USA. There had been six bond issues in the Swiss market since 1989. The initial placing of the shares on the Swiss market in the summer of 1988 was cautious. S. G. Warburg Soditic managed and underwrote a placing of 2.5m – 1 per cent of PPI's total share capital.

The main decision, however, that Asil Nadir had to make during these weeks was who, if anyone, should succeed Tony Reading as general manager. Reading had said publicly that his job was about to be diluted. As things turned out, Asil Nadir planned not to dilute it but to break it up. At the end of August, he revealed that Reading's functions would be divided between the four chief executives of the Polly Peck's food, textiles, electronics and leisure divisions.

Radar Reshad, who had advised Asil Nadir to go into the citrus business a decade earlier, was made head of the food division; Joe Harris was placed in charge of textiles; Norbert Wirsching was appointed head of electronics; and Tahsin Karan took over leisure. Whether Karan was happy to be moved sideways was doubtful, but in practice he remained in charge of the electronics operations in Turkey. Similarly, Wirsching's role was confined mainly to the Far East: his appointment as group electronics overlord never became a reality. In fact there were already some signs that Polly Peck's two electronic empires, Vestel in Turkey and Capetronics in the Far East, were at least as likely to compete against each other as they were to complement each other's activities.

At the same time the group created a new corporate development group to be headed by Mark Ellis, who had been running Polly Peck's American operations for the previous year. The changes were announced by Tim Wood, who had briefly become a high-profile figure in the group. In the aftermath of Tony Reading's departure, Asil Nadir had brought Wood back from South Audley Management to become head of the investor relations department, and the press reported that he would soon become a director. This looked like a rebuff to David Fawcus, who had been responsible for Wood's original departure.

Back in the plush surroundings of 42 Berkeley Square, however, Wood no longer felt as happy about working at Polly Peck as he once had done. He was uneasy about the group's borrowing and foreign exchange losses and in conversations with colleagues he let his worries become known.

Whenever criticism of this sort was heard within the building, it almost always became known to Asil Nadir very quickly and would be followed by an unpleasant discussion in his office, with accusations of disloyalty. Wood's remarks, made one afternoon in the boardroom, were followed by an angry confrontation with Nadir.

The appointments of managers, mostly old faces, could not disguise the fact that Polly Peck had become a one-man band again. But perhaps it did not matter. Inside the company, Asil Nadir and his advisers were aware that they were within days of pulling off a masterstroke.

Their moment came on 7 September 1989. Asil Nadir announced that Polly Peck had bought the Del Monte fruit businesses, the biggest brand-name in the fruit industry. The deal was instantly applauded as the greatest triumph of his career and it brought him, at least temporarily, the recognition and acclaim in the City which he had always longed for, as well as wiping out memories of Tony Reading's departure.

The announcement had been preceded by several days of rumour on the Stock Exchange. The whisper was that Polly Peck was about to make a big acquisition, but the market was not encouraged. Polly Peck had been mentioned among the more remote possibilities as a buyer for Del Monte, but the business as a whole seemed too large. It would draw Polly Peck into borrowings that it could not afford: the share price sagged a little in anticipation.

Another school of thought had it that Polly Peck was about to take a minority stake in Lonrho. Had Asil Nadir not always said that there were immense business possibilities in sub-Saharan Africa? There had long been attempts to compare Polly Peck and Lonrho as overseas traders, but this speculation had proved false. All else apart, Asil Nadir and 'Tiny' Rowland would not have made a plausible working team. And Rowland was also, of course, the owner of the *Observer*, the paper which had seared its way into Polly Peck's corporate memory with its salvoes against the group in 1983 and afterwards.

Del Monte Fresh Fruit had come on the market in February 1989 in the wake of Kohlberg Kravis Roberts' [KKR's] epic $25 billion take-over of RJR Nabisco. KKR's plan was to help finance the largest takeover in history; to Asil Nadir, it seemed the opportunity of the century.

Del Monte Fresh Fruit was the largest distributor of fresh pineapples in the world and the third largest distributor of bananas. In 1988 it sold more than a million tons of bananas and 275,000 tons of fresh pineapples, mostly in the USA and the countries of the Pacific rim, making a trading profit of £79 million on sales of £382 million. When KKR placed it on the market, the company had hoped to sell Del Monte as a single unit, combining both its fresh and processed fruit activities expecting to make $1.5 billion. Asil Nadir, at least for a time, thought that Polly Peck might be able to buy both.

For there were some arguments against buying the fresh fruit business alone. More than 85 per cent of the profits came from bananas: growing, shipping and distributing them. But it was agreed that this business had matured. Its profits had peaked in 1986 and Del Monte depended heavily on three countries – Costa Rica, Guatemala, and the Philippines. It was vulnerable to competition from elsewhere.

Against that there was the expectation that Polly Peck fruit sold with the Del Monte label on it, and perhaps distributed directly by the company, would bring much higher profits. The benefits did not stop there. The injection of highly skilled management that would come with Del Monte was also very welcome to City opinion. So if some Del Monte executives were given jobs at the top of Polly Peck, the market would be pleased.

Polly Peck had been steadily pushing its way into North America, even before Del Monte. The previous spring, there had been the purchase of Prevor and Mendelson Zeller. Del Monte would be a very much bigger operation and there was no way of acquiring it without borrowing heavily. Indeed, in the early stages, Asil Nadir hoped to be able to buy the entire Del Monte business. Tim Wood, in a series of intense arguments, gradually persuaded him that the company could not raise the finance to do this. But in June, David Fawcus, spent a day with the management of Del Monte's businesses, and discussed a preliminary bid for both the fresh and processed fruit activities. The following month, once Polly Peck was definitely on the short-list (there were reputed to be seven other serious bidders), David Fawcus flew out to Central America to visit the Del Monte plantations and factories.

A purchase would give Polly Peck not only a thriving business, but, more importantly, a supermarket brand-name – something it had always lacked. That depended on Polly Peck being able to persuade KKR to sell them the fresh fruit business without the processed fruit side, while allowing the British company to retain the Del Monte brand-name for the fresh fruit. Del Monte sold about 60 per cent of its produce direct to supermarkets. If it could by-pass the wholesaler, why should Polly Peck not do likewise? Fruit distributors in the UK and Western Europe were finding the going increasingly tough. Retailers – mainly the giant supermarket chains – were getting larger and larger and so better able to impose their terms on suppliers. They demanded ever-higher quality and certain technical improvements such as control of the temperature at which the fruit was stored throughout the distribution operation.

The problem for Asil Nadir and his advisers was that the fresh fruit business alone would cost somewhere between $800 million and $1 billion, certainly more than the company could afford at that time. Polly Peck was already heavily indebted. Bank borrowing by itself would not be possible on that scale. But it was less than a year since the group's last rights issue and it had given shareholders a clear undertaking not to approach them for another cash call for several years. How would the market react if Asil Nadir now went back and asked for cash?

Early in August Credit Suisse–First Boston, a bank which had lent regularly to Polly Peck over the past three years, signalled that it would be able to arrange a £350 million loan. The balance would have to come from a rights issue. The deadline for submitting bids was Tuesday 15 August. As the closing date drew near, the Polly Peck negotiators began to detect signs of nervousness in KKR and to interpret this as meaning that they were the strongest contender. Other possible bidders were thought to include Castle and Cooke Inc., the US company which sold pineapples under the Dole brand, and United Brands Co. with the famous Chiquita brand. But these contenders faced a snag which Polly Peck did not: US anti-trust laws.

David Fawcus, Mark Ellis and Anil Doshi – now described as the group's merger chief – flew to New York on 14 August for a round of talks at the offices of Simpson Thatcher, the law firm which represented KKR. After four and a half days of negotiations, the deal was clinched. Del Monte Fresh Fruit would be added to the Polly Peck empire for £557 million ($875 million). When the world heard about the deal a few weeks later, it was universally applauded as a master-stroke.

It then remained to thrash out a detailed arrangement. One provision on which the bankers insisted, which within a year assumed a significance that no one could have foreseen, was the setting up of a 'financial ring-fence' insulating Del Monte Fresh Fruit financially from the rest of the company.

During the negotiations, Brian Haycox, the Del Monte Tropical Fruit chief executive, had asked some probing questions of the London company. One of the points which struck all observers was that although Del Monte was a much older and more experienced company, dominating its chosen markets, it had much narrower profit margins than Polly Peck's fruit business.

There was also the brand-name, in itself worth anything up to £250 million. True, it had to be shared with the processed fruit arm of Del Monte which Polly Peck was not buying, but there could be ways around that. For example, the two companies could jointly set up a third which would own and administer the brand.

Certain features of the deal attracted especially admiring comments. Asil Nadir had paid a $30 million deposit but it was refundable if the deal did not come off. The market had plunged less than a year ago and investors were still fearful of a possible second crash. Asil Nadir wanted to be sure he did not have to face angry shareholders.

There were also nine ships, refrigerated cargo vessels, included in the deal. Del Monte had ordered these for its shipping line, which already had thirty vessels, dwarfing the PPI fleet of only nine ships. When the nine were completed, they could be sold and leased back, reducing the debt burden by about $200 million. So although Polly Peck's gearing would rise back into three digits again, to around 108 per cent, it might not do so for very long.

A deal announced on 14 May the following year did indeed dispose of the nine refrigerated ships. They were sold off to a Norwegian consortium, and would then be leased back to Del Monte for ten years. Six would be sold to the consortium on 30 June. As a result of this transaction, David Fawcus was able to announce that the price paid for the Del Monte acquisition had dropped from $875 million to $640 million. 'It was a very cheap price to pay for a brand-name of that stature,' he commented.

One slightly unusual feature of the deal was that the finance for the Del Monte operation was 'ring-fenced' from the remainder of the Polly Peck group. Head office would have no access to any of the funds generated by Del Monte until all the loans involved in buying it had been paid back to Credit Suisse–First Boston. Capital investment was allowed, but anything above an agreed level had to be approved by the banks. No dividends would be transferred to the group from its profits and any dealings between Polly Peck and Del Monte Fresh Fruit had to be carried out on a strictly formal basis, allowing the banks a full insight into what was happening.

Two weeks later, on 25 September, KKR found a buyer for the other side of Del Monte, selling the processed fruit business to a consortium which included the Del Monte management, Kikkoman, the Japanese soy sauce producer, Merrill Lynch and Citicorp Capital Investors, for a total of $1.48 million. The news was announced the day that Polly Peck investors gave their approval to the purchase of Del Monte Fresh Fruit at an extraordinary general meeting.

Along with news of the deal came the latest sets of half-year figures. It turned out that the fruit operations which Polly Peck had bought in Spain and Germany were loss-makers and the textiles business was not doing much better, with profits down from £2.1 million to a mere £200,000, but overall the picture was bright. Pre-tax profits rose to £64.4 million, with electronics making £13.5 million. Capetronics had done particularly well. Sales of computer VDUs had doubled its profits. The star, of course, was the fruit and vegetable business. Its pre-tax profits were up from £37.7 million last time to £50.7 million.

All reservations melted away. There was the first rush to buy Polly

Peck shares for six years. In two days the share price went up 98p to
413p, something much closer to the level everyone said the company
should have. The p/e ratio rose to 8, still modest but definitely more
respectable.

But amidst all the applause, there was a small grudging note in the
Observer on 10 October. It warned that the Stock Exchange might once
more be investigating Polly Peck share-dealings made just before the
announcement of the Del Monte purchase and the £283 million rights
issue. Rumours of the deal had swept through the market on the Wednesday, the day before it was made known, and there had been a sharp
fall – 14.5p – in the share price, with large numbers of investors getting
rid of the shares.

If they had kept them a day longer, they would have been vastly
better off. Why had they sold? Part of the explanation was what
early reports of the Del Monte deal suggested: word of a new rights
issue had leaked out or investors had thought that Polly Peck was
about to overstretch itself by buying the whole of the American company. A less savoury explanation was that there might have been
what the market calls a 'bear squeeze', with some dealers putting the
pressure on unwary investors to sell their shares ahead of the good
news. But the article passed almost unnoticed. After the events of the
last six years, no one expected kindly words about Polly Peck from the
Observer.

With the acquisition of Del Monte, Polly Peck had taken its place as
third largest fresh fruit company in the world. Nor had the company's
run of good luck yet been exhausted. A few days later Hurricane Hugo
wiped out most of the Caribbean banana crop for that year and added
up to £2 to the cost of a box of bananas. Del Monte Fresh Fruit was
one of the main beneficiaries.

Seven weeks after the triumph with Del Monte, Polly Peck achieved
another sensation, this time in the Far East. On 27 October 1989, Asil
Nadir proudly revealed at a press conference in Tokyo that he was
buying a 51 per cent stake in Sansui, an ailing but relatively well-known
audio and consumer electronics group, for Yen15.6 billion (£69 million).
The Sansui take-over was hailed as the brain-child of Norbert Wirsching and his partner in Capetronics, who was himself Japanese, a fact
which proved an asset in the negotiations.

Sansui had been in the red since 1985. Sales sank steadily from
Yen35.5 billion in 1986 to Yen26 billion (£115 million) in the year to
October 31 1989, and a loss for that year of Yen6.4 billion (£28.3
million). That meant there would be a cumulative deficit of Yen13.8
billion (£61 million). With figures like these, no Japanese buyer could

be found for Sansui, and unless a foreign buyer stepped forward, the prospects for the company seemed grim indeed.

What had gone wrong? Sansui clearly belonged to the same stable as Japanese market leaders in hi-fi and consumer electronics. The company had been set up in the late 1940s by Kosaku Kikuchi, around the same time as the other Japanese electronic giants. Sansui began as a maker of transformers for radios and audio equipment, but in the 1950s it had entered first the audio and later the radio business. By 1961 it was listed on the Tokyo Stock Exchange.

In 1967 came a US offshoot, Sansui Electronics in New York and later New Jersey, and three years later it moved into Europe via Belgium. By 1975 there was a British offshoot, Sansui UK, and it went on to expand overseas, but in the early 1970s, it was plagued by union problems. When Communists in the union demanded places in the management, Kosaku Kikuchi, the company's founder, quit, and the company subsequently lost its sense of direction. Instead of building on its earlier reputation as a maker of high-quality audio gear, which meant moving into a new market for mini-component products and portable players, Sansui failed to widen its product range. Its sales and income lagged behind its competitors, and in due course Sansui did not have the cash to shift its operations overseas when the rest of the market decided that production in Japan was no longer competitive and moved their operations to South-East Asia.

Finally, Sansui was blown completely off course by exchange rate fluctuations between the yen and the dollar in the first half of the 1980s. It was less diversified than the large corporations and thus more vulnerable to changed conditions. 'We found we had lost sales and faced shrinking margins at the same time,' recalls a top Sansui official. So for several years, Sansui paid no dividend and tried a series of rescue measures. Five banks, led by the Bank of Tokyo, helped keep it afloat, but they could not be expected to do so for ever.

Some production was shifted from Japan to Taiwan, to cut costs. It began to diversify into new businesses, such as car audio production, industrial electronics and computer peripherals, and musical electronics. Real estate was sold, but it was clear that without an outside partner the group faced a bleak future.

'We were searching for possible partners because we saw great difficulty in making the turnaround on our own resources,' says Mr Koichi Enomoto, Sansui's deputy general manager. Several possible partners were approached before March 1989, when contact was first made with Polly Peck. The Japanese management of Sansui had never heard of the company, but they did know of Capetronics as a Taiwanese components supplier. Negotiations started in March and continued until October, although basic agreement had been reached by July, round about the time when Tony Reading was leaving Polly Peck and the Del Monte negotiations were getting into full gear.

The talks were the swan-song for Ryosuke Ito, Sansui's president, who was to retire in June 1990, six months after the deal became effective. Norbert Wirsching spearheaded the talks, but all the key decisions had to be relayed back to London for approval by Asil Nadir, though he took a backseat for most of the negotiations. Also taking part was David Fawcus, who impressed the Japanese as a typical English gentleman.

When the Japanese company began to examine its prospective new parent in London, it found that it liked what it saw. 'We were much impressed by Polly Peck International at the time,' recalls Mr Enomoto. 'The company had a splendid balance sheet, and I understood that it was one of the fifty largest in the UK and the number one as far as fast growth was concerned. We had no hesitations at that time about it.'

Sansui was a smaller purchase than Del Monte, but in a way it was comparable. It would give Polly Peck's electronic operations the chance to sell goods across the world under a well-known brand-name and through established distribution channels. It was particularly good news for Capetronics. At last it was going to be able to link up with an international brand-name of its own.

In Tokyo, Asil Nadir basked in the glare of TV studio lamps, enjoying the adulation of the media. It was his first ever visit to Japan and he was bowled over with enthusiasm for the country. He had arrived before the negotiations, conducted by Norbert Wirsching, Tim Wood, and Barry Buttifant, were finalised. Wirsching had refused to take any calls from him until the deal was completed, but Asil Nadir was, understandably, fearful of arriving in Japan to find that the deal had gone flat while he was in the air.

Despite a call from Wirsching saying the time had come to fly to Tokyo, Asil Nadir arrived to find that talks were still going on and their outcome was in doubt. There was another snag. He had wanted to stay in the best hotel in Tokyo, which for Norbert Wirsching meant the Imperial, the Japanese capital's grandest hotel. But there was a motor exhibition under way in the Imperial when Asil Nadir arrived. The manager recommended a brand-new hotel, the Royal Park, as an alternative in which Wirsching's chairman could stay. Despite Wirsching's hesitation, Asil Nadir graciously accepted the new hotel without demur and went out to dinner while Wirsching completed the negotiations.

At this point Nadir once more showed his resourcefulness. The previous day Norbert Wirsching had arranged that Asil Nadir should meet the Bank of Tokyo, which was Sansui's main backer. A courtesy call had been paid and all the proper gifts were exchanged in the enormous boardroom of the Bank of Tokyo. While discussions were going on, one of the senior Japanese bankers told Asil Nadir that he had been called by a reporter on NHK, the Japanese broadcasting company, who had disclosed that he knew all the details of the Sansui deal and would be going public with them the following morning. This upset all Wirsching's detailed plans, right down to the seating arrangements, for a signing ceremony in the boardroom the following afternoon just after the Tokyo stock market closed.

'Asil, you know what he is asking you, he is asking your permission to tell NHK that they can release the story. You may have to jump on him,' whispered Wirsching.

Asil Nadir was completely unruffled. 'Very well, then, we will sign the deal tomorrow morning at seven o'clock,' he told the meeting.

'Asil, that is impossible. I can't get a place or the necessary people together and it's all been organised,' said Wirsching with alarm.

'If they want to announce early, we must sign so that we don't have to deny the story all through the day until the afternoon comes,' repeated Asil Nadir.

A frantic evening followed of booking a basement banqueting room in the Royal Park and getting everything in place. The meeting was held even before most Tokyo office workers were at their desks next morning.

For Japan, the take-over was a national event. More than 200 journalists were present and the news made the front pages of the Tokyo press. There were welcome messages for Asil Nadir from the Minister of International Trade and Industry and the Minister of Overseas Trading. Fluent, charming, self-confident, he delighted the Japanese as he had never been able to charm the British on a public occasion. 'Today is almost an historic landmark in the relationship between Japan and other trading nations. The myths that Japan is not open to companies from foreign countries have been demolished at a stroke,' he declared proudly.

'The grim demeanours of Sansui's directors at a joint news conference here left little doubt that this was not the company's finest hour,' observed the Wall Street Journal's reporter, noting that Sansui had once been one of Japan's premier makers of expensive, high-quality stereo gear.

The deal was only the third ever foreign take-over of a quoted Japanese company. T. Boone Pickens, the US entrepreneur, had battled furiously to get a 26 per cent stake in Koito. So how had Polly Peck succeeded in buying a Japanese company when most other Western bidders had failed? According to Ryosuke Ito, Sansui's chief executive, the reason was that Polly Peck had made its advances with the delicacy that the Japanese expected in such matters. This was probably a coded way of saying that Capetronics played a crucial role in the deal, though it is true that the other two foreign take-overs in Japan had also been friendly affairs.

A less attributive explanation was that Sansui was something of a basket case, an ailing firm with which the Bank of Tokyo and other large Japanese companies had grown impatient. Mark Ellis assured reporters that the take-over was not a rescue operation, but it was hard not to see it at least partly in that light. 'If you find sound, healthy companies in Japan, they are not for sale,' remarked one Japanese stock market analyst drily.

There was some discussion about the Sansui board after the merger. Could new directors be nominated to it or would Polly Peck have to wait until there had been a shareholders' meeting? In Japan, directors can only be elected at a meeting of shareholders. In the end it was agreed that new directors would join the board in December 1989, in the interval between the news of the deal being made public and January 1990 when it took effect.

Meanwhile, Yen15.6 billion was injected into the company. From July 1990 Capetronics was going to be 100 per cent owned by Sansui and the real changes would begin to work only after that date, when the new group structure was in place. Sansui would then have two plants in Japan, three in Taiwan, and one each in Hong Kong and Malaysia, with a work-force of over 6,000, as well as subsidiaries at Freemont California in the USA and Imperial, a manufacturer of large TV screens in Milan. At the same time Sansui embarked on changes which were intended to change its market profile drastically, producing video recorders and moving from hi-fi into the portable unity market. The relationship with Vestel would take longer to work out, but Sansui already had links with Cyprus: it exported to the Greek south of the island.

Other Sansui shareholders – mostly Japanese banks and life assurance companies – did not do too well from the deal, but they probably no longer expected to. Polly Peck was to be issued new shares at approximately one-third of their quoted value. But the value of their investment went up sharply. For months Sansui's shares had been languishing between Yen600 and Yen800 on the Tokyo Stock Exchange. News of the deal sent the shares leaping upwards from Yen775 to Yen1,270, but it was to be a short-lived recovery. A year later, while the Japanese equities market was in the throes of a crash, Capetronics was eventually to be absorbed into Sansui as a subsidiary – which meant that it would remit some of its profits in the form of a dividend to help strengthen its new parent company in Tokyo. Capetronics would also have an internationally famous brand-name to use for the first time. 'A good move, but no more than that,' Lex's verdict in the *Financial Times*.

Polly Peck had a recent precedent in its history for this sort of purchase: despite having been the UK's best-known make of electric kettle, Russell Hobbs still languished under Polly Peck's ownership, and its famous brand-name had not been put to work. The same was to prove true of Sansui. The obvious place to use it would have been in Turkey. But there the Vestel brand-name was already several years old and had managed to achieve a reputation for good quality with local consumers. So there would have been little to gain from replacing it with a relatively down-market Japanese brand-name.

On the other hand, the Sansui name could be put on TVs, video-cassette recorders and microwave ovens destined for export markets. These were already being sold under the brand-names of other companies. And Sansui's engineering department and research and development could be harnessed for Vestel. This implied integrating the Far Eastern business with the Turkish electronics operation. Asil Nadir promised that Sansui would be given any capital injection it needed to enable it to become a top-class player in the global battle for the consumer electronics market.

Dominick Henry, then Polly Peck's business support manager, warned that Capetronics would probably lose some business with other large Japanese consumer electrical manufacturers whom it supplied with components. But the major downside of the deal was that it left Polly Peck with a vast debt burden. Total borrowings equal to about 125 per cent of the group's net assets. Had Asil Nadir overreached himself? As things stood, Polly Peck's profitability would also be partly eroded by Sansui's losses until the company was turned around.

One less welcome result of the Sansui acquisition was the need to raise even more cash. More bank borrowing would be unwise: Polly Peck's gearing had once more shot up to precarious levels as a result of the Del Monte purchase. Another cash call to UK shareholders was also clearly out of the question less than three months after the £283 million Del Monte rights issue. Instead, it had been decided that Polly Peck would place some of its shares with international investors, especially in the Far East. On 11 December, the company announced a convertible preference share issue for $110 million (£69 million).

Meanwhile, Polly Peck set out to turn around Sansui's fortunes. A new chief operating officer was to be brought in from Toshiba's consumer electronics division, and Sansui was to be integrated with Capetronics and the PPI operations in Taiwan, Turkey and Malaysia. On 22 May, the restructuring of the group was announced: Sansui issued new capital, worth £310 million, to pay for Capetronics and Imperial, and Polly Peck's stake in the company went up to 70 per cent. And a dividend remitted from Capetronics later the same year, helped push the newly constituted Sansui Group into profit, even though Sansui itself was still trading at a loss.

But was Sansui, one of the most notorious laggards on the Tokyo stock market, in fact a good buy? For months afterwards, Asil Nadir could be heard angrily denouncing the suggestion that the Japanese had let him buy Sansui only because it was in trouble. 'Gossip and hearsay,' he told reporters the following February. 'We don't buy things that people all want to buy and we don't refuse to buy things which people don't want to buy,' he said, promising that Sansui would become profitable again in the second half of 1990. Polly Peck had not got where it had over the last decade by listening to gossip and making wrong decisions. No fewer than forty new products would soon be appearing from Sansui, ranging from mini-stereos to compact disc players and perhaps even fax machines.

Asil Nadir had arrived in Tokyo at the end of January 1990, fresh from his holiday in the West Indies. The Japanese media were fascinated at the idea of a foreign entrepreneur willing to take them on in their own markets. Was he driven by anything more than bravado?

Not for the first time in his career, Asil Nadir emphasised his caution to the Japanese. He had bought Sansui because it would fit in well with Polly Peck's existing electronics operations, such as Capetronic, Imperial, and Vestel, creating a new global force in the electronics industry. Japanese investors were favourably impressed. On the Tokyo Stock Exchange, Sansui's shares rose again.

On 22 May, at the Polly Peck annual general meeting, Asil Nadir announced the next stage of its plans for turning Sansui around. Capetronics and Imperial, the Milan-based TV manufacturer, would join the Sansui group. In return Polly Peck would receive £30 million in cash and increase its shareholding in Sansui from 51 per cent to 70 per cent. Since Capetronics was strongly profitable, it alone should be able to propel Sansui back into the black by remitting earnings to its new parent. Asil Nadir said that Sansui was in any case on course to move into profit in the second half of the year. It was a matter of reaffirming his faith in the company and showing that Polly Peck wished to be a long-term investor in Japan.

In November 1989, Polly Peck sold off its Hong Kong textiles division for £38 million, though it netted only £27.5 million from the deal. The sale helped boost the company's cash flow in the wake of the Del Monte and Sansui acquisitions which had left Polly Peck with debts equal to 108 per cent of shareholders' funds.

1989 ended with two new faces on the board. Peter Compson became director of human resources; he was to play a key part in the events of the following year, as did Brian Haycox who was to become chief executive of Del Monte Fresh Fruit. At the end of this year, Asil Nadir was personally far richer than he had ever been before. Trade union researchers discovered that in 1988 he had been paid more than £6 million in dividends from his shareholdings in Polly Peck, although he was only in fourth place in the league table of tycoons making millions out of dividends, coming far behind David Sainsbury of the supermarket chain, who was said to have made over £17 million or 'Tiny' Rowland, the Lonrho chairman, who had received £9 million. It was even rumoured that Nadir was planning another take-over. Perhaps his next move would be to take over Geest, the Dublin-based banana group.

Stories also began to circulate that Asil Nadir was planning a demerger of the group. The parent company would remain in overall control, but there would be a New York flotation for its food operations, including Del Monte Fresh Fruit, while the Far Eastern electronics operations, including Sansui, were to be floated in Tokyo. In Turkey, part of Vestel could also be sold on the Stock Exchange.

In fact the Vestel flotation, which took place in June 1990, was the only one of these plans which was actually carried out. Meanwhile, Asil Nadir's purchases had brought him a degree of respect which he had not enjoyed in London for many years. But while the markets gazed at Del Monte and Sansui, much of his attention was devoted to ventures in Istanbul and Cyprus where a second Nadir empire, largely unnoticed in the Anglo-Saxon business world, was growing rapidly.

10 · The Turkish Empire

Since the late 1970s, the Nadir family had had their own privately owned businesses in Cyprus. Asil Nadir's decision to move into Turkey in his own name rather than Polly Peck's came much later. Turkish newspapers and businessmen tended to ignore the distinction between a large, publicly owned corporation and a group of companies owned and operated by a powerful industrialist. As Asil Nadir's profile rose ever higher in Turkey, he was drawn steadily further into its business life until in Turkish eyes had become one of that country's most powerful tycoons.

This was largely because his purchases in Turkey had concentrated chiefly on press and publishing, ensuring that, for good or bad, he had become a figure everyone in the country was aware of. He responded by lavishing a good deal of his attention and emotional energy on his newspapers, and on the publicity and controversy that went with being a press baron. 'The press bug has got him,' murmured one of his aides in the summer of 1988. By 1989 he was in discussions to buy *Hürriyet*, then Turkey's largest-selling daily, and it seemed that his share of the market might soon top 40 per cent.

Newspapers were not Asil Nadir's only targets. After the disappointment several years earlier over the proposed purchase of the Ottoman Bank, he had finally bought his own bank in Turkey. This was Impex Bank, a small bank specialising in foreign trade finance and investment advice, which had been set up in 1984 by a group of industrialists who, seeing that the small one-branch 'boutique' operations set up by foreign banks in Turkey were making spectacular profits, hoped to do likewise. Three branches were swiftly established, close to Turkey's main foreign trade centres.

Nadir's chance to enter the banking market came when the high hopes of Impex Bank's founders turned out to be wrong. The bank was renamed and new management was put in place. Asil Nadir seemed to have turned it around: in 1989, it made profits of TL3.6 billion ($1.5 million) on total assets of TL255.3 billion ($110 million). In the summer of 1990, the bank became one of the advisers to a new Turkey Fund, for foreign investors in the Turkish Stock Exchange. A year later, it was famous for a different reason. Asil Nadir had sold it in December 1990 to raise cash, but it remained at the centre of a bitter series of legal disputes in England and Turkey.

But the acquisitions which made Asil Nadir a national figure in Turkey were his newspapers. By the summer of 1990, according to IBS, the top consultancy firm in Istanbul, Asil Nadir is believed to have paid around $90 million to buy three of Turkey's top publishing groups.

On 6 July 1988, he had announced a much more ambitious purchase, buying *Günaydın*, a brightly coloured tabloid daily, renowned for its shrieking headlines in a newspaper world not conspicuous for sobriety. *Günaydın* had been ailing for several years and its heyday lay back in the 1960s and 1970s, but it was still one of Turkey's best-known newspaper titles, and although its circulation of 237,000, around a quarter of the largest-selling dailies, was low by British standards, it was a solid platform on which to build. However, the purchase did not come all that cheap. In Istanbul it was assumed by other papers that Veb, the company which owned *Günaydın*, must have cost Asil Nadir around $40 million. In fact it may have cost even more than this. 'Some other newspaper owners believe that this represented at least 30 per cent above what any [one else] would have paid, showing that he [Nadir] paid a considerable price for good will,' wrote IBS.

Having bought the paper, Asil Nadir then went on to woo readers, partly by improving its quality. There was heavy investment in new equipment: $1 million was spent on installing an ultra-modern fax transmission system. Top journalists were hired from other papers. To boost the circulation, the paper's price was held down below that of the competition, and circulation duly rose to a healthier 400,000 by 1990.

Buying newspapers in Turkey was relatively cheap by UK standards. It was a market that was easy to enter and a foreign entrant, equipped with international technology and media marketing skills, might find it easy to make headway against the existing competition.

In Turkey, the entry of Asil Nadir into the national newspaper market provoked both excitement and alarm. But it was good news for the Turkish premier. Almost the entire Turkish press establishment disliked President Özal, just as industrialists did, viewing him as an upstart whose economic philosophy clashed with the defensive nationalist views of almost all other Turkish politicians, right- or left-wing. *Günaydın* evolved into a loyal advocate of the president and his policies. For the government, the turnaround must have been very welcome indeed. It was the first time any Turkish mass circulation daily had come out permanently in support of Özal. Until then he had enjoyed the consistent support only of an artificially created new right-wing mass daily which was known to have the backing of an underground religious order close to the president's family.

Along with *Günaydın* came a miniature press empire with six regional dailies, another national daily, and nineteen publishing companies belonging to the Veb Ofset group. A statement from Polly Peck made it clear that the deal was being done in the name of Mr Nadir alone and not the company.

Over the next few years, Asil Nadir was to build up a substantial press operation, mostly in Turkey but also including a chain of local newspapers in the UK. The aim of the UK operation was quite simply to gain experience. Who knew what acquisitions might lie ahead? There was a moment when Asil Nadir had his sights on one of the large dailies, the *Independent*.

In Turkey, however, the purchase of *Hürriyet* fell through. The Simavi family then launched talks with the late Robert Maxwell and for a time there seems to have been a real possibility of a sale. Whatever the Turks may have thought about Asil Nadir, there was no doubt in their minds about Robert Maxwell: as everywhere else, he was detested, and a press conference on the *Lady Ghislaine*, moored in the Sea of Marmara off Istanbul, ended with the press poking fun at Maxwell's painted hair and his gruff attempts to lecture the Turks on the benefits their political leaders, especially Turgut Özal, had brought them.

AN Graphics, an ambitious publishing and printing operation in Northern Cyprus, was potentially the most significant of Asil Nadir's private companies. The company was set up in Cyprus and, like his other press operations, had no connection with Polly Peck, although, rather confusingly, there was an unconnected mainland Turkish company of the same name which did belong to the group and was later replaced by Mediaprint.

The idea behind AN Graphics was that a top-quality printing company, capable of supplying all of the Middle East and much of Europe, could be set up in Northern Cyprus, in the same way that similar operations in Singapore served the countries of the Far East. Among other things, AN Graphics could make a good living if it simply won contracts to print glossy labels for the Polly Peck companies throughout the world.

A 30,000 square-metre site outside Nicosia was selected and state-of-the-art computerised printing presses were ordered from abroad. Despite opposition from his directors, Asil Nadir insisted that the whole building should be air-conditioned at an additional cost of £800,000.

At the same time the press could be used to print a new Turkish-language daily newspaper in Northern Cyprus. Here again personalities played a part. The Turkish Cypriot opposition accused Asil Nadir and

his associates of backing the National Unity Party in the 1984–5 elections. In fact Asil Nadir's commitment to the NUP at that stage seems
to have been much less intense than it was in the elections of 1989, but
the accusation stung him and, once goaded into action, he began to
see a Turkish Cypriot newspaper as the best way of countering his
critics.

Why did he own these publishing and printing operations personally
rather than include them in the Polly Peck group? One frequently given
explanation is that the shareholders in the UK might have been alarmed
to see him entering uncharted territory, though in the past his admirers
had not reacted in such a way. In fact, although the newspapers were
loss-making, there was strong reason to suppose that they could be made
into active profit centres within a few years. The income would come
partially through advertising but also through marketing the products of
associated companies. The large Istanbul dailies generated money for
their owners by acting as the hub of marketing operations in a country
with a large population, rising incomes and growing consumer demand,
but a relatively undeveloped tradition of marketing for consumer industries. There was an obvious fit, for example, between the consumer
electronics activities of Vestel, and owning a national newspaper.

In January 1989, Asil Nadir moved further into the Turkish press
world by buying Gelişim Yayınları, a publishing group which included
eleven magazines, including a business weekly, an encyclopaedia, a
men's magazine, *Erkekçe*, and *Nokta*, a glossy political weekly aimed at
radical but well-to-do younger Turks.

Erkekçe was in bad shape. It had lost its place in the market a year or
two earlier when fundamentalists in the Motherland Party had persuaded Turgut Özal to pass a law obliging any magazine which might
be harmful to minors to be put in a black polythene bag and sold with
a heavy surcharge.

Nokta was a much more enticing prospect. It had a good income
from advertising. Fashion companies, car makers, electronics firms and
cosmetics houses all liked to advertise in its pages. There was another
and frankly political side to the purchase. *Nokta* had emerged in the
early 1980s as Turkey's military dictatorship had begun to relax its grip
on the country. It began life as one of a group of opposition magazines
and remained left-wing in flavour throughout the first five years of the
Özal government.

Nokta had frequently probed into areas where the prime minister
thought it should not go. When Özal visited London in February 1986,
he told an audience at the Royal Institute of International Affairs that
Nokta was not a serious magazine. It also got itself banned – the hallmark

of any self-respecting Turkish periodical – from time to time, and had various court cases pending against its journalists.

All this had made *Nokta* by common consent the most exciting development in Turkish journalism in the 1980s. Its founders, a group of left-wing journalists, had caught a change in direction in Turkish society to which the daily newspapers had been unable to respond. Young people might still be left-wing, but as a result of several decades of relative prosperity in their country they no longer dreamed of overthrowing the world economic system by joining tiny Marxist coteries – they wanted consumer goods.

None the less, the politics were important. *Nokta* was a prime source of weekly information on taboo topics such as police use of torture which the daily newspapers were not able to match. It also poked fun at the powerful in a country where irreverence had previously not been permitted. In fact it was the magazine which six years earlier had portrayed Asil Nadir on its cover as a cowboy-hatted Turkish-style J. R. Ewing, and the Nadir family's life-style as Istanbul's answer to 'Dallas'. Another of its best-selling numbers contained a cut-out cardboard doll figure of President Kenan Evren, the former general who ruled the country between 1980 and 1989, along with several different costumes to stick on him.

Selling the magazine to Asil Nadir, a close ally of Turgut Özal, signalled a change of political direction. But if it lost its political spiciness, would the readers stick with the magazine?

Here, some of the skills which Asil Nadir had used years earlier in other take-overs in other countries came to his aid. He persuaded the existing management of the magazine that he wanted them to stay. Just what formula was arrived at was never made public. *Nokta* remained spicy, but somehow from 1989 onwards, it shifted its attention away from politics towards society, sex and fashion. The readership stayed with it, more or less, and so did the profits.

Later in the year came an altogether new venture in the publishing world. Metin Münir, the Turkish Cypriot journalist who had worked as Turkey correspondent for the *Financial Times* and later the *Independent*, and as the BBC's stringer in Turkey, rejoined Nadir's entourage in the middle of the year. He now worked directly for Asil Nadir's personal interests rather than Polly Peck and, with the encouragement of Elizabeth Forsyth, began to work on new newspaper and magazine projects.

A more fundamental purpose was to launch Turkish and English language papers on Cyprus. *Kıbrıs*, a Turkish language daily, began to appear in the summer of 1989 printed and published by AN Graphics. Mehmet Ali Akpınar, a former Reuters stringer and one of the best-

known correspondents on the Turkish side of the island, was brought
in as editor-in-chief. A tubby, jovial man, Akpınar had a wide range of
friends and contacts among international journalists. He was also among
the staunchest of Nadir's lieutenants in Cyprus at this point, and
belonged to the inner ring of Turkish Cypriots surrounding him, though
his friendship with Nadir went back only as far as 1983. Ultimately he
was a Rauf Denktaş man.

Kıbrıs was launched a few months before the Turkish Cypriot elections. It strongly backed Rauf Denktaş, the incumbent Turkish Cypriot
president, and the National Unity Party (NUP) which he had founded,
against challenges from the left. Nationalist sentiment and self-interest
coincided for Asil Nadir on this point. The Turkish Republic of Northern Cyprus owed most of its identity to the work of Rauf Denktaş over
four decades. While Denktaş was in power, there was not likely to be a
settlement with the Greek Cypriots except on terms which gave the
Turkish Cypriots their own territory and political and economic self-
determination. The opposition parties would not be anything like as
strongly dedicated to maintaining the status quo. Some of them were
committed to a settlement with the Greeks and the early reunification
of the island.

Although the opposition parties tended to cloak their discussion in
left-wing political rhetoric, the underlying argument was that Turkish
Cypriots were Cypriots, not mainland Turks. The growing influx of
workers and settlers from the mainland meant that sooner or later the
original Turkish Cypriots were doomed to become a minority once
again in their own country, this time dispersed among settlers from the
mainland.

Although the exact number of settlers is a state secret in Northern
Cyprus, everyone in the north knows that it is in fact well above 40 per
cent – some mainlanders and Turkish Cypriots can be heard saying in
private that it is already above 50 per cent. As a result, the contest in the
Turkish Cypriot elections has partly become one between indigenous
Turkish Cypriots in the opposition parties and settlers who favour the
NUP, which is increasingly the party of minor officialdom and administrative convergence with the mainland. In Denktaş's view, there is less
of a special Turkish Cypriot identity than a Turkish Islamic national
one, shared with the mainlanders.

To counter the opposition, therefore, *Kıbrıs* and the NUP put out a
simple message: an early settlement with the Greeks would reopen old
wounds and probably mean the end of the physical security which the
Turkish Cypriots had enjoyed ever since August 1974. Did they want
to return to a life under siege once more?

The very strong backing given to the NUP left a sour taste in the island. Some ordinary Cypriots said there had been cheating in the elections, though no serious evidence for this has ever been advanced. Instead, the opposition parties felt that Asil Nadir, the one millionaire in the north, had used an unfair advantage and that the elections would in any case not have gone the way they did if the mainland immigrants had not voted en masse for Denktaş.

Metin Münir and Mehmet Ali Akpınar drew up the plans for the Turkish newspapers and they were approved by Asil Nadir. Münir would handle the English-language paper and Akpınar the Turkish one. English staff were to be recruited, as Münir wanted an English editor. Thirty journalists were interviewed before a suitable person was chosen. There was a training programme for Turkish Cypriots selected to work on the paper.

The paper was launched at a reception attended by 1,000 guests – a vast number for Northern Cyprus. Asil Nadir was not present, however. He seems to have decided to stay away after hearing that a last-minute technical hitch had made it doubtful whether copies would actually roll off the printing presses at all that day, so instead Safiye Nadir, Elizabeth Forsyth and Bruce Matthews, Asil's adviser on press affairs, presided. They held their breath, uncertain for the first hour of the reception whether President Denktaş and the other guests would get copies of the paper. But after an hour *Kıbrıs*'s commemorative supplement for the paper's first issue arrived, followed an hour later by the newspaper itself. Behind the scenes there were gasps of relief. Most of the previous twenty-four hours had been taken up with efforts to get a broken component in the printing press mended. Nadir's private plane had to be despatched at 4 a.m. from Istanbul to The Netherlands to obtain a new component, and meanwhile a Turkish engineer had tried to improvise a replacement.

Setting up the newspaper was a slow process and getting the printing equipment to the island took much longer than hiring people. In the interim an entire new Nadir publication was born. Elizabeth Forsyth and Metin Münir decided to establish a new English-language glossy magazine, to be published by the end of 1988, which would reflect the cultural life of Turkey and Northern Cyprus. The magazine, called *Turquoise*, ranged across the world of fashions, antiques, history, travel and haute cuisine. Was it a coincidence that it was given the name of the former Nadir home in Hampstead? No expense was spared. Colour separation was done at top studios in the West End. It was intended to promote Turkish fashion, gastronomy, interior decoration and archaeology, aspects of Turkey and Northern Cyprus which had not previously

reached an international audience, and puffery was kept more or less
under control, though from time to time articles appeared which
betrayed the magazine's origins – a sympathetic portrait of Bilge Nevzat,
Asil Nadir's sister, for example, or a look at the little-known poets of
Northern Cyprus. Contributors were mainly Western journalists or
travel or fashion writers with connections with Turkey. Under John
Scott, Münir's successor as editor of the magazine, the present author
wrote periodic book reviews for *Turquoise*.

When the magazine was being planned, the Turkish government,
anxious to improve the country's international image, had retained
advertising and management consultants Saatchi and Saatchi as public
relations advisers. Asil Nadir seems to have hoped that *Turquoise* would
play a major part in the bid to raise Turkey's image in the UK and
other countries of Western Europe. In a sense it was to be the in-flight
magazine for the country's cultural image on its voyage westwards.

In many ways *Turquoise* was a typical Nadir production, eye-catching,
expensively produced, but without much apparent control or fore-
thought, growing rapidly as a result of its ambitious goals and its consistent emphasis on the most expensive and the most chic. Asil Nadir
himself seems to have kept involvement with the magazine to a minimum, unlike the newspapers where his background presence was always
strongly felt, particularly on editorial issues such as Cyprus coverage.
But Turkish Cypriots took a special pride in their glossy magazine.
Travellers arriving at Ercan airport in 1990 found its name displayed
on the luggage trolleys. Educated Turks working in Western Europe
and North America in the professions especially loved it. 'At last I have
something about my own country which I can put in my waiting-room
alongside the National Geographic for my patients to read,' said one
Californian Turkish-American surgeon.

But he was not able to do so for very long. Like almost all of
the Nadir publishing ventures, *Turquoise* was a loss-maker. It kept few
accounts, but towards the end, when its advertising revenue from outside
the group was beginning to take off, it seems to have been earning
around £45,000 an issue while costing £65,000. This was perhaps
a relatively modest price to pay for a magazine which transformed
international readers' views of Turkey – but when *Turquoise* fell upon
hard times along with all Nadir's other press operations towards the
end of 1990, Turkey's semi-official foundations for promoting the
country's image showed little interest in keeping it alive in its original
form.

Kıbrıs quickly achieved the status of the main Turkish newspaper
both in Northern Cyprus and within the Turkish Cypriot community in

the UK. A clean tabloid with elegant lay-out and high-quality graphics, it had little in common with the older generation of Turkish Cypriot newspapers. Part of its success was due to the appointment in June 1989 of Bruce Matthews, who had been chief executive at News International, the right hand man of Rupert Murdoch, and had been introduced to Asil Nadir and Elizabeth Forsyth through Rawlinson and Hunter, Nadir's advisers. He was brought in to build up Nadir's papers and his decisions sometimes had far-reaching effects.

Next on the agenda came an even more radical plan. It was decided that Asil Nadir would establish a quality daily newspaper on mainland Turkey. Turkey has only one such newspaper, *Cumhuriyet*, with a slender readership base of little more than 120,000, even in good times. *Cumhuriyet*'s readership was left of centre, with Kemalist traditions that stretched back half a century and strong beliefs in government control of the economy. Was there room for another paper which would be broadly speaking liberal, but in a Western sense? Nadir was persuaded that there was and decided to embark on the daunting and expensive task of creating a rival to *Cumhuriyet*. Starting up an entirely new daily was ruled out; instead, in the autumn of 1989, he opted to buy an ailing middle-market newspaper, *Güneş*, which had been trading at a loss for several years, and take it upmarket.

Bruce Matthews decided that Metin Münir, the former *Financial Times* and *Independent* correspondent in Turkey, was the obvious person to become editor of the transformed *Güneş*. Although Münir had only limited editorial experience – he had edited Turkey's only English-language paper two decades before – he was a Turkish Cypriot with flair and imagination and was in regular contact with the international press.

The new-style *Güneş* emerged in late 1989. It wooed readers with lavish supplements and angled for *Cumhuriyet*'s readership by launching a human-rights page, the first of its kind in a Turkish daily, which broke long-standing taboos. For several months sales were at a low ebb, however. Competitors claimed that *Güneş* was selling only 40,000 copies a day. It was certainly making heavy losses, but as 1990 went on, circulation began to creep back upwards as *Güneş* found its readership. Brushes with the authorities helped win the paper street-credibility. Before the winter months were out, the paper had one day's issue banned by the Özal administration for writing an article questioning the need for conscription.

Not all Nadir's entourage were impressed by this show of independence, however. There was some incongruity in the idea of Metin Münir working in an organisation which had several retired policemen in its

senior echelons, for in his days at the BBC and as *Financial Times*
stringer in Turkey, Münir had been periodically harassed by the authorities who at one time had even begun a court case against him, based on
a news despatch to the BBC. A prompt and overpowering international
outcry ensured that the prosecution was instantly dropped, but not all
foreign correspondents working in Turkey in the early 1980s were so
lucky. Weariness at such harassment nevertheless seems to have played
an important part in Münir's decision to leave journalism in 1983 to
work for Polly Peck.

In the much freer atmosphere of the spring of 1990, *Güneş* and its
sister papers in the Nadir press empire were widely criticised in the rest
of the press when it emerged that orders had been given that journalists
working on newspapers owned by Asil Nadir were expected to follow
the 'national' Turkish line on Cyprus. Just who this order emanated
from and why it was issued remains unclear. The Turkish Press Council
– a fairly new and shadowy body – issued a condemnation, leading to
protest resignations from that venerable body by Nadir loyalists.

Relations between Münir and his ex-policemen colleagues were
reputed to be strained at times. Fahri Görgülü the former Ministry of
the Interior official and police chief who acted as Asil Nadir's deputy in
Istanbul and was also chairman of Meyna, the Polly Peck fruit exporting
business in Turkey, had a veteran civil servant's concern with detail.
Münir found the ex-policeman's emphasis on security and detail irk-
some. Sometimes it seemed that all the directors' mental energies were
being devoted to questions of who should sit on which side of Asil Nadir
when travelling with him by car, so that they could act as a human shield
in the event of an assassination attempt. And though Metin Münir was
strong on editorial direction and product design, he was not a hands-on
editor and he could be impatient. The clashes between the two men
mirrored many earlier personality clashes over the years in Polly Peck's
London headquarters.

The Turkish newspaper world had, to put it mildly, very mixed views
on Asil Nadir, and these were shared by some parts of the Istanbul press
establishment and the business world. Attacks on Asil Nadir began to
be stepped up in some newspapers and magazines and, from 1988, his
friends and admirers would murmur among themselves that he had
made a serious mistake by becoming involved in the press.

The strongest attacks came from *İkibine Doğru* ('Towards 2000'), a
radical weekly which had originally been Maoist and was permanently in
trouble with the authorities who were forever prosecuting its proprietor,
Doğu Perinçek, and attempting to sentence him to one massive jail
sentence after another. The magazine's purported exposés of Asil Nadir

went well beyond anything *Private Eye* had ever dreamed of. Beyond branding Nadir as the 'finger which stirs Turkey', the magazine seemed to have no incontrovertible evidence to go on when it alleged one dark thing after another against him. Its strongest attack seemed to be testimony from a driver said to have been formerly employed by Asil Nadir. His accusations, centring on mutterings of drugs and guns, were described as sheer fabrication by the Nadir entourage. They are also dismissed outright by independent observers in Northern Cyprus who know the individuals concerned.

A series of old-fashioned personal attacks on Asil Nadir and his family in *Sabah* was probably more damaging. The Turkish public is quite used to the spectacle of sparring newspaper proprietors and understood perfectly well what was going on. The root of the problem, however, may have been that familiar trait in those hostile to Asil Nadir: a sense of disappointment by Dinç Bilgin, the owner who had built *Sabah* into the country's best-selling newspaper in less than half a decade, at joint venture plans which came to nothing.

By the autumn of 1990, Asil Nadir had a powerful position in the Turkish press. *Güneş* appeared to be well on the way to becoming established as the main quality daily in Turkey, with a voice which was taken seriously. Circulation crept up to 120,000 (a figure which suggested that it was pulling level with *Cumhuriyet*). When Iraq invaded Kuwait, *Güneş* threw its weight behind Turgut Özal and his pro-Western foreign policy in the following weeks with two signed editorials on its front page.

Güneş's staff now included many of the most famous journalists in the country, but it had not yet moved out of the red, and when Asil Nadir's personal wealth disintegrated after the share-price collapse and Polly Peck's slide into administration, the flow of funds into the newspapers ceased. It fell to Birol Nadir, Asil's elder son, to discover a profitable niche in Turkish journalism. Birol opened *Fotospor*, an illustrated sports paper which sold fairly well and covered its costs.

By the end of 1988 Asil Nadir was already spending more time on his newspaper interests than many of his executives thought was good for him or for Polly Peck. Few people in London seem to have understood that the Turkish newspapers were not only time-consuming, they were also a serious drain on Nadir's personal cash flow.

Perhaps because of this, one of Asil Nadir's final ventures into the Turkish media was done via Polly Peck. By 1990 satellite TV was becoming big business in Turkey. Star-1, Turkey's first satellite television station, had opened – without formal official permission – in the autumn of 1989. It quickly emerged in the Turkish press that one of

the main backers behind it was Ahmet Özal, the president's son. Nadir
was not involved in this venture.

Soon after this, however, he got together a group of backers for his
own satellite TV station, Turkish–German TV, which, unlike the press
ventures, was to be part-owned by Polly Peck. The TV station would
operate from studios in Germany, but have many of its production
facilities in Istanbul. Nuri Çolakoğlu, a well-known radical Turkish
journalist, was hired as general manager. His career had taken him from
being a celebrated Maoist dissident and torture victim in the early 1970s
to a brief spell as deputy director-general of Turkish State Radio and
Television until he was howled out of office by the nationalist far-right
wing. In between had come a spell in exile in Britain after a hurried
departure from Turkey when the generals seized power in 1980. But
the station never came to anything. Before its first transmission had
gone out, Polly Peck was in administration and it was among the earliest
subsidiary operations to be closed.

Was Asil Nadir seeking profits or power and influence through the
media? Nothing in the way any of his media operations was run suggests
that they were expected to make money even in the medium term,
though his editors argued that the long-term outlook was bright. How
much money they lost is anyone's guess. IBS claimed that the annual
losses of Asil Nadir's printing operations in Turkey were estimated in
1990 at up to £20 million. Inside his own entourage, informed guesses
sometimes ranged as high as £50 million. Even if these figures are
exaggerated, a lot of money was being spent.

Costs on this scale could be met only through borrowing. In the final
throes of the company on the Stock Exchange in September 1990, it
would emerge that a good chunk of Asil Nadir's shares in Polly Peck
had been pledged against personal borrowing from the banks two years
earlier, at the time when he had been moving into journalism and publishing in Turkey and Cyprus.

Long before then it had become apparent that the Turkish newspapers needed better management. In the summer of 1990, a single
managing director for the Istanbul press operations, Mehmet Bayraktaroğlu, was appointed at a salary believed to be around £10,000 a month.
Highly regarded in Turkey, Bayraktaroğlu had turned around other
publishing operations and there were great hopes for what he would
achieve at *Günaydın* and *Güneş*. But he was not given much of a chance.
By December the newspapers were struggling desperately to survive and
Bayraktaroğlu and the new managerial team had been replaced by a
long-term Nadir trusty with fewer managerial skills but who was more
suited to this emergency. Fahri Görgülü took the helm.

Güneş's circulation rapidly fell away after 1990 and the departure of Metin Münir as editor. Starved of cash, it nevertheless managed to linger on until early 1990, a shadow of its former self, despite frequent protests from staff who said that they were being asked to work without pay.

Asil Nadir's Turkish press empire glittered for only a few months during 1990, although its achievements were undeniable. After the collapse of Nadir's personal fortune, some papers were quickly sold off. Others lingered on for months, with their staff waiting in vain for good news, including their monthly pay check. The better publishing assets eventually became part of the cat-and-mouse game between Asil Nadir and his creditors in the aftermath of Polly Peck's collapse. Yet for a while he had set standards of journalistic and publishing professionalism which seem unlikely to be rivalled in Turkey for some time to come.

11 · The Way to the Forum

Somewhere in the early scenes of most tragedies comes a moment of foreboding or a hint of the future, even if it is not always delivered by a doom-ridden soothsayer. The downfall of Polly Peck was no exception. Asil Nadir had his warning. But, like Julius Caesar on his way to the Forum, he took no notice of it.

1990 began well. As the new decade opened, Polly Peck was acknowledged as the best performing share of the 1980s, and it seemed on course for even greater things in the 1990s with Sansui and Del Monte Fresh Fruit on board. The share price surged upwards once more to 428p. The Sansui deal, giving Polly Peck 51 per cent control of the Japanese company, was completed on 5 January. 'I am confident 1990 will be an exciting start to a second decade of growth,' wrote Asil Nadir in his chairman's statement in the 1989 company report. Like other UK businessmen, he seems to have had no inkling that the market was about to slide into its worst recession in decades.

In such a climate of optimism, a vague warning of possible trouble ahead hardly bothered him. In any case the alarm signal came not from City analysts, but from Ankara, and whether it was really based on any serious information remains questionable. He was probably right to ignore it.

Right at the beginning of 1990, sources in Turkey close to the government warned Asil Nadir to prepare himself for an onslaught against his company later in the year. 'He took no notice,' says the former Turkish official who delivered the warning. Instead, Asil Nadir departed in January for another holiday in the West Indies, again accompanied by Joanna MacKay. He liked to take his holiday in winter. Holidays in Cyprus and Turkey in the summer always involved work, with a constant stream of people expecting to be seen and telephone calls to be taken. He had reached a point in his life where he wanted to relax at least once in a while. Perhaps, too, he was now a little more out of reach of the stern influence of his mother than he had ever been before: after the breakdown of her marriage plans for him he went his own way.

Nor was there any particular reason to take the warnings too seriously. Like any prominent figure, Asil Nadir received them periodically, along with threats. But his Cypriot background made him more vulnerable than the chairmen of other large companies, and he regarded threats of assassination or violence against him seriously – hence his famous bodyguards and the security with which he constantly surrounded himself.

He was well aware, too, that in some quarters hostility towards him was increasing as his power and wealth grew. He was now an important figure in the politics of the Eastern Mediterranean. Early in the New Year, his Cypriot entourage wondered whether he had not added the USA to the list of his enemies. Their fears were based on a meeting a week or two after Nadir's return from Jamaica with Nelson Ledsky, the US State Department official responsible for following the Cyprus dispute. Ledsky was doing the rounds in preparation for a possible international conference on Cyprus and hoped that he could persuade Asil Nadir that he and the Greek Cypriot president, George Vassiliou, were business-minded people who could do a deal. Implicit in this was the suggestion that Asil Nadir might break with Rauf Denktaş, the Turkish Cypriot president and his ally of many years.

The elections in Cyprus the previous autumn had been acrimonious. Asil Nadir's lieutenants had thrown all their weight behind the National Unity Party which Denktaş had established and still backed. After the poll was over, the Turkish Cypriot opposition parties boycotted the new assembly – as they still do. Most of those parties, and the newspapers supporting them, were hostile to Asil Nadir. There were small but telling signs of his unpopularity: vandalism against Polly Peck signs was fairly common in Northern Cyprus.

Under these circumstances, it was not very likely that Asil Nadir would pick this moment to ditch Denktaş and propel Cyprus towards a settlement which might remove most of the economic advantages enjoyed by the Turkish Cypriots in the last decade and a half: the orange groves in the north would have been among the first things claimed by the Greeks in any settlement negotiations, along with much other Polly Peck and Nadir property.

So Ledsky was politely but coolly received. Nadir's views were summed up in a position paper given to the State Department which stuck rigidly to the official Turkish Cypriot line of President Rauf Denktaş. Its author was Çavlan Süerdem, the former Turkish official in Nicosia who had been passed on to Asil Nadir as a political adviser by President Denktaş. In private Asil Nadir told his colleagues at Polly Peck that he was not opposed to a settlement in principle. He thought that one would come eventually, but it was still a few years away. In the meantime, he hoped to transform the economy of the north so that much of the inequality between the Turks and the Greeks in Cyprus would have gone by the time of the settlement.

There were obvious risks in adopting a hard line towards the Americans. The USA was a close military and diplomatic ally of both mainland Greeks and Turks. And although Asil Nadir was a close ally of Rauf Denktaş, he was at least as dependent on the much more powerful figure of President Turgut Özal in Turkey, who was a loyal friend of the Americans. His priority was to build strong political links with the USA as part of the groundwork necessary for turning Turkey into a prosperous merchant state.

When Özal had first come to power as prime minister in December 1983, he moved to reduce the annual subsidy from the Turkish mainland, on which the Turkish Cypriot economy had largely depended ever since the 1974 invasion.

With Asil Nadir to generate economic activity on the island, the withdrawal of the subsidy could be plausibly presented as yet another example of shifting a burden from the state to private enterprise. Asil Nadir and those around him were quite open about their hopes: another few years of investment and the Turkish sector would finally become self-sufficient economically and as wealthy as the Greek south of the island. This would mean that the Greek Cypriot dream of reuniting the island on their own terms would vanish for ever, although Turkish Cypriots sometimes added that it might also mean that a different sort of settlement based on equality between the two communities would become easier in a few years' time.

Meanwhile, there was a mild cloud over the relationship between Özal, who wanted progress towards a settlement, and Denktaş, who warned of its dangers. The nationalist right among the Turkish Cypriots warned continually that a Cyprus settlement could mean the end of the decade and a half of physical safety for Turkish Cypriots, possibly even renewed attacks by the Greek Cypriots. This message had been vividly spelt out in the election material which Asil Nadir's lieutenants in Cyprus prepared for the NUP, Denktaş's party, during the 1989 elections. 'By doing so, Asil explicitly identified himself as one of the obstacles to a behind-the-scenes deal over Cyprus. He was not against a settlement, but he thought that it should not happen for a few years. 1990 or 1991 would be too early,' says one former Polly Peck director.

In London, there were other signs of impending trouble. Early in January, Tim Wood finally left Polly Peck amidst serious bad feelings on both sides. There had been many departures from the company over the previous decade; Brian Handicott's in 1985 and Tony Reading's in 1988 were only the most celebrated examples. But whatever had led up to these departures, leave-taking from Polly Peck was usually graceful, with subdued final expressions of regret and goodwill on both sides, and Asil Nadir courteously accepting any advice he was offered. Severance terms for senior figures were almost always generous. As a result, the world heard nothing more about Polly Peck from those who left the company. Although Asil Nadir's defenders in the City believed that the press campaign against him came from disgruntled former executives, this seems to have been completely unfounded. As far as one can tell, the former directors of Polly Peck remained completely silent, and indeed to this day many of them refuse to discuss the company and the time they spent there.

Tim Wood's case was rather different. He left Polly Peck a disappointed and saddened man. He also felt uncertain about the way Polly Peck operated and was convinced that he simply did not know enough about the subsidiaries and how they worked.

Yet he had contributed powerfully to the growth of the company. Without Wood's skills as a financial engineer, most of Polly Peck's borrowing in the last phase of the company's life would not have materialised. The Del Monte and Sansui purchases would not have been possible. In the process, Polly Peck's borrowings had risen by more than £700 million. Hurt and upset, Wood withdrew to his house in the Home Counties, looking for a new job. He did at least have a generous financial settlement from the company with which to console himself.

Soon after his departure, Ersin Tatar, a Cambridge-educated Cypriot who had been his deputy, arranged another Swiss Fr.150 million deal on the Zurich Stock Exchange, brought to the market by Warburg Soditic with a coupon rate of 8.75 per cent, and due to mature in 1997.

David Fawcus now set in train other moves to restructure the bank's finances. The aim was to concentrate Polly Peck's borrowing – spread among sixty banks, in a much smaller banking group. Each bank would make up to £30 million available for three to five years. If this process had been completed, the year might have ended very differently.

One thing the group did not now have to worry about was its ability to attract fresh talent. After the Del Monte acquisition Polly Peck found it increasingly easy to attract big names. On 17 February 1990, it announced an especially glittering catch from the leisure industry. Manfred Nissan, manager of twelve hotels for Swissôtel and a former senior vice-president of Sheraton until 1984, arrived in the group. Was Polly Peck going to concentrate on the leisure business from now on? Asil Nadir liked the industry, partly because it fitted in well with his long-term ambitions for Cyprus and Turkey. The rest of the board were mostly much less enthusiastic, but they were not the ones at the driving-wheel.

Around the same time – February 1990 – Kroll Associates, the US firm of private investigators, launched a probe into Polly Peck. When Asil Nadir got wind of this, he and his entourage were immediately convinced that the investigation was another manifestation of Greek Cypriot hostility. Later, Nadir and his allies would suspect that there was an overlap between the investigation and some of the hostile press coverage which erupted in the autumn. Yet this seems not to have been the case. Later in the year, Kroll would confirm that there was indeed an investigation, but claimed that the clients on whose behalf it was carried out were a group of international banks contemplating lending to Asil Nadir. An investigation of this sort would have been by no means unusual. Despite these assurances, many of the people around Asil Nadir believed and still believe that some of their foes in the press were journalists who doubled as researchers for private investigation agencies.

There was nothing to alarm bankers or investors in Polly Peck's 1989 results when they were published on 29 March 1990. Far from conveying a foretaste of disaster, they contained very good news for investors. The rise in pre-tax profits was the greatest for many years: they had shot up by 44 per cent to £161.4 million, including a £2 million contribution from Del Monte Fresh Fruit – made during the one month of the 1989 financial year in which it had belonged to Polly Peck.

Half the growth came from companies bought during the year, and the average profit margin had actually slipped a little from 25.7 per cent a year earlier to 22.4 per cent – a level well above the industry average. Food still made up about half the group's £1.16 billion sales worldwide.

Interest charges had risen to £66.1 million, twice what they had been in the previous year, but this did not look unreasonable in the light of the gains Polly Peck had made from the Del Monte and Sansui takeovers. They had brought a formidable-looking mountain of borrowing with them for the group: debt was up from £255 million in 1988 to £850 million, which meant that even after a doubling of shareholders' funds, the company's gearing was still around 103 per cent. The total dividend for the year went up handsomely, from 9.5p to 13p.

The burden of debt revived mutterings among the sceptics. The debt level would fall, Asil Nadir said, to around 80 per cent after the sale and leaseback of the nine ships bought from Del Monte.

There was no profit or loss figure from Sansui as the deal had been completed only in January 1990, but Asil Nadir vouched that Sansui would at least break even during the year. That was to prove a vain hope. Sansui's losses over the next two years were destined to grow even larger, as the company was hit by the recession in several markets.

Come early February, however, the news generally still looked good. On the market, Polly Peck was now trading at 414p, an improvement for which Hoare Govett, the stockbrokers, were partly responsible: they said that Polly Peck was still undervalued. Later in the year, first news of a demerger of the group could be expected, and that would be a real 'kicker to the rating'.

It was announced that Del Monte's chief executive, Brian Haycox, would join the board of Polly Peck from July. PPI Del Monte executives had visited Polly Peck's fruit operations in Turkey and declared themselves impressed. A merger of the American and Near Eastern food operations was under discussion. By 1993 Meyna would have been integrated with PPI Del Monte.

Polly Peck itself was now the world's number three in bananas. Norman Angling, the British manager who had set up the Niksar water-bottling plant, was despatched to Madagascar to see if Malagasy bananas (free of insect predators, but small, pink and good only for a single day) could be crossed with other strains to make a variety suitable for British markets.

Throughout the spring and the summer of 1990, the mood in Polly Peck remained cheerful. Asil Nadir continued to be on the look-out for new companies which he could buy or lines of business to go into. There was expansion in the USA. The purchase of Standard Fruit and Vegetable (SFV) of Texas for $30 million, announced on 1 March, meant that Polly Peck now had annual fruit sales of over $500 million in the USA. Given that the company was now up to its eyes in debt, the purchase was something of an achievement. In fact, the SFV deal was typical of Polly Peck acquisitions in which no cash was actually paid out and so the company avoided having to borrow. SFV was paid through an issue of new shares which were placed with institutions and other investors.

Fruit, tourism, and electronics were not enough, however. Asil Nadir had always wanted to be in the automobile industry, and in Turkey Polly Peck was engaged in talks with Peugeot, the French automobile group, and the Çukurova Group, a leading Turkish banking and industrial company, to set up a joint venture which would produce Peugeot 405 cars, a relatively new model by Turkish automobile industry standards since it had come into production in Europe only in 1988. It was clear that the joint venture with Peugeot would have to move fast, as two rival ventures led by Toyota and General Motors were also under way. Turkey had a small and highly protected motor industry, but the new investment might eventually produce 100,000 or more cars a year, a scale which had not been seen previously in the country where total car sales in 1990 would be little more than 150,000, including imports. The venture that succeeded would probably not only capture a rapidly expanding domestic market, but would also be well placed to compete in the international markets. Was Asil Nadir now poised to become the Henry Ford of the Eastern Mediterranean?

During the spring, he negotiated a more personal purchase, buying Zeytin Adası (the Isle of Olives) in the Gulf of Fethiye on Turkey's Aegean coast, for around £1 million. The island was agreed by yachts-men to be one of the finest in the Turkish Aegean. 'You can't sail past it without a twinge of envy for its owner,' as one Istanbul yachtsman put it. No investment plans were announced, and it seemed obvious that the island would make a perfect holiday retreat for Asil Nadir and his friends and family. Just as Aristotle Onassis owned Scorpios in his day, it seemed somehow appropriate that Turkey's first internationally famous millionaire should likewise have his own private island.

Recognition in the UK seemed to have arrived at last. Asil Nadir was profiled in the *Tatler*. In the *Sunday Times*, Valerie Groves drew a sympathetic portrait of him as a businessman, living almost like an athlete as he paced himself against a gruelling schedule, as a connoisseur of the arts, and a patron and supporter of charities.

In this last respect, Asil Nadir's most famous donation was to the Spastics Society. He had sat at home one evening watching a TV docu-mentary on spastic children which touched a raw nerve and made him weep. 'I think it is fairly clear from the way he was affected by the programme that he must have known a crippled child somewhere in the past, perhaps in his Cyprus years,' says one of his entourage at Berkeley Square. A gift of £1 million to the Spastics Society was announced. The money was to be used to help build the Oak Tree Project, a £5 million treatment centre to be opened in 1992 near Milton Keynes for adoles-cents and young adults with challenging behaviour. News of the donation provoked comments from his enemies that Asil Nadir was trying to buy his way into respectability with gifts to charities.

Perhaps this was so, but the cynics tended to overlook first, that the Nadir family had long believed in making gifts to charities – an orphan-age on the outskirts of Famagusta was the earliest of a series of these – and second, that Asil Nadir himself loved to give things away and to push his generosity well beyond what would have been necessary to buy affection. He could sometimes be extremely tight-fisted towards employees inside the company, at least in the early years, but in public he seems to have believed – as many others in the Near East have done before him – that part of the point of having money is to be able to give it away in grand gestures.

He also gave money to the Conservative Party: his donations, totalling £1.5 million, did not become public knowledge for nearly a year after Polly Peck's collapse. The gifts were by no means unusual for the chairman of a leading company – John Latsis, a Greek shipping million-aire, gave £2 million, as did businessmen from as far away as Hong Kong. But if Nadir was hoping to soften establishment attitudes towards him by these donations – which some people interpreted as an attempt to woo favour with an eventual knighthood in mind – he was dis-appointed. Mrs Thatcher and her ministers kept their distance.

Meanwhile, throughout the summer of 1990, the market was watching to see what Polly Peck would do next, not yet realising that events such as the collapse of British and Commonwealth in May and a set of atrocious half-year results from the clearing banks two months later had effectively marked the end of the Thatcher boom years. As June passed, the market began to sense that any Del Monte flotation in New York was still some way off. On 8 June, Polly Peck shares climbed to 462p – as it turned out, the highest level they would ever reach – but within a week the market's appetite was blunted by new rumours. This time, it was claimed that Polly Peck might be thinking of buying Dixons, the UK high-street consumer electronics chain. There was nothing in the rumours, but they were sufficient to drive the share price back down to 456p.

In fact, Asil Nadir's board was pressing him quite strongly against more acquisitions. In particular, it was felt by several senior directors, including David Fawcus, the finance director, and Sir Michael Sand-berg, who had recently joined Polly Peck after retiring as Chairman of the Hongkong Shanghai Bank, that Polly Peck should withdraw from the leisure business and get a restructuring operation under way which would dispose of its leisure operations. They believed that the choice was between a massive expansion and concentration on the industry or a divestment of its hotel operations. A resolution committing Polly Peck to moving away from the tourism business was duly approved by the board during the summer.

Asil Nadir, however, was not easily convinced. The hotel business had proved highly profitable for Hilton and Sheraton in Turkey and there was plenty more potential for growth. It was an industry which generated a lot of hard currency and required relatively little cash to run once the start-up costs had been covered, and the development of tourism made particular sense in Northern Cyprus. Turks and Turkish Cypriots alike felt that tourism was more than just a money-spinner: it helped promote enduring good will and affection between a country and its visitors.

During the spring of 1990 Asil Nadir seriously considered making an offer for the International Leisure Group, a tourism company with its own airline, Air Europe. Other directors and some of his senior executives were horrified. They fought a hard battle to deter him from making such a move.

A slick presentation by ILG's American banking advisers was followed by a three-week scramble by Polly Peck to collect detailed information on the travel group. There were investigations into the market, the company itself, its operating practices, the ownership of its fleet of aircraft. Stoy Hayward did what was reckoned to be an outstanding job in probing the ILG accounts, and a leading aviation specialist produced a twelve-volume report on the company and its operations.

At the end of the three weeks, there followed a second presentation, this time by Polly Peck's lawyers and accountants and corporate finance team. Their recommendation was clear: buying ILG would be fraught with risks and Polly Peck should not attempt it. There was also a presentation to brokers at Standard Chartered. They too were against the idea, fearing that the market would react badly to the deal.

Asil Nadir watched carefully and nodded in agreement. For the first time Polly Peck seemed to be functioning smoothly, like any other well-run large corporation in which decisions were taken on the basis of professional analysis. And the advice was indeed sound. The following spring, ILG and Air Europe collapsed and went into receivership. But by then, of course, Polly Peck was itself in the hands of administrators.

The market knew nothing of these and similar episodes. But other rumours of possible take-over bids continued. No doubt leaks from the company sometimes helped keep the market primed about what was being planned. But most of the rumours on the market during the summer of 1990 do not seem to have fallen into this category and were merely irritants: they had an unsettling effect on the share price. Somehow life inside Polly Peck always seemed uneasy.

Later in June there was a market whisper that Polly Peck was planning a bid for Granada, the television company. It was not true and a denial was issued on 13 June.

Meanwhile, however, there was one flotation which Asil Nadir did intend to proceed with – but it was in Istanbul, not London. Vestel was now the undisputed star of the rapidly burgeoning Turkish consumer electronics industry. In a fast-expanding market, it had managed to overtake existing producers and drive its way to a 30 per cent market share within three years. These figures aroused some scepticism in

London, but they were accepted in Turkey, even by Vestel's rivals.

Most Turkish industrial groups closely resembled Polly Peck in that they were owned through holding groups, often controlled by trusts, which were dominated by first-generation entrepreneurs and their families. In the late 1980s, the stronger of these groups had dipped their toes in the new capital markets by selling off substantial minority stakes of up to 30 per cent – though never enough to endanger the control of the founding family. Vestel was an obvious candidate for an operation of this kind, raising the visibility of the group and producing some cash for Polly Peck.

Its profits were rising impressively. It had made TL30.5 billion in 1989, up from TL10.62 million in 1988. Asil Nadir had retained Impex Bank and Finansbank, a leading Turkish merchant bank owned by Mr Hüsnü Özyeğin, to handle the Vestel flotation for him. Only part of Vestel – its manufacturing and exporting end – was covered by the sale. Its distribution operation, Vestel Limited, supposed by analysts in London to produce considerably more profit, but which also ran the risk involved in advancing funds to retailers to make it possible for them to sell their goods on instalments, lay outside the deal.

On 7 June, the sale of Vestel closed oversubscribed. Just over 18 per cent of the company had been sold, rather than the 15 per cent planned, apparently owing to a failure of arithmetic by some of the bankers involved. This, the Turkish market believed, had not entirely delighted Asil Nadir. The flotation put a value of around £460 million on Vestel and it raised about $90 million. Roughly two-thirds of the shares sold went to thirty-eight foreign investment funds and financial organisations from abroad.

On 27 June, the shares were floated at TL13,250 for each TL1,000 share. But strangely, the Turkish market turned out to have almost as little appetite for Asil Nadir's shares as its London counterpart had had for most of the 1980s. Although the shares rose briefly to TL15,250 on their first day's trading, in the following weeks they drifted down on the market back towards their flotation level, to which they returned on 27 July, exactly a month after the float. It was a fall of over 13 per cent, Turkish analysts noted, in a sharply rising market. At the end of August, the market was up by 20 per cent, but Vestel's shares were still doggedly stuck slightly below the flotation level, even though Turkish public opinion had virtually no inkling of the storm which was now breaking over Polly Peck in London.

What was the problem? Perhaps there was no very sinister explanation. Turkish investors are used to trading in blue-chip companies, and Vestel, however familiar its products were from the shops, was a novelty.

A feeling that Asil Nadir, if not an interloper in the Istanbul business world, was at least a newcomer seen by some people as a British capitalist, may also have played its part.

The proceeds of the sale for Polly Peck were £82 million. It was widely assumed that part of the money would be put to use reducing the group's international debt. However, that seems not to have been the case.

Hardly was the Vestel flotation completed in Istanbul than the London market began speculating once more on a flotation of Del Monte Fresh Fruit. The idea now was that Asil Nadir would raise $1 billion by floating 49 per cent of PPI Del Monte in New York. The appointment of Bob Fisher from the Dole Food Company seemed to point directly at such a move. At Dole, Fisher had worked on plans to spin the company off from its parent, Castle and Cooke, until they were abruptly put on the shelf in April 1990. Fisher was an obvious man for a similar move at Polly Peck.

There could also be another flotation in Turkey. Meyna, Polly Peck's fruit and vegetable subsidiary in Turkey, was thought to be at least five times more profitable than Vestel. Some analysts believed that it might be making profits of more than £70 million a year – the main cash-cow in Polly Peck's £161 million pre-tax profits in 1989.

As for British investors who wanted to tap the potential of the infant Turkish market, Asil Nadir had shown them the way in June 1990 by helping to set up the Turkey Trust, Britain's first investment trust specialising exclusively in Turkish securities, when he bought a stake in Colonnade Development Capital. It had come on to the market as an offshoot of British and Commonwealth, the financial services group whose collapse the previous month had been one of the most spectacular débâcles yet seen on the British Stock Exchange.

Inside Polly Peck, meanwhile, a major shake-up was under way. Once again, the board was being given a face-lift. David Fawcus had been finance director for over three years and his decision to stay with Polly Peck when Tony Reading resigned had been of immense assistance to the group in a time of crisis. But Fawcus was a generation older than most of the other executives at Polly Peck and had to endure a good deal of badgering. The City and the press still set great store by Fawcus, from whom a word was often enough to reassure sceptics. Now he was to be gently sidelined by 'promotion' to the new position of deputy chief executive, while Reg Mogg, newly appointed to the board from Maxwell Communications, where he had been finance director, would succeed him as finance director. Typically, the decision seems to have been taken unbeknown to Fawcus himself.

In some ways it was a curious appointment because everyone expected that as soon as Mogg arrived he would try to set in place a tight system of financial reporting controls. David Fawcus and Vi Jansen had tried to do just that and had been thwarted in their attempt. It was almost as if Asil Nadir had a split personality on this issue. Senior employees welcomed Mogg's arrival, though privately some wondered how long he would last before running into a confrontation with Asil Nadir, just as his predecessors had done.

None the less, the outlook at Polly Peck had never been more buoyant. As an international trader, with most of its income coming from subsidiaries abroad and its bankers outside the UK, the company did not even have to be particularly concerned about the looming recession which was rapidly bringing the Thatcher era in Britain to a close.

One day in July, Peter Kleeman, one of Asil Nadir's oldest friends in the City, found himself chatting with Mark Ellis in Polly Peck's elegant New York offices. Kleeman recalled all the turbulent years since 1972 when he had first met Asil Nadir during the Wearwell flotation. The company seemed finally to have piloted its way into calm waters. As Kleeman looked out over the New York skyline, he murmured to himself: 'What could possibly go wrong now?'

12 · A Fatal Error

August 1990 began with a thunderclap for the world as Iraq invaded Kuwait. Suddenly, the whole of the Middle East seemed in jeopardy from Saddam Hussein – and, as it became clear that there would have to be some sort of armed conflict in the Gulf before stability could be restored, the optimism which had followed the ending of the Cold War abruptly disappeared.

For Asil Nadir and Polly Peck, the month opened badly too, with a small bump on the stock market. On the last day of July, Polly Peck's share price had tumbled 12p back down to 434p as 3.5 million shares changed hands, but there was nothing especially unusual or alarming in this, as the share price was still not all that far from its all-time peak.

With its half-year results only six weeks away, Polly Peck looked on course for a sharp increase in its profits, perhaps to over £100 million at the half-year and £240 million for the year-end, and the point at which it would begin to reap the rewards for its acquisitions in the previous two years could not be far off. Meanwhile, the company seemed to be cruising uneventfully far above the altitudes of a few years back. Did another small share price tumble mean anything? 'A lot of the time this is a stock driven by pure rumour, since hardly anyone has a clear idea of its financial position,' an analyst told the market reporters at the *Financial Times*. There were more than a few people inside the company who privately agreed with him about that.

For most of the summer, the rumours had been upbeat, with suggestions that Asil Nadir was planning fresh acquisitions. The worst investors had to fear was that the company might overreach itself. From the start of August, however, the rumours became sinister suggestions of approaching trouble. There was talk of tax investigations, a possible downgrading by the analysts, of stock placed on the market and failing to find a buyer.

Where did these rumours come from? The reports of an investigation by the Inland Revenue were true. The previous autumn, a senior figure in the Revenue had talked to both Stoy Hayward, the group auditors, and Coopers & Lybrand, Asil Nadir's tax advisers, about the chairman's position. Some of his questions involved the problem of Nadir's domicile for tax purposes: he was resident in the UK but his country of origin was not the UK, and his tax liabilities, in particular his worldwide assets, were disputed between his advisers and the Inland Revenue.

But the investigator also touched on other matters with the people he talked to: suspect dealings in Polly Peck shares by small companies in Switzerland. Here, more than just potential tax liability was at stake: if they were made using company money and by company personnel, they would be a clear breach of the law. These names and details were to surface in public for the first time ten months later in the Sunday papers. But some people in the two accountancy houses were aware of them throughout the year and the auditors drew the attention of the chairman to the claims, but did not inform the rest of the board.

Cyprus and Turkey – still, despite all claims to the contrary Polly Peck's main areas of operation – were too close to Kuwait not to feel the effect of the Middle Eastern crisis immediately. Iraq was one of Turkey's main trading partners: throughout the Iran–Iraq War, Ankara had discreetly done what it could to keep the Iraqi economy alive. A double pipeline through Turkey was one of the main outlets for Iraqi crude oil on its way to the West. Within a few weeks, Turkey had shut it down as part of international sanctions and the Turkish economy plunged into a recession.

All this hit Polly Peck's share price hard. The rumours of a tax investigation did not in themselves amount to very much as far as investors were concerned. Since the group was thought to be on course for profits of £245 million by the year-end, up from £161 million in 1989, there seemed to be no obvious reason for the alarm. None the less, the following day the share price fell again, this time dropping 16p to 418p, more or less wiping out the gains made since the first two months of the year.

Matters were not helped when Noble Raredon announced losses of £970,000 for the half-year, attributed by Asil Nadir's sister Bilge Nevzat, the company chairman, to the costs of making new investments. Polly Peck continued to fall on the market, although the news of David Fawcus's impending appointment as deputy chief executive and the arrival of Reg Mogg as group finance director might have been expected to encourage shareholders.

By the end of the first week of August, Polly Peck's share price had fallen from 453p to 410p. The group's market value was down £200 million. By now there were stories on the market of investigations into irregular share dealings: it was not always clear who was supposed to be doing the investigating. Some accounts said the probe was being

carried out by the Inland Revenue. Others thought it was the Stock
Exchange or even the Serious Fraud Office at work.

The *Sunday Times* reported that it had been telephoned by anony-
mous 'tipsters' offering to give it the inside story about Polly Peck.
Asil Nadir was unruffled. Asked to comment, he merely said that he
was very comfortable with analysts' profit forecasts of £240 million.
'As far as I am concerned, it is all systems go,' he told the *Sunday
Times* on 3 August.

But the following week made it clear that the tension in the Middle
East was having a dramatic effect on the share price. By 9 August, Polly
Peck stood at 388p, having touched 381p. The group put out a statement
saying that the proportion of turnover generated in the Near East and
the Middle East had been only 25 per cent in 1989 against 80 per cent
in 1986, but it made little difference. Inside the company, as in many
another corporation that week, the finance director and other top executives began to consider ways of battening down the hatches in case
things went seriously wrong that autumn. It was at this point that David
Fawcus and Reg Mogg decided that the best way of guaranteeing the
confidence of the banks and investors would be to hold a large amount
of cash, say £50 million, on deposit in London.

At 42 Berkeley Square, Asil Nadir stared uneasily at the screens on
his desk. Among his executives, hopes were still fairly high about the
prospects of his succeeding in bringing back £25 million from Cyprus
in the next few weeks to meet the group's forecast cash-flow shortages.
It was already clear that its earnings in Turkey could come under threat
if that country, Iraq's neighbour and close trading partner, became
embroiled in a war in the Middle East.

Analysts began contemplating downgrading their profit forecasts for
the year and switching their recommendations from buy to hold. The
interim results, due on 25 September, were now only six weeks away.
Another set of good results would cheer the market up.

Within the company, there was one bright spot on the horizon. The
Antalya Sheraton Voyager hotel had taken more than a year longer than
expected to build. Now it was almost complete and there was to be an
opening ceremony early in September.

Towards the end of the second week in August there was more
trouble, however. Late in the week, Asil Nadir was told by Bill Grosvenor, his London PR man, that the *Sunday Times* was planning an
article into suspicious dealings in Polly Peck shares. This meant that
the market would be given a fresh scare just at a time when the share
price was already very weak. Bad publicity was nothing new for Polly
Peck, but it seemed to mark some sort of reversal in Asil Nadir's dealings

with a paper which not all that long ago had published a favourable profile of him.

On Saturday, Asil Nadir had an even more astonishing piece of news for David Fawcus. He had finally decided to take the company off the Stock Exchange by buying out the other shareholders, an idea he had been toying with for several years. If London did not want him, it need not have him. He would withdraw to Switzerland and run the company from the headquarters that he had been setting up there. In due course Polly Peck's subsidiaries could be floated on the US and Japanese stock markets.

The news of the planned article in the *Sunday Times* came at almost exactly the same time as Asil Nadir's decision to take Polly Peck private. After Polly Peck's final slide towards administration had got under way, it was sometimes claimed – particularly by journalists – that the buy-out idea was a panicky response to the *Sunday Times* news.

A little earlier that day, Norbert Wirsching, who was passing through London, met Nadir in his office. Wirsching was full of plans for carrying the electronics investment in the Far East a stage further. Capetronics and Imperial had now been sold to Sansui, so the next step was to turn Sansui into a profitable concern which could pay a dividend and in due time raise more finance. But as Wirsching talked to Asil Nadir, he realised that his mind was on other things. 'I have to go abroad,' said Nadir. So the two men exchanged a Turkish-style farewell embrace and Wirsching flew on to New York. On Saturday morning, to his astonishment, Wirsching was called by Nadir and asked to return to London for a board meeting.

Meanwhile, on Friday evening, Asil Nadir had been talking with Elizabeth Forsyth and his other advisers about his approach to the board. Since the bid was being made by Asil Nadir personally, he was told that he should seek lawyers and accountants who had not previously worked with Polly Peck. Elizabeth Forsyth called Philip Pettijohn of Rawlinson and Hunter to a meeting in Switzerland the following morning. It was to be held in the Royal Suite of the Richmond Hotel in the centre of Geneva, whose elegant reproduction antique decor appealed to Asil Nadir. Legal advisers to the bid were to be S. J. Berwin, a leading City firm of solicitors, with which Asil Nadir had not previously dealt. It was the beginning of an association which would last for over a year, for Berwin would handle Asil Nadir's affairs during the upheavals of 1990 and through 1991 until he was declared a bankrupt in November that year.

The day in Geneva was spent toiling over papers, drinking endless cups of coffee. At the end of it, Asil Nadir and Philip Pettijohn flew back to London for meetings early on Saturday evening and on Sunday morning before Asil Nadir spoke to the board. 'He had made his mind up and as far as he was concerned all that now remained was to persuade them of his plans,' says one of his advisers.

In the course of the day, a fax reached Elizabeth Forsyth from her secretary telling her that Michael Gillard of the *Observer* wanted to speak to her about Swiss companies which he believed she was involved in. She rang Polly Peck's press office to see what the enquiry was about, only to learn that they had been contacted by the *Sunday Times* the same day with similar questions.

Returning to 42 Berkeley Square, Asil Nadir faced warnings and questions about the course he was taking. He was asked again and again whether he had the necessary money to go ahead with the bid. 'I don't give a damn what they think. I am going to go ahead and do it,' he declared angrily in his office. But he seemed to have no game plan, and although there are those who think that he did have the money in place, it has never been satisfactorily established that this was so. What he certainly did have were tentative expressions of interest from a number of banks, but this was far from actually having the money guaranteed. Late on Saturday, David Fawcus was told by Asil Nadir that he wished to call a board meeting on Sunday at which he would put his offer to them.

When the directors assembled the next day for the meeting, only seven of the complement of thirteen were present. The others could not attend because of the short notice at which the meeting had been called. This point was later to be fiercely criticised by the Stock Exchange.

One director who was present was of course Norbert Wirsching of Capetronics who had flown through the night from New York in order to be back in London in the early afternoon. He had decided to come straight back as soon as he learned that Asil Nadir was bidding for the company. Like everyone else, Wirsching wanted to know how Asil Nadir would raise money for the bid. Nadir said that he was very insulted that the seriousness of his intentions was being questioned.

The directors at the board meeting endured a double shock that day. Apart from the news which Asil Nadir had to give them, the Sunday newspapers contained the fiercest attack on him since Michael Gillard's 1983 broadside. It came from the *Sunday Times*, which claimed that the Inland Revenue was investigating the beneficial ownership of several Swiss-based 'letterbox companies' that had traded in large volumes of Polly Peck shares over a four-year period. They were Riverbridge Investments, registered at a post office box number in Geneva airport,

Gateway Investments, with a similar Geneva airport address, and Tristan, which shared a Zurich address with Fairweather Investments, a company through which Bilge Nevzat controlled Noble Raredon.

Was there any link between the two developments? The *Sunday Times* claimed there was. David Fawcus said soon afterwards that Nadir had approached him with details of the buy-out before the question of the *Sunday Times* allegations was raised with him. Bill Grosvenor, Polly Peck's spokesman, was categorical: 'There is no connection between Gateway, Riverbridge, Tristan and Polly Peck, or between them and Asil Nadir.' A day or two later, David Fawcus said that Nadir was frustrated and exasperated by the reports. But that is not the same thing as being driven by them into making the most momentous decision of his business life.

For the time being, news of the buy-out proposal eclipsed everything else, including hostile articles in the weekend press. The concept of the buy-out was simple. Polly Peck would become a pure holding company, and its fruit businesses would be floated, probably under the PPI Del Monte name in New York, while the electronics business would float on the Tokyo stock exchange. The holding company, and Asil Nadir, would move to Switzerland, where a headquarters had already been selected, at Fournex near Geneva, in a £35-million villa occupied by Jason Davies, a twenty-seven-year-old former stockbroker and friend of Asil Nadir's son Birol.

The concept might be simple, but finding cash for it was not going to be. For a start, Nadir had to find the money to buy out the shareholders who owned the 74 per cent of Polly Peck which he did not own. In order to take the company private, he would have to hold 90 per cent of the shares, the level at which he could force any recalcitrant shareholders to hand over the remainder to him.

Polly Peck's shares had closed at 393p the previous Friday, giving the group a market valuation of £1.6 billion. The buy-out price would have to be well above any previous share price. That meant finding perhaps £1.3 billion. A £5-per-share bid was probably the minimum price at which the board would conceivably have felt itself able to recommend shareholders to accept. It would have valued the company at £2.14 billion, implying that Asil Nadir would have to find about £1.6 billion.

Against this, there was the fact that Asil Nadir was already the main shareholder with 26 per cent of the shares. Even if the break-up value of Polly Peck was placed at 650p a share, Asil Nadir was still in a very strong position to determine the course of events, provided he could find the necessary money.

But the need for cash would not stop there. Asil Nadir would also have to refinance the company's entire debt. At the end of the previous year, this had been around £1.3 billion. So a total sum not far below £3 billion was involved. First in line would be £256 million of guaranteed bonds raised through Warburg Soditic and $110 million of convertible preference shares, all of which contained clauses in their agreements allowing the investor to redeem them at face value if one person ever took more than 50 per cent of the Polly Peck voting rights.

Where would Asil Nadir find money on this scale? By comparison, finding the £50 million which Reg Mogg had told him earlier in the week would be needed by Polly Peck over the next three months was a minuscule task. How on earth was such a sum going to be raised?

Next, the two sides picked their advisers. Asil Nadir planned to retain Hambro Magan, the mergers and acquisitions specialist, as his financial adviser for the bid, and Shandwick as his public relations consultant. In fact he never concluded an agreement with either firm. He had contacted Hambro Magan during the previous week to alert them to his possible intentions and had been told that a lot of preparatory work would be needed. On Saturday, he called them again to let them know how his plans were going, and was again told of the large amount of preparation and planning that would be needed. When George Magan discovered on Monday that Asil Nadir was actually going ahead with a whistle-stop bid, he was horrified and withdrew.

Polly Peck's board planned to hire Morgan Grenfell, the City merchant bank, as its advisers. One thing the directors were able to do was bring forward the date announcing the half-year results from 25 September to 6 September. David Fawcus took over as acting chief executive of Polly Peck until the bid was resolved. Meanwhile, the directors had to decide who their financial advisers for the bid should be. Five non-executive directors on the board, led by Sir Michael Sandberg, would now play a crucial role.

They would have to put some value on each of the businesses which made up the group's assets. How much, for example, was Sansui worth? Or Vestel, a strong but new Turkish company, whose shares were traded on a fledgling stock market where prices soared and sank without warning? Del Monte Fresh Fruit was acknowledged to be a good business, but it had been purchased cheaply, chiefly because selling it to anyone else presented problems. And what was Asil Nadir's own worth to the group? Had it reached the stage where it could proceed without the man who had built it up and was idolised by the shareholders? Polly Peck without Asil Nadir was hard to imagine. This was the main reason why hitherto there had never been any serious risk of a predator appearing for the group.

'Mr Nadir's prospective buy-out must be taken seriously and he in turn must offer a seductive and serious price once the half-way results are revealed on September 6,' said *The Times*, adding that the deal was shadowed by the prospect of some sort of formal investigation into trade in Polly Peck shares by Swiss shelf companies over the past few years. 'Both Mr Nadir and his sister have denied involvement, but smoke takes some time to clear.'

On Monday morning, the market learned of the intended buy-out of Polly Peck by Asil Nadir. For a while this seemed to put a whole new complexion on the share and demand for it resumed. In one of its busiest days ever trading in Polly Peck shares, 14 million shares changed hands and the share price briefly touched 450p. By the time the London market closed on Monday evening, the share price was well above the 400p level at 417p, even though in the course of the day some holders of the stock became increasingly doubtful about what the buy-out news might really mean, particularly when taken in the light of the previous day's newspapers. Was this not perhaps a golden opportunity to say goodbye to the stock on favourable terms?

On 14 August, the market turned again and the share price slipped back down to 408p. There was beginning to be serious uncertainty about whether Asil Nadir would be able to fund the buy-out.

These fears were well founded. If it is possible to pinpoint an exact moment when Polly Peck began its final slide towards disaster, this was at 3.27 p.m. on Friday 17 August, when Polly Peck's board released a brief statement from Asil Nadir. The buy-out offer had been abandoned.

Asil Nadir said that he had given up, not because he did not have the funds needed but because key investors had signalled that they were not willing to sell. 'Since the time of my letter to the board, I have received approaches from significant institutional and individual shareholders who indicated that they would not wish to see Polly Peck become a private company and wish to see it progress and develop as a public entity. Therefore, I have decided to discontinue my approach made last Sunday and do not intend to proceed with the possible offer.'

The important point was that the funds had been available for a buy-out. David Fawcus explained that, as he understood it, Asil Nadir had the funds to proceed with the bid, but had realised that there was a sufficient volume of opposition to the sale to make it impossible for him to pick up the 90 per cent of voting rights which he needed.

Which investors had indicated that they would not sell was not clear. To this day accounts differ. Friends Provident, one of the largest Polly Peck shareholders after Asil Nadir himself, with 5 per cent, said afterwards that it had not come out against a buy-out. However, David

Fawcus says that he was told early that week that they were unlikely to accept the offer, and Asil Nadir therefore had no option but to withdraw it. Until the offer price was known – and it was not due to be revealed before the interim results on 6 September – it was hard for many investors to express a view one way or the other.

The greatest mystery, which remains unresolved, was where the £1.5 billion minimum needed for the bid would have come from. Rich as he was, Asil Nadir did not have funds of his own available on this scale. Bank borrowing would seem to have been the only alternative. But from which banks? 'The board understood that such funds were mainly to be provided from Turkish sources,' the Stock Exchange enquiry later reported.

Again, what sources could these have been? £1.5 billion ($2.7 billion) is a vastly larger sum than any Turkish bank, or group of banks, has ever lent inside the country – whose GNP, it must be remembered, was around $100 billion in 1990, and which had a large external debt of more than $40 billion to service each year at a cost of $7 billion. A loan on the scale needed to buy Polly Peck would have had an extraordinary effect on Turkey's balance of payments.

Even if Asil Nadir had some sort of government-backed financing for his buy-out, it would have been an impossible burden. Nor, in the months that followed, could any Turkish banker be found who had been approached to take part in a financial package for the buy-out – not even those bankers, such as Hüsnü Özyeğin at Finansbank, who had worked closely with Asil Nadir earlier in the year.

The worst fears of Polly Peck's sceptics seemed to be coming true. On the Stock Exchange, the share price plunged to 324p as 18 million shares changed hands, with investors scrambling to get out of the stock. In one hour's trading, the share slipped by more than a pound, losing more than 25 per cent of its value. 'To say that Mr Asil Nadir has slipped on one of his Del Monte banana skins would be a pitiful under-statement,' said the *Financial Times*'s Lex column as the week ended. It suggested that the best thing Asil Nadir could now do would be to wait two and a half weeks until the interim figures appeared and then make a tender offer for perhaps 10 per cent of Polly Peck stock. This suggestion assumed that Nadir would now be able to find the cash for such a purchase and that he would have been allowed by the Stock Exchange to waive the rule under which he had automatically to make an offer for the entire company when his share-holding rose about 30 per cent.

Lex also suggested that the Stock Exchange might seek some further explanation of what had happened. The hint was superfluous. The Stock Exchange had already publicly announced that it had asked Polly Peck's advisers, including Barclays de Zoete Wedd, the securities and merchant banking arm of Barclays Bank, Lehman Brothers, Morgan Grenfell and Chartered WestLB, what was going on. Late on Friday 17 August, it launched an investigation into share price movements during the days of the abortive bid. The first meeting between the Exchange and some of the advisers was to take place on the following Monday. 'We have done everything in line with the rules. They won't find anything unusual,' said David Fawcus. But the Sunday newspapers were already on the trail.

Thousands of miles away from the crisis in London, Ayşegül Nadir gave a grand masked ball in Istanbul on 18 August in the Saadullah Paşa Yalısı, the splendid wooden palace on the eastern coast of the Bosporus which had been the last home that she and Asil shared. The party was attended by the British Ambassador and his wife, down from the embassy in Ankara, and other dignitaries. Also present were most of the younger generation of the great industrial dynasties of Istanbul, including the Koç family. The trees in the gardens were spangled with light from star-shaped lanterns which sparkled on the waves of the Bosporus outside the eighteenth-century drawing-room. Some of the guests already knew that something had gone seriously wrong for Asil Nadir in London, but Ayşegül herself had no idea that anything untoward had taken place. Champagne and caviare flowed abundantly, and a sense of carefree extravagance hung delightfully on the summer night air. 'My wife is crazy. She has brought four dresses just for a single night,' declared one guest, just in case anyone had not noticed his wife's changing costume as the evening progressed.

Ayşegül's family thought it was by far the best ball she had ever given. They were not to know it was also to be her last for a very long time. Towards five in the morning, the music stopped playing, the musicians folded their instruments and went away, leaving the wooden palace and its garden to the sound of the waves and the passing ships of the Bosporus.

The following morning in England, readers in more than a million homes woke up to find that the *Sunday Times* had returned to the attack. For the first time it mentioned Jason Davies and South Audley Management, the small company owned by Nadir family trusts and set up to manage their properties.

Davies, formerly of Saffron Walden, was now living in the Vaud on the north shore of Lake Geneva. He was a director of Nadir Investments and a former director of South Audley Management. When he first met Birol Nadir, Davies had been director of A. J. Bekhor in the City, a firm of stockbrokers which was now closed, but he was still a representative of Paul E. Schweder Miller, another London stockbroker. He has always denied any illegal share-dealing and no charges have ever been brought against him.

According to the *Sunday Times*, Davies and South Audley Management were at the centre of Stock Exchange and Inland Revenue enquiries. This provoked a swift denial from Bill Grosvenor, Polly Peck's spokesman, that suspect share-dealing was involved in the stock market enquiries – and indeed those interviewed by the Stock Exchange the following week later said that they were not questioned about the Swiss companies and share-dealing allegations.

The Stock Exchange's concern was whether Asil Nadir's conduct in the previous week might not have created a false market in the shares and infringed its investor protection rules. Meetings between the Stock Exchange's Quotations Panel Committee and the professional advisers involved in the Polly Peck buy-out stretched through Monday and Tuesday. On the market, Polly Peck's shares rallied and on the 21 August ended the day at 310p, though they had been briefly below 300p. That day the committee, under its chairman Graham Kennedy, saw Asil Nadir and George Magan of Hambro Magan.

On the afternoon of the 24th, the Stock Exchange authorities announced their findings. There was little the committee could do in practice other than rebuke Asil Nadir, for any other moves against the company would have punished its shareholders, the very people who had suffered most from the extraordinary changes in the share price around the time of the buy-out offer.

The committee said that it was critical of the lack of preparation to normal standards of the bid, and noted that only one professional adviser, S. J. Berwin, had been retained – and only on 11 August, when Asil Nadir had already summoned Polly Peck's board to meet the following day to discuss the bid.

'Mr Nadir's apparent decision was to ignore advice received, albeit on an informal basis, from Hambro Magan (a merchant bank) that any formal notification of his intention to make an offer was premature and should not be made.

'If Mr Nadir had chosen to consult fully with financial advisers at an early stage, he may have recognised that any offer made, at the kind of premium which he evidently had in mind, was unlikely to achieve the level of acceptance which would be necessary to take the company private.'

Perhaps the most startling finding of all was the suggestion that although Asil Nadir had been thinking of taking Polly Peck private since

1988, he had not discussed the possibility with outside professional advisers or any third parties before Saturday 11 August – the day before he put the proposal to the board.

The report was passed on to the Department of Trade and Industry and the Serious Fraud Office. The move was not necessarily more than an unfriendly gesture, but it was the first time that the SFO had been officially mentioned in connection with Polly Peck.

What the investigation failed to do was to discover any evidence that Asil Nadir had known from the outset that he would not be able to go through with an offer for Polly Peck. If that had been established, it might have opened the way for a prosecution under Section 47 of the Financial Services Act and a jail sentence of up to seven years. The Lex column of the *Financial Times* pointed out witheringly: 'The shares are still at the same level relative to the market as they were at the start of the year. Logic suggests they ought to fall further.'

Peter Wilson-Smith in the *Independent on Sunday* was even more scathing: 'The revelations to emerge from the Stock Exchange's quotations panel leave the impression that Mr Nadir's buy-out was little more than a fantasy of his own invention.'

Inside Polly Peck, there was fury at the behaviour of the Stock Exchange. The text of the statement had been sent to the company late on Friday afternoon, giving almost no time for a reply to be issued. A brief rejoinder from the board said merely that the company was committed to continuing to maximise its shareholder value. A few days later the interim results were again brought forward by three days to 3 September.

Three questions remained unanswered. Where would the money have come from? Who were the 15 per cent of the Polly Peck shareholders who had told Asil Nadir that they objected to the buy-out? Above all, why had he rushed into the move in the space of twenty-four hours over a weekend? To this day, no clear answers have emerged.

The next step seemed likely to be a Department of Trade and Industry Inquiry to establish the full facts. The weekend brought fresh bad news. The *Sunday Times* was now openly writing about the possibility of a sophisticated share-support operation, along the lines of the Guinness affair. It pointed out that unauthorised use of a company's money to purchase its shares was a criminal offence under Section 151 of the 1985 Companies Act. DTI inspectors, armed with far greater powers than the Stock Exchange, would be able to get further.

The *Sunday Times* said that the Stock Exchange enquiries had been triggered by an Inland Revenue investigation into Asil Nadir's personal tax status. This investigation centred on the tax treatment of Asil Nadir's assets outside the UK. Although Nadir was domiciled in Britain, his country of origin was outside the UK, and if he died, his assets world-wide would become liable to inheritance duties in the UK. This fact seems to have been one of the reasons why Nadir had been preparing for several years to move his domicile from the United Kingdom to Switzerland. He had in fact already completed the formalities for Swiss residency in 1989, adding Swiss residency documents to his British, Turkish and Turkish Cypriot passports. To all this, Asil Nadir responded in due course with the threat of a libel action. He strenuously denied any wrong-doing.

How had the dispute leaked out to the press? Did it really have any connection with investigations by the Stock Exchange? Asil Nadir and his entourage were convinced that the leak had come from Greek Cypriots working inside the Inland Revenue, though no evidence to support this claim was ever produced. The dispute with the Inland Revenue itself had little directly to do with the fierce controversy now raging around Polly Peck and its chairman. When Asil Nadir's lawyer, Peter Knight of Vizards, had conversations with the Revenue in the ensuing weeks, he was able to elicit polite expressions of regret for the possibility that the Revenue's investigation might unintentionally have caused problems for Asil Nadir on other fronts. The text of a memorandum written by Peter Knight on his conversations with the Inland Revenue was shown to some Polly Peck employees as a morale-booster in the weeks that followed.

The Sunday newspaper reports focused attention on Polly Peck's problems. Nadir strongly denied the allegations and threatened libel action. But the papers had not created the basic problem: the aborted bid approach overshadowed the market. The shares sagged to 247p at one point on 30 July, to close that day at 265p, 15p down. Without the appearance of US buyers, evidently willing to boldly go where UK investors would not, it would have fallen further. The June peak of 462p seemed a world away.

Could the damage to the company be repaired? If so, how long would it take? The outside world knew nothing of Polly Peck's looming cash-flow problems. Asil Nadir's enemies, however, sensed that a denoue-ment might now be not long distant. Polly Peck had seen plenty of crises before, but the bid episode was perhaps the most damaging so far. For while, in earlier crises, it had always been possible for his defenders and admirers to portray Asil Nadir as an entrepreneur of genius, this time there was no obvious optimistic interpretation of events.

The facts then known about the buy-out suggested that at the very least Asil Nadir had acted extremely impetuously at one of the key moments of his business career and had erred disastrously. Those observers who suspected that he had not been able to find the funds he needed to buy out the other shareholders were left with an even less favourable set of explanations to choose from. One view was that by delisting Polly Peck on the London Stock Exchange as a result of buying out the other shareholders, he had hoped to reduce the degree of public scrutiny on himself and his company.

None the less, Asil Nadir's admirers felt that he had been treated with undue harshness by the Stock Exchange, even though they did not know what had been the exact position of the institutional investors. The offer had collapsed, and that was all there was to the story. But this version – which is in any case vehemently rejected by those inside the company who were close to the events – still left some questions unanswered, not least how Asil Nadir would have been able to raise the vast amounts of cash involved.

It also gradually emerged that on earlier occasions he had approached financial advisers about a possible buy-out, and had done so in a much less hasty fashion than on 11 August. Nor had the recipients of these earlier approaches been contacted on the later occasion. All in all, there seemed to be an impenetrable aura of mystery around his recent conduct, whichever theory one chose to adopt, and certainly it was impossible to devise any explanation which enhanced his reputation as a shrewd entrepreneur.

Bilge Nevzat said that she thought her brother had been inspired to buy out the company by the examples of Richard Branson of Virgin Records and Andrew Lloyd Webber. 'When he makes his mind up about something, he just goes ahead,' she said. Ayşegül's account is even less informative. 'Asil did explain to me afterwards why he had done it, but I don't remember the exact reason he gave,' she says. 'It went in one ear and out the other.'

In Turkey, Asil Nadir's troubles were followed with some puzzlement and little appreciation for the seriousness of his position. Insider dealing did not formally become a crime on the Istanbul Stock Exchange until legislation on the subject was introduced in 1992, and it was hard for many Turks to see what the uproar was about – or to understand that it really was capable of bringing down the Nadir business empire. President Özal is believed to have phoned Asil Nadir towards the end of the month, expressing his support for him. That at least was something to be grateful for. It was generally assumed inside Turkey that Asil Nadir's problems were the result of a Greek Cypriot campaign against him. Turkish officials made their backing clear.

The Greece and Cyprus Department of the Turkish Foreign Ministry was particularly strong in his support, urging that strong representations should be made to the UK government to help Asil Nadir. The Turkish Embassy in London, closer to the events, was less eager to be involved, but eventually representations were quietly made to Downing Street by the Turkish Ambassador. They do not seem to have cut much ice with Mrs Thatcher and her entourage, despite Asil Nadir's regular donations to the Conservative Party.

As the month ended, Asil Nadir – persuaded by friends in Turkey and seemingly in particular by Metin Münir – agreed to an interview with the *Financial Times*. He seldom saw journalists. Some of his friends and admirers thought that this remoteness from the press was one of the reasons for his isolation, others that it was simply a trait he shared with other entrepreneurs. In the UK, Michael Walters of the *Daily Mail*, the early sceptic who had later become a firm believer in Polly Peck, was one of Asil Nadir's few regular contacts in the press. His contacts among Turkish journalists were fairly numerous, but the Turkish journalists to whom he spoke were usually his employees.

Sitting in his first-floor office in 42 Berkeley Square, amid his antiques and evergreens in vast pots. Asil Nadir gazed at his visitors, chain-smoking Silk Cut, the cheap cigarette brand which he preferred. He spoke quietly but vehemently, still smarting under the sense of a recently suffered injustice. What he had to tell the *Financial Times*, however, did not carry the story very much further. He parried questions rather than offering explanations, least of all any which would make sense out of the disorder of the month's events.

According to Asil Nadir, the root cause of everything was the stock market's failure – the failure of most investors, despite a wonderfully loyal minority – to recognise Polly Peck's achievements. As a result, he said he was preparing to counter parts of the Stock Exchange report. He would like to float parts of Polly Peck in the USA and Japan – this idea was far from new – but private ownership of Polly Peck would have given his company the freedom to move into new areas without attracting the criticism which had dogged him over the past decade. He had envisaged paying a price of 500p or slightly above it, but it turned out that this was not what the shareholders would accept. Now that this option was closed to him, he would go ahead with a global restructuring of the company, shelving the idea of taking it private for the foreseeable future. As for his failure to consult a larger number of advisers well ahead of the bid, Asil Nadir said that he had felt that the only help he needed at the initial approach stage was from experienced corporate lawyers.

A sense of resentment at the way the market undervalued Polly Peck ran through everything he said. As for the question of whether a Sunday board meeting was unusual or not, 'In my case, the seven days are all similar, a Sunday is no different from a Monday,' was his response. 'I know that here in Britain you think of your working week as Monday to Friday and then you have your Saturday to Sunday holiday. That is not the case in this company. It is a living entity,' he told the slightly sceptical journalists (they were not to know that he did in fact normally work at the office on Sundays). 'Committee meetings or board meetings take place at a day's notice or a morning's notice,' he added to reinforce his point.

Meanwhile, he was aware that his own personal finances were coming under increasing pressure. On 31 August, five of the banks which had lent him money began selling shares which they held – the *Observer* later wrote – to meet margin calls triggered by Polly Peck's share-price collapse. Under these circumstances, there was little chance of Asil Nadir's coming up with assistance from his personal wealth in the UK or Western Europe. The only possible funds left to tap appeared to be those in Turkey and Cyprus.

The weekend and the end of the month arrived with Polly Peck's share price limping at 291p, 25 per cent down on where it had been at the beginning of August. It had taken a very severe dent, but it was not comparable to the share price collapses of 1983 or even 1985. Every time this sort of thing had happened in the past, Asil Nadir had always recovered. Perhaps this would be so again.

Amidst the furore created by the abortive buy-out offer, David Fawcus and Reg Mogg's cash-flow forecasts had been lost sight of inside Polly Peck. Perhaps it was understandable that with so much else on his mind, Asil Nadir had not as yet managed to bring back any of the £50 million needed by the company from Cyprus.

13 · On the Brink

When Asil Nadir's business partners called him from Polly Peck's operations around the world in late August and early 1990, they were
invariably surprised at how calmly he seemed to be taking the recent
dramatic reversal in his fortunes. Asked how he felt about this, he would
reply with a mixture of jauntiness and exasperation, 'These things are
sent to try us,' and then move on to business as usual. As the crisis
facing Polly Peck got steadily more serious, Asil Nadir remained serene
and outwardly unaffected by the alarm which gripped many of those
around him. His calm, unworried demeanour recalled his confidence in
a similar crisis a decade and a half earlier when Wearwell had tottered
on the brink of bankruptcy.

There were some signs of tension: sitting in his armchair in his office
at 42 Berkeley Square, he chain-smoked throughout the day. But this
was nothing new. Depending on the particular perspective of those who
talked to him, his calmness in the face of the storm seemed either deeply
inspiring or another sign that he was slightly remote from events. Either
way it was slightly uncanny.

But while some of Asil Nadir's self-confidence rubbed off on those
working with him, the market was much harder to reassure. Once again,
Polly Peck tried to get out of a tight spot by unveiling a glittering set of
results. On Monday 3 September, the company published its interim
results for the half-year – the last full set of trading results it ever
announced. As on previous occasions in the last decade, Asil Nadir and
his advisers hoped that news of a good performance would soothe at
least part of the market and restore the company's credibility. It was to
this end that the date of the interims had been twice brought forward
during the last three weeks of August. If the buy-out and its aftermath
had not happened, the figures, which unlike year-end results did not
have to be independently audited, would not have emerged for another
three weeks.

More than fifty analysts – by London standards, a very large number
indeed – crowded into 42 Berkeley Square to hear Asil Nadir discuss
the results. They knew that this set was certain to be good. They would
be the first profit figures to reflect the purchase of Del Monte Fresh

Fruit. In Turkey, Vestel was known to be having a very good year. But would all this sufficiently impress the market to make it forget its other worries?

Pre-tax profits had indeed risen. They were up by an astonishing 72 per cent, from £64.4 million to £110.5 million. Good news was festooned everywhere. The food division had achieved turnover of £572.2 million, which was higher than the entire year's turnover in 1989. Food profits were up, though less sharply, at £86.8 million, from £50.7 million. Del Monte contributed a robust £29.6 million.

The electronics businesses followed the same trend, though not as strongly, with £18.9 million pre-tax profits from Vestel, five times up on the previous year. Sansui's contribution to group results was a mere £6.1 million loss, but even that was said to be an improvement on what had been expected. Other divisions were operating around the level of the previous year. But collectively the electronics division's turnover was £281.5 million, up from £195.1 million.

Even the leisure division made a contribution to profits, albeit a small one, of £500,000. Gearing was 93 per cent, but it would fall in a few weeks when the Del Monte ships were finally sold and Capetronics and Imperial were merged with Sansui.

The analysts did, however, note that interest payments on debt were sharply up.

As for the events of the past month? 'I regret that anything I did could be the subject of any criticism,' said Asil Nadir, using words which he had evidently carefully selected in advance. However, he felt that some of the statements from the Stock Exchange had been inaccurate and he was endeavouring to have the record put straight.

If Asil Nadir thought that these results would appease his critics, he was wrong. By now what people wanted to know was not so much the trading position of Polly Peck, but what – if anything – lay behind the claims that the Serious Fraud Office, the Inland Revenue and the Stock Exchange were investigating the group. According to some newspapers, it was not just the last few months, or even the last few years, which was now under scrutiny. The investigators were looking through all Polly Peck share-dealing over the last decade – 'since the company was founded in 1979', wrote one journalist who should have known better.

For a few days, however, things seemed to quieten down. By the 11th of the month, when Polly Peck prepared to open the Sheraton Voyager Hotel in Antalya, the mood in the company was once more cautiously optimistic. The disastrous aftermath of the abortive bid offer seemed to be fading. Perhaps, Polly Peck executives told each other, the worst was now over.

In this hopeful mood, they departed for Antalya and a weekend of triumphant festivity organised by Nil Adula, head of Asil Nadir's PR in Istanbul. Noble Air flew guests direct from Luton to Antalya. The plane taking many of the directors left four and a half hours late, but that did not dampen the spirits of the passengers, well oiled by a crate of champagne which had somehow been discovered by Nick Dow of Dox, Polly Peck's media consultants. The most alarming moment of the flight – a thunderous noise as a heavy object shot past Sir Michael Sandberg – proved to be nothing more than the ill-judged effects of opening a champagne bottle at 30,000 feet.

Once at the Sheraton Voyager, the guests sat in groups on their balconies, sipping champagne in safer circumstances and watching the sun set over the haunting outline of the Lycian mountains at the western end of the bay of Antalya. Like Peter Kleeman a few months before in New York, they asked themselves whether it was possible that anything could now go wrong.

On the seventh floor of the hotel was the Sultan's suite, reserved for Asil Nadir himself. Not one but two nights of festivity had been organised for the opening. For two nights, Asil Nadir was sultan and the Sheraton was his palace, and he relished his triumph as much as any pop star.

His appearance was carefully staged. On the first evening, Sezen Aksu, a well-known Turkish singer, was in mid-act when Asil Nadir and his entourage made their entry. The entire room burst into wild applause and the guests stood to cheer him. The applause was not entirely spontaneous, however, for as Asil Nadir advanced across the floor, he was preceded by Nil Adula, who, in an impressive blending of high Ottoman courtly fashion and TV showmanship, walked backwards, not taking her eyes off her master, and clapping in time with the music as she went. Asil Nadir went over to his mother's table, kissed her and then sat down with the Minister of Tourism and President Rauf Denktaş, the Turkish Cypriot leader.

For the British members of the party, however, the festivities were overhung with storm clouds. Over glasses of champagne and whisky at different tables and in different rooms, conversations kept returning to the dangers threatening the group. One of these conversations was itself to add a new twist to the crisis.

On the second morning news came through from England that there had been a further round of unfavourable articles in the Sunday papers. The *Sunday Times* suggested that Asil Nadir was planning to move to Switzerland. He immediately responded by holding a meeting with some of the journalists who were present in the party. 'I deny ever having considered a move to Switzerland,' he told reporters. Polly Peck was setting up an office in Switzerland, but this was no different from its other representative offices in London, Hong Kong, Tokyo and New York. And Jason Davies, the stockbroker, who seemed to be at the centre of the press reports? He was not in charge of the move, came the reply.

One of the puzzling things about these replies is that somehow – perhaps because these contacts were nervous and hurried – the press reports failed to bring into focus the exact connection between Asil Nadir and South Audley Management – a failure which would harm him considerably over the next few weeks. Some newspapers reported that he denied knowledge of it, others that he claimed it was a family business. In fact South Audley was a property and management services company, controlled by a complex circle of family trusts, but whose function was to handle the Nadir family's properties and other financial affairs. A similar company, Marmara Management, was later set up in Istanbul (though registered in the Cayman Islands) and existed to handle property in Turkey, run by an unhappy American whose main job appeared to consist of sending a stream of faxes to London warning Asil Nadir that his enterprises in Turkey were spending far too much money and complaining that he was never listened to.

Asil Nadir also denied the by now fairly widespread and entirely untrue rumours in London that the Del Monte flotation in New York was being held up by investigations by the US Securities and Exchange Commission.

On the second night of the festivities, the keys of the Sheraton Voyager were symbolically handed over to the Sheraton company as a sign that from now on it would be in charge of running the hotel. At this point the party ended. Asil Nadir flew back home to London and disaster.

He did not yet know it, but his problems had been considerably exacerbated by a conversation in the small hours of Sunday morning in the hotel between David Fawcus and Dennis Robertson, the senior partner of Stoy Hayward. Conversation turned to the share-dealing allegations against Polly Peck in the papers, a topic which naturally worried David Fawcus a great deal. Robertson, however, had news which horrified him. It emerged that the previous October, Stoy Hayward and Coopers & Lybrand had been visited by a Mr D. Cook, an official from the Holborn special office of the Inland Revenue.

Fawcus rose from the table, trying to pick his words carefully. He was very angry indeed, but it was late at night. He was doubly worried since this was not the only piece of bad news he had heard during the previous few hours. A senior journalist on close terms with the company over the previous decade had told him over an earlier drink of a large tranche of Polly Peck shares which was bought on Friday 10 August – the last trading day on the Stock Exchange before the buy-out was announced – and sold the following Monday. There was no suggestion that anyone in the company had been involved, but none the less it was enough to make a conscientious finance director's hair stand on end.

Angry and worried, Fawcus returned to London, having already decided on the course of action that he must take. He would fix up a meeting between himself and Peter Compson, the personnel director, and Stoy Hayward, the group's auditors. Then, if necessary, he would go to the Serious Fraud Office.

Several factors lay behind the bad press Asil Nadir was getting. One accusation was that he had been illegally buying Polly Peck shares to keep up the price of the stock on the market. There was no direct evidence for this claim. But the share-dealing allegations seemed to be firmly linked to something else – an investigation by the Inland Revenue into Asil Nadir's tax liabilities. This went back several years, but during the summer and autumn of 1989, the Revenue, acting through Cook, had stepped up its investigations.

The exact nature of the Inland Revenue's interest in Asil Nadir's affairs has never been made public, but a dispute over how his tax liabilities were defined was a major part of the problem. He had been advised by Rawlinson and Hunter that if he died, his world-wide assets outside the family trusts, including in particular the Turkish newspapers, would be subject to a rate of 40 per cent inheritance tax residency and domicile. If South Audley Management handled any of his overseas interests, they would immediately become liable to UK tax. So his overseas interests had to be managed from somewhere outside the UK.

As the overseas private operations had begun to expand, the plan had been for Elizabeth Forsyth to resign from South Audley Management and take up residence in Switzerland, from where she would have been able to direct Asil Nadir's overseas businesses, almost certainly working alongside her master.

Switzerland is a notoriously difficult country when it comes to getting residence permits. To speed up a process which might have taken as long as five years, in 1989 Asil Nadir had bought for cash a small computer assembly company, called Alptech, believing that its computers could be used in Harland and Simon, the printing industry control systems company in which Birol Nadir, his eldest son, had bought a controlling interest using money given to him by his grandmother. A Swiss holding company, Nadir Investments, was then set up at the village of Givrins as a possible holding vehicle to control several companies.

As things turned out, it owned only one company, Alptech. Jason Davies, who worked part of the time at Nadir Investments, was loosely described as a personnel officer.

When journalists began to arrive at Givrins in pursuit of Jason Davies and the Polly Peck story, they were predictably impressed with what they found: as usual, Asil Nadir's predilection for attractive settings was in evidence. Flowers bloomed in immaculately tended gardens around the villa, set between well-trimmed hedges. Jason himself lived in an apartment at Fournex, a short car journey away. He was not at home in the days after 23 September when a stream of hopeful journalists began to arrive at his front door. They quickly established that on 14 May, Davies had become a director of Nadir Investments, while M. Jean Heim, a lawyer who sometimes acted for Asil Nadir, was the chairman.

When the press had begun to link Jason Davies with suspect dealings in Polly Peck shares, Nadir Investments said that they had asked him to explain what was going on in a report, but by 26 September (so an unidentified spokesman who talked to the press that day said) Davies had not submitted this and the company was unsure of where he actually was.

There were other curiosities in Switzerland which puzzled the press. One of them was the revival of a small Polly Peck company called Elbise – the Turkish word for dress – which had been transferred from Fribourg to Domaine de Leydefour, the Givrins farmhouse which was the offices of Nadir Investments. It had originally been a textiles company, but now its proposed activities covered food trade and electronic goods as well. However, John Botfield, one of its two listed officials, said that it was only an international transport company.

Early in the week came another piece of bad news. The *Daily Mail* claimed that a senior police officer, Chief Superintendent Colin McMurray, was being probed by his superiors for allegedly helping his wife, Isabel, to set up Asil Nadir's team of bodyguards. Mrs McMurray was indeed a security consultant on a two-year contract to Polly Peck, but the company denied that her husband had been in any way involved in her work.

By 19 September, two days after the end of the party at the Antalya Sheraton Voyager, Polly Peck's share price was down to 243p. This was about 200p lower than its peak level, but it was not yet back to its lowest point for the year.

Inside the company, David Fawcus was still trying to pursue his own enquiries. He and Peter Compson met Dennis Robertson that evening at a dinner in the Savoy Grill. Notes were taken at the meeting and Fawcus prepared a memorandum which was sent to Stoy Hayward. The approved version was sent back on Friday morning to Fawcus. What Compson and Fawcus did not know as they sat at their meeting with Dennis Robertson, was that earlier the same day the company's fortunes had just taken a sharp turn for the worse. By then Polly Peck was reeling after the greatest body-blow in its history.

Early on the morning of the same day, Wednesday 19 September, after weeks of speculation in the press, the Serious Fraud Office had finally moved in. A team of policemen and accountants appeared at South Audley Management and began to go through its accounts and records. Elizabeth Forsyth, the company's chairman, was not there: she was travelling in Europe. But she was among the first to learn of the raid when she called her secretary.

Alarmed and uncomprehending, the girls who worked for the company were confined to an inside room for the duration of the raid. Most of them lived in the plusher districts of London or the Home Counties and were not the sort of people who ever imagined they could find themselves on the wrong side of the law. For weeks they had watched unhappily as their company rocketed from obscurity to notoriety in the Sunday newspapers. Now they were being busted.

Although Asil Nadir must clearly have been aware of what had happened the previous day, he was his usual cool self on the morning of 20 September. Barry Buttifant had arrived from the Far East, and when he saw Asil Nadir that morning, the chairman's sights were on a possible new hotel deal in the Far East. The rest of the board may not have liked the leisure industry, but Asil Nadir was still very interested in it.

On the stock market, however, news of the raid was leaking out. The share price quickly began to signal that some disaster had taken place. Polly Peck's shares went into their final and most spectacular plunge in a decade full of such disasters. Dealing had opened at 243p, but as reports of the raid began to spread, investors rushed to sell.

As the price began to plunge, another danger for Asil Nadir came into view. At least a quarter of the 28 per cent of Polly Peck's shares which were owned at that point by Asil Nadir himself had been pledged as security through Restro, the Nadir family trust, against lending from the banks. If the shares fell below a certain price, the bank would automatically jettison them. Most of the lending had been arranged two years earlier, so the shares had to fall a long way before the alarm bells would begin to ring. A share-price collapse was a different matter.

On the market extraordinary rumours came and went. Asil Nadir was dead: he had shot himself in Hong Kong, said one version. No, said another, he had been gunned down by a Middle Eastern death squad. He had been arrested.

One rumour did have some substance. According to the press, callers who rang the SFO were told informally that a raid on South Audley Management had taken place the previous day. This was deeply alarming news to the market. The information was given out to callers while the shares were still being traded.

In offices across London and far beyond, the sudden plunge in the Polly Peck share price on Reuters screens was more than enough of a danger signal to the outside world. Something had obviously gone seriously wrong. Investors who had been holding on to their shares hoping for yet another recovery decided to dump them.

When the shares reached 210p, Citibank placed its holding on the market. A sell order for 7.9 million shares placed by Shearson Lehman, the company which had absorbed L. Messel, proved the last straw. Ironically, Shearsons were also the brokers through whom Polly Peck was trying to ask the Stock Exchange to suspend its shares. The 7.9 million was bought by UBS Phillips and Drew, the London stockbroking arm of the Union Bank of Switzerland, which of course lost heavily as a result when dealings in the share were suspended soon afterwards. A few weeks later, stockbrokers at UBS Phillips and Drew would be ruefully joking that the purchase might have cost them their Christmas bonus. When news of this sale appeared on the Seaq ticket, the price plunged by a pound.

In all, 36 million shares were sold during the afternoon of Thursday 20 September. To this day Asil Nadir's advisors suspect that they were the victims of some kind of plot aimed at creating a share-price collapse by fomenting panic on the market. They point to a news agency report that day of the assassination of Asil Nadir. They say that it took three requests from their brokers before the Stock Exchange suspended the shares.

Asil Nadir was by no means alone in feeling that there had been undue delay in suspending the share. For days afterwards he claimed that if the company's wishes had been acted on promptly, the share price would have been suspended long before it got anywhere near the 108p level.

The only way forward now was for Asil Nadir to talk directly to the SFO and refute the suspicions surrounding him. In the afternoon, he drove round to their grey stone headquarters in Elm Street, just off Gray's Inn Road, where he was questioned for nearly three hours. From his later remarks on the subject, it appears that the SFO's enquiries were basically confined to the share-dealing allegations and matters linked to them, such as his connection with South Audley Management and its precise method of working.

The visit to the SFO marked a momentous change in his fortunes. Among Nadir's enemies, there was ill-concealed glee. Rumours and reports of what was happening raced around London. 'They've got him under Section Two and he is singing like a bird,' market reporters were told by their sources. Both assertions were wrong. Asil Nadir was not questioned under Section Two, the regulation which permits the SFO to question a witness without the right to silence, and his ability to deliver fluent answers did not desert him.

As he faced his interrogators, perhaps his thoughts passed from time to time to his native Cyprus. At the very hour that he was being interviewed, the Jasmine Court Hotel, the flagship of his leisure industry investments on the island, was being opened. In the weeks that followed, he was to stay many nights in its splendid buildings outside Kyrenia, originally built by the Greeks but refurbished by the Turkish Cypriots.

When he emerged from the Elm Street building, amid flashing cameras and the glare of television arc lights, Polly Peck's fortunes had been shattered and the City was in uproar. On newspaper stands across London, the *Evening Standard* trumpeted the news of the share-price collapse and (an hour or two later) of Asil Nadir's interview at the SFO.

Towards the end of the afternoon, Ayşegül was coming out of Harry's Bar in the West End, her favourite meeting-place for lunch.

'Did you see the papers?' asked her driver.

'What papers?' said Ayşegül. He pointed to the *Standard*, which said that the shares were going to be suspended. She was astonished. For months she had been out of contact with Asil and had no idea of the difficulties he and Polly Peck were in. When she went home, she rang him up for the first time in almost a year and they arranged to meet.

As a result of the day's events, many investors – not least Asil Nadir himself – were very much poorer. Though it is difficult to forecast the impact on the market of an event such as the SFO raid, particularly when it affected a company which had lived through extraordinarily turbulent events in the past, the share-price collapse seemed at the time a somewhat excessive response. It suggested that many shareholders had put their money into Polly Peck despite their awareness that if things ever went wrong, it might collapse like a house of cards.

The Lex column commented: 'The market has reached the end of its tether with Polly Peck. Whatever one's views of fresh fruit, Cypriot hotels or the prospects for Turkish electronics, they fade into the background compared to the sheer chaos of yesterday's events. The shares plunged so fast, and in circumstances so bizarre that Polly Peck's market price has lost all contact with fundamentals.' At 108p, the prospective p/e was only 2.3 and the gross yield 19.8 per cent. It was, said Lex, a death-bed rating that companies reach only when nearly bust. 'But that surely is not Polly Peck's position,' the writer remarked.

Lex suggested that Barclays de Zoete Wedd and Lehman Brothers should resign as brokers, because they had not been informed of the SFO raid on South Audley until Wednesday evening. This would have been something of a doomsday gesture of doubtful benefit to Polly Peck shareholders, for without its familiar professional advisers, the company's chances of handling the crisis ahead of it would have been even smaller.

The same evening, news emerged for the first time of approaches by President Özal to Mrs Thatcher through the Turkish Embassy in London on Polly Peck's behalf. The Turks insisted that Polly Peck was the victim of a British press conspiracy masterminded by the Greek Cypriots and their advisers. The Turkish Ambassador, whose job it was to advance this message, received a politely glacial response. Other British officials in the Foreign Office and the Bank of England were scornful about the approach, which they felt had been conducted in a very ham-fisted manner. A week or two later, they would get their chance to make their attitude plain in a letter to the Turkish authorities, rebuffing the Özal administration's final request for help for Polly Peck.

Meanwhile, the share price was stuck at 108p, a level which it had last touched in 1986. For Asil Nadir, an especially bitter irony in the crash was that the previous Friday, he had bought 500,000 shares in the company at 247p and another 750,000 at 248p, taking his stake in the company up to 28.14 per cent at the time of the crash.

Not everybody had yet lost faith in the company, however. In the USA, on the New York unofficial third market in which British shares are traded, Polly Peck shares were still changing hands at between 125 and 140p as the day ended. But in London, the nervousness of Polly Peck investors was infectious. Apart from the goings-on at Polly Peck, the UK was beginning to realise that it was in the grip of the worst depression for more than a decade. The stock market as a whole had fallen sharply, dropping 48.9 points to 2016.9, its lowest level in sixteen months.

On Friday 22 September, the Zurich Stock Exchange halted trading in the six Polly Peck International bond issues and Polly Peck shares. The bonds were Tim Wood's legacy to Polly Peck. They had raised Swiss Fr.665 million ($460 million) in seven issues for the company, and helped it pilot its way through the cash shortages in 1987 and 1989. S. G. Warburg Soditic, the lead manager bank for the bond issues, protested that there was no need for trading to be suspended, but the price of the bonds on the market was already dropping steeply when the order went out.

Responsibility for the survival of the company now rested on all its directors. Without a clear statement from the board about what was going on, the Stock Exchange would not allow trading in Polly Peck shares to resume. The non-executive directors in particular had a considerable weight on their shoulders. The board's task was not simply to provide a convincing account of the odd events of the last few weeks which demonstrated that Polly Peck's subsidiaries were functioning normally. Equally important, the directors must guarantee that the group's finances were in good shape and its cash flow was adequate to sustain normal trading. Although as yet the newspapers had no inkling of the financial crisis, by 21 September it was much the more serious problem. The directors could not give any assurances about Polly Peck's financial good standing because its sources of bank funding were starting to dry up rapidly.

The first serious problems with the banks had arisen in late August. As events unfolded ever more grimly through the early weeks of September, they became steadily more unwilling to risk their money even on normal daily commercial business with Polly Peck. One particularly alarming moment had occurred when a large German bank wrote to the company in mid-September saying that it had lost confidence and did not wish to do any more lending to the group. This provoked serious alarm among some of the executive directors. The share-price collapse and the SFO raid on South Audley Management had been the last straw. Until the bankers were reassured, Polly Peck was in the grip of a cash-flow crisis and might face possible collapse.

Day after day, including the weekend, the directors of Polly Peck gathered in the downstairs boardroom of Polly Peck, drinking endless bottles of sparkling water and trying to find ways out of this situation. Reg Mogg and David Fawcus had been proved right. It would have been sensible to keep a large amount of cash on deposit in London. If Asil Nadir had brought back even part of the £25 million he had promised in early August, there would have been nothing to worry about from the banks.

As it was, Polly Peck must look to its overseas subsidiaries for cash. The meetings to discuss this were professional and businesslike, with operational directors reporting on how much each of them might be expected to raise. Since the overseas subsidiaries were mostly known to be cash-rich, there should be no insuperable problem in raising a substantial amount of money from them. But most of the subsidiaries were in Turkey.

Tahsin Karan of Vestel was the director in charge of electronics (Asil Nadir handled everything else in Turkey and Cyprus). But Karan was not present at the meetings, feeling that he could not get away from Vestel's operations, including the one which eventually placed the company in administration.

By the doorway in Berkeley Square, the Ottoman sultans stared gravely down on the directors' deliberations from a seventeenth-century French print. Inside the room, eyes shifted from time to time to the portrait of an Art Nouveau puma's head, painted in gold and black ink, ready to spring from the wall.

Far from being able to offer the rest of the world enlightenment on their company's dramatic recent history, the directors themselves were most uncertain about what was happening. 'We kept asking what was going on. Was this something to do with the company?' recalls one who attended the meetings. The answer given, usually by senior figures in the company and its advisers, was that the problem had nothing directly to do with the company, nor was it a reflection on the chairman.

As the weekend drew to a close, Asil Nadir proposed one option on which the board could agree. Late on Sunday 24 September, the company formally asked the DTI to launch an investigation into the events of the previous week and the share-price collapse. This was not wholly bravado. Many executives at the top of Polly Peck felt there were some questions to which the company could reasonably expect answers. For example, how had a secretive organisation like SFO allowed so much news of its raid on South Audley Management to seep out so fast, when trading in Polly Peck shares was still continuing on the market? And why had trading taken so long to get stopped? If the price had been suspended around 250p, the situation for Asil Nadir and the company would have been very different. Citibank would not have placed its shares on the market, because its threshold would never have been reached. Asil Nadir would have been a much richer man, and the task of restoring an orderly market in Polly Peck shares would have been far easier. Those who believed that some sort of press conspiracy was behind Polly Peck's troubles naturally hoped that a DTI investigation would confirm this.

But the DTI did not want to launch an investigation at this stage. Investigations had a way of dragging on for years and generating endless political controversy. The recently published inspectors' report into the House of Fraser was a case in point. Besides, the DTI was not usually invited by a company to investigate it in order to give it a clean bill of health. Since a report usually took anything up to two years to produce, it was difficult to see it being of much benefit to anyone in the short term.

But John Redwood, the corporate affairs minister, swiftly put paid to the idea of an enquiry on the following Monday. His reply did not arrive at 42 Berkeley Square until 4.15 p.m. The DTI, Redmond said, had no intention of conducting an investigation, and if Polly Peck wanted one, it would have to pay for the probe itself, which could well exceed £1 million. It would also have to provide more reasons about why it wanted one at all. Redwood added that the SFO was already looking to Polly Peck share-dealings and their possible connections with Asil Nadir's business interests, and if court action were to follow, then the DTI report could not be published until after it was over. It was the first time the government had openly admitted that the SFO was investigating Polly Peck.

On Saturday morning, David Fawcus took the plunge which he had known was imminent for the previous week. He rang the SFO. Unfortunately it was Saturday morning and there was no senior figure there to take his call. He left a message saying that he wished to call again on Monday because he wanted to come in to the SFO and discuss certain matters with it.

In Berkeley Square, the by now deeply dejected and weary Polly Peck directors considered their options in the light of this dispiriting reply. Much of the time, the meeting was split into two parts. In one room Asil Nadir sat with his lawyers, drinking Turkish-style glasses of tea, making long telephone calls to friends, allies and family, and exuding an eerie sense of simultaneous calm and hyperactivity.

In another room were the directors and their advisers. By Monday 25 September, they had even more grounds for being gloomy than was apparent to the world outside. That was the day Polly Peck missed its first debt payments. News of this failure was bound to leak out before very long and when it did, it would plunge the whole future of the company, with its borrowing somewhere between £840 million and £1 billion, into immediate question.

David Fawcus and Reg Mogg were aware that they were no longer fighting simply to clear Polly Peck's name and restore confidence in its shares. Some sort of additional financing – either fresh money or an agreement with creditors – would have to be worked out soon. The rest of the world still assumed that Polly Peck was basically a going concern, but the fight for survival had already begun. Could any company or group of men be reasonably expected to fight off disaster on so many fronts at once?

News of the debt problems was kept under wraps for a few days. Meanwhile, the directors faced a bleak agenda. If Asil Nadir was not to be replaced as chairman, and there was to be no DTI enquiry, what else could be done to boost the public's confidence in the company?

As the discussions advanced, several different groups emerged among the directors. One consisted of Asil Nadir and his two oldest colleagues on the board, Mark Ellis, the corporate development director, and Radar Reshad. They were usually backed by Norbert Wirsching, the entrepreneur from the Far East who had joined Polly Peck at the time of the Capetronics purchase. David Fawcus, Peter Compson, Reg Mogg and Brian Haycox of Del Monte Fresh Fruit formed another group. The non-executives headed by Larry Tindale and Sir Michael Sandberg were trying to find a diplomatic middle way.

In a series of anguished boardroom meetings, different solutions were proposed and rejected. An obvious one in the wake of the recent press allegations was for Asil Nadir to stand down as chairman. On 22 September, David Fawcus and Peter Compson went to see Sir Michael Sandberg to try to persuade him that the non-executives should co-operate with them to insist that Asil Nadir was now a liability to the company and should at least take a sabbatical from his job. Asil Nadir had already agreed that when the time was ripe, he would step down, but Fawcus and Compson did not succeed on this occasion, perhaps partly because Sir Michael was reluctant to step into the breach himself.

The City was aware that a change of chairman was under discussion. All sorts of names were suggested. There was even wild talk of former US presidents Richard Nixon or Ronald Reagan being persuaded to take the job. A more realistic choice would have been a man like Sir John Harvey-Jones, the former chairman of ICI-turned television personality, though it is doubtful whether he would have taken on such a task. But feelers were put out to some other City notables. Sir Norman MacFarlane (now Lord MacFarlane), former chairman of United Distillers, was among those to receive a discreet approach. By Monday evening the directors had come up with several drafts, but there were always objections. Either one or other of the directors declined to sign, or the Stock Exchange Quotations Panel rejected the form of words employed. The idea of a new chairman began to fade.

Instead, the board decided to appoint an outside firm of accountants to investigate the company's affairs and report to shareholders. The obvious choice was Coopers & Lybrand. Both sides would know each other well. Though Coopers had never been Polly Peck's auditors, they had helped Asil Nadir plan his strategy on many occasions, right back to the Wearwell float, as well as being his tax advisers, and they had a strong presence in Turkey. A favourable report from them would perhaps restore the group's credibility with the world. In any case, Coopers had also been selected to advise the group if it became unable to trade and had to go into administration. In the event, the original Coopers' mandate lasted less than five days. It was quickly apparent that the readers who mattered would be not the Polly Peck board but the sixty banks to whom the company owed money.

Things were moving on other fronts. Wednesday 19 September was also the day that Tim Wood, the former Polly Peck treasurer who had left the company the previous January, went to the headquarters of the SFO. He did so against the advice of his lawyer, and with some misgivings.

Tuesday arrived with the Polly Peck board still stuck in its marathon meeting and wrestling over the difficulties of drafting a statement. At this point there was a further shock. News emerged of the first definite irregularity in Polly Peck share-dealings. It was only a technical irregularity, but to this day it remains the only one that has been uncovered – and the puzzles it poses have never been resolved.

Blade Explorations was a Swiss front company which had been buying and selling Polly Peck shares for several years. It was run from small offices next to the World Trade Centre in Geneva, by a little-known company called Rhone Finance with a British managing director, Ian McNeil. After the Stock Exchange made its enquiries, Blade Explorations sheepishly admitted on 14 August that it had sold a large parcel of shares just three days before Asil Nadir withdrew his abortive bid offer.

Blade Explorations had sold 200,000 shares at 417p and 250,000 at 410p – a deal worth £1,859,000. Whoever had sold the shares had taken his profits while the stock was fairly close to its peak August value, and well ahead of the price collapse which was to follow Asil Nadir's bid withdrawal. Blade Explorations should have disclosed details of the transaction by 12 o'clock the following day, 15 August, but it had not done so. When the Stock Exchange was monitoring Polly Peck share-dealings around the time of the bid, it quickly detected these deals and asked for details from the stockbroker concerned. They revealed that Blade Explorations had owned more than 1 per cent of Polly Peck on 14 August.

So who was behind Blade Explorations? Behçet T. Ali, came the reply. But who was Behçet Ali? Apparently a Turkish Cypriot millionaire, capable of buying and selling £2 million of shares on a single day, and Turkish Cypriot millionaires are a scarce species. In a world where everyone knows everyone else, Behçet Ali's identity was – and is – a mystery. The name is almost certainly a *nom de guerre*. Behçet Ali itself is a fairly common combination of first names, like Jean-Paul in French. Since there is no surname, he is presumably Turkish Cypriot rather than a Turkish mainlander. What, if anything, the middle T stands for, is another mystery. Whether he is Turkish or Turkish Cypriot, Behçet T. Ali has never stepped forward to explain his happily timed share purchases. Another theory put around soon after the event in some quarters was that Mr Ali was actually a Greek Cypriot who did not spell Turkish very well. But there is no evidence for this.

Mr McNeil of Rhone Finance, who appears not to have realised that the name would be publicly released, would not give the press any details beyond saying that he had 'no dealings' with either Asil Nadir or Polly Peck. He had been unfamiliar with the UK rule, introduced in the wake of the Guinness share support operation, which obliged all deals by a shareholder owning more than 1 per cent of a company to be disclosed the next day.

One fact shone out: on Polly Peck's share register, there was no mention of Rhone Finance or Blade Explorations, even though the latter had owned more than 1 per cent of the company – and still held 3.9 million shares. And, of course, there were the earlier unanswered questions. Who was behind Riverbridge, Gateway and Tristan, the companies which had been at the centre of the suspect share-dealings publicised in August?

When UK shares are held in the names of off-shore nominee companies, it is likely to be difficult or even impossible to identify the true owner. Companies uncertain of who their shareholders are, and worried that a predator may be trying to build up a stake, have the power to demand information about the identities of their shareholders under Section 212 of the Companies Act. If they do not get the information they need, they can under some circumstances penalise over-reticent shareholders by asking the courts to remove some of their rights, including dividend, voting and sales rights. Finding the ultimate owners, if they are hidden behind three or four screens of nominee companies, is laborious – and seldom of obvious benefit.

In the case of Polly Peck, it now turned out that the company did not even keep a complete register of directors' shareholdings, an important requirement under the Companies Act. Without information of this kind, investors had little chance of understanding who really owned a company.

Details of the nominee companies, such as Restro of Jersey, through which Asil Nadir owned his shares, should have been published but had not been. As the month ended, Polly Peck's luckless director of investor relations found himself scrambling to bring the records up to date.

While news of the unusual share-dealings at Blade Explorations was
leaking out, the Polly Peck board was spending its sixth day trying to
devise a statement which would satisfy the Stock Exchange and get Polly
Peck's shares back in the market. By now, by no means the entire board
was caught up in the marathon. Mark Ellis and Brian Haycox were in
New York, and Sir Michael Sandberg was on his way back from a
business trip to the same city. A draft statement had gone to the Quotations Panel of the Stock Exchange on Tuesday morning, but agreement
on it had not been forthcoming.

Other institutions linked with Polly Peck were beginning to suffer.
On Tuesday 26 September, the share price of Standard Chartered, one
of the banks on which Polly Peck depended most heavily, fell by 10 per
cent. It was known to have lent the group about £50 million and had
been one of its main advisers during the Del Monte purchase a year
earlier; it had also helped handle the 1988 rights issue.

Other UK banks mostly only had slight exposure, with one exception.
Lloyds, the smallest of the 'Big Four' clearers and the bank which
described itself as a 'thoroughbred among banks', had lent Polly Peck
£20 million. This embarrassing misjudgment remained a secret throughout the weeks of the company's collapse.

Barclays, the largest UK bank and the one which had been expanding
its lending most aggressively in the late 1980s, turned out to have no
exposure at all to Polly Peck. The news raised some eyebrows. Barclays'
merchant banking and securities offshoot, Barclays de Zoete Wedd, was
a joint broker to Polly Peck. It looked very much as if someone had
given the company the thumbs down somewhere along the line.

Another bank with no lending to Polly Peck was BCCI, the Bank of
Commerce and Credit International, which was to be closed down a
year later in an even bigger financial scandal. Over the years it had
politely declined approaches from Polly Peck to lend it money, despite
the fact that Turks and Pakistanis were supposed to be close Muslim
friends and allies. Just why it would not lend to Polly Peck is not clear.
'I used to think BCCI were pretty shrewd when I discovered that they
would not lend to us, but we never discovered what the reason was,'
says one disillusioned former Polly Peck executive.

Wednesday morning came and the board finally agreed on a statement
which was sent round to the Quotations Panel. It was returned at
5.45 p.m. Exasperation on both sides was now passing any previously
imaginable levels. Tension was heightened by the fact that on the same
day, David Fawcus had a meeting with the SFO. The outside world
assumed that he was being summoned, but the meeting was of course
at his own request and he told the other directors so. He was questioned

by the SFO in Elm Street in a bleak room with a stripped pine decor where Ernest Saunders, his erstwhile colleague at Guinness, had been grilled in the course of the Guinness scandal, fascinating his interrogators with the sharpness of his mind.

These developments spurred Asil Nadir to try to take the initiative again. In a bid to stem the torrent of criticism and innuendo now appearing in the press, he announced that he was starting High Court actions for alleged libel against the *Observer* and the *Sunday Times*. In each case three articles were involved, and there were two injunctions to prevent the publication of further articles. The move was welcomed by his friends, who thought that much of Polly Peck's share price collapse might have been averted if he had taken an aggressive line against his critics at an earlier stage.

A second initiative was even bolder. It was a last-ditch effort to find the finance which would save the company and involved going on a long and highly public journey. On Friday 28 September, Asil Nadir rose early at his home at 3 Aldford Street. After another morning of arguing with the board, he left the office in the afternoon, and drove in his limousine to Heathrow. He planned to fly to New York on Concorde with British Airways.

It seemed on the face of it astonishing to City opinion, unaware of the mounting cash crisis inside Polly Peck, that Asil Nadir should leave the country at this point in the proceedings. After more than a week of struggling, Polly Peck had still not come up with its draft statement. But as he stared out of the car window on his way to the airport, Asil Nadir's thoughts were no longer primarily focused on the statement. The reason why the tension had gone out of the process of drafting it was that it had become a side-issue compared to the main problem now facing him and the company. Polly Peck was already in the throes of the greatest liquidity crisis in its history, a crisis which would certainly destroy it unless new financial support could be found somewhere. The only chance of obtaining it lay in this dash to New York and a meeting with the one man he now regarded as a possible saviour for Polly Peck.

Asil Nadir had always hated flying and he had little taste for Concorde, knowing that on a scheduled flight he would be quite likely to experience air turbulence at some point. One of the attractions of having your own private jet was that the pilot could detect turbulent weather on his screen and alter course to avoid it. Asil Nadir had suffered from turbulence on Concorde in the past, and he greatly disliked it. A journey in his own jet would have been more comfortable, but slower, hence his decision to fly on Concorde rather than in Polly One.

As for the board's proposed statement, after a week of deadlock, the fight seemed to have gone out of both sides. The bones of the statement had been more or less decided. David Fawcus and the lawyers were at work on a version which seemed likely to be satisfactory. Asil Nadir would make his own separate statement, rejecting the allegations against him and clarifying his relationship with South Audley Management. That left four executive directors and two non-executives, the latter including Larry Tindale, the deputy chairman of 3i, struggling to get something produced by the weekend.

There was no split among the directors, but no one was too sure what the future might hold. Polly Peck's lawyers advised the non-executive directors that they should consider retaining their own separate legal advisers in case their interests started to conflict with those of the company.

As Friday wore on, it became clear that there would be no statement that day either. No one now thought of preparing it over the weekend, and the optimists in Polly Peck began to tip the following Tuesday as the most likely delivery date. But the statement by itself would not be enough. Polly Peck's institutional shareholders were now quietly making it plain that the price of their continued support of the company, once trading started again, would be a new chairman.

Asil Nadir had already offered his resignation, only to have it unanimously rejected by the other members of the board: many of them felt that Polly Peck would not stay together unless he was at the helm, and no one else could remotely approach his influence in Turkey and Northern Cyprus.

The following Monday, 1 October, was going to be a most disagreeable day anyhow. It was the day payment was due for anyone who bought Polly Peck shares in the last stock market account period. The cash would be handed over for purchases that were now virtually worthless. City stockbrokers UBS Phillips and Drew were thought to have made a £7 million loss on shares bought in the final hours of trading in Polly Peck, but the worst-hit casualty of all would be Asil Nadir himself. It was already known that he was going to have to pay out at least £3,095,000 on 1.25 million shares bought on 14 August that were now worth only £1.35 million at the suspension price of 108p. In fact he had made much larger purchases than this. The deals were entirely legal but they ran up debts of tens of millions of pounds and left him with shares which could not be traded. In a few weeks, the stockbrokers involved would be suing him in the bankruptcy court.

Concorde flight 001 was on time when the plane touched down at New York. Reporters from the British press were on the lookout for

Asil Nadir at JFK International, but they had a long and fruitless wait at the arrivals barrier from which they expected him to emerge. For having cleared his documents in London, Asil Nadir had taken a helicopter straight into town, to East 60th Street, from where he rode in a limousine to Polly Peck's New York offices on West 57th Street. The British press initially assumed that he was travelling to some US bank or corporate finance advisers to seek a rescue package.

Towards evening, Asil Nadir went out again, to a reception at the Peninsula Hotel given by the man he had flown across the Atlantic to meet and on whom all his hopes of saving Polly Peck now appeared to hang. This was not a figure that would have occurred to the chairman of any other large corporation in London to regard as a possible last-ditch saviour. He was neither a New York banker nor a corporate finance specialist but no less than President Turgut Özal of Turkey. Accompanied by his usual plane-load of Turkish ministers, senior bureaucrats, businessmen and bankers, Özal was in the USA for the annual conference of the International Monetary Fund and a UN-sponsored meeting of children from across the world at which he was due to meet, among other people, Mrs Thatcher.

News of Polly Peck's liquidity crisis broke in the Sunday newspapers on the last day of September. The *Sunday Telegraph*, which had evidently been well briefed by sources within the company, thought that Polly Peck probably needed between £80 million and £120 million to tide it over the crisis which involved placating forty-three creditor banks. It believed that Polly Peck had the cash in Turkey and Cyprus, and that the problem was persuading the Turks to allow it to remit the funds. In fact Turkey's foreign currency reserves were over £12 billion and the Turkish lira had been declared a fully convertible currency by the IMF earlier that year.

The *Sunday Times* claimed that at least six Polly Peck executives would be interviewed by the SFO in the week ahead. It disclosed that Tim Wood, Polly Peck's former treasurer, had been interviewed by the SFO the previous Friday, the day that Nadir flew to New York. In fact by then he had had several meetings.

Meanwhile, on the other side of the Atlantic, Asil Nadir talked endlessly with his closest allies in the Turkish political establishment, Çavlan Süerdem, the political adviser he had inherited from Rauf Denktaş, and with Bülent Şemiler. Şemiler, an adviser to the president, a Turkish Cypriot by birth, and a close family friend of the Nadirs, was in New York as part of Özal's entourage.

When Asil Nadir returned from his meetings with Turkish officials to the anxious party of Polly Peck officials waiting in his New York hotel, he was in up-beat mood. He was now confident, he said, that funds would arrive at agreed times.

The Turkish president was certainly concerned about the possible collapse of Polly Peck. When he met Mrs Thatcher on his New York visit he briefly mentioned the Polly Peck affair to her, but how direct these approaches were and how far they went is a matter of some uncertainty.

Officially, all decisions on Polly Peck were taken not by President Özal, a non-executive head of state under the Turkish constitution (though in practice the driving force in the government), but by Güneş Taner, Minister of Economic Affairs and a former Citibank executive in Istanbul. A week or two later, Taner would insist that Asil Nadir's plight had not been directly raised with Mrs Thatcher by President Özal. The president had merely insisted that Asil Nadir should not become the victim of a possible Greek plot. Nevertheless, a letter to the British government on Asil Nadir's behalf was certainly despatched to London by the Turkish government that weekend.

In seeking help of this sort, the Motherland Party government was of course seriously miscalculating. In public, Thatcher and Özal affected to be soul-mates, emissaries of the revolutionary free market philosophy that had distinguished the 1980s from its predecessors. They had even been born on the same day of the year. But when Turgut Özal warned that the Polly Peck affair could harm relations between Turkey and Britain, the Turks asked Mrs Thatcher to explain whether there were any proven allegations of wrongdoing by either the company or Asil Nadir, and got a cool response. Mrs Thatcher told him that the question was not one for the British government but for the SFO, which was in charge of the investigation. Perhaps her patience was wearing a little thin.

The Turkish letter to the British government went out at the weekend. Signed by Güneş Taner, it was intentionally or otherwise couched in blunt terms which raised hackles when the letter was read in Whitehall, especially in the Bank of England. To British officialdom, Asil Nadir and Polly Peck appeared as something of an irritant, a company which had courted suspicion. Asil Nadir was not only at the centre of serious allegations; he had also brought down disaster on his own head with the abortive bid for the company.

To Turkish official eyes, in marked contrast, he seemed a great businessman whose misfortunes on several occasions had demonstrably been the work of Greek Cypriots. The idea that Asil Nadir's problems were the result of a conspiracy between the Greek Cypriots and the Western press received a boost that weekend when the Greek Cypriots announced plans to investigate and perhaps try Asil Nadir *in absentia* in the south of Cyprus for fraud and theft in his use of property in the Turkish Cypriot north of the island.

This move was a piece of theatrics. Nadir was not subject to Greek Cypriot jurisdiction and the Greek Cypriots had been making this sort of complaint against him for more than a decade. Nevertheless, some newspapers automatically reported this news under headlines such as 'Cyprus to investigate Asil Nadir for fraud'. Others reported Nadir's own claims that he had turned the corner: 'Things are going very well,' he said on Sunday 30 September. 'We are working hard to prepare a very comprehensive statement which will clear up everything. It will not be long now. I am sure we will get back to normality.'

But seen at close quarters, Asil Nadir no longer looked so calm. At the reception in the Peninsula Hotel given by President Özal, guests had noted that beads of sweat were pouring down his face, and he gave the impression of a man trying hard to appear relaxed.

His future hinged on the goodwill of Özal and Güneş Taner. Though Asil Nadir had probably forgotten it, he could expect little personal sympathy from Taner. He had stood him up for lunch in the past and there was little warmth between the two men. When they met in New York, the Turkish minister had been non-committal and a little distant. He asked Asil Nadir outright whether he was guilty of the allegations against him and listened in silence to his reply.

Taner did not say no directly, but played for time. He told Asil Nadir that at least a week would be needed to assess his request. But to others he struck a much less certain note. 'I'm not sure what we should do. We don't know these people. We don't know much about them at all,' he told one British journalist. It was an odd way of referring to the best-known Turkish businessman there had ever been, but Bülent Şemiler and others among Asil Nadir's Turkish allies told him that this did not matter too much, that Taner was not very much more than a glorified office-boy doing the bidding of his master, the president. This evaded the main point.

However Taner couched his words, the underlying reality was clear. Turgut Özal had decided not to weigh in on Asil Nadir's side. Polly Peck's prospect of avoiding financial collapse suddenly looked very bleak indeed.

14 · Into Administration

Asil Nadir flew back to London on the night of Sunday 30 September. He brought no cash with him, so the meeting of the board the next morning had to rule out any hope of an instant solution to the company's cash problems. The tightening squeeze from the banks meant that there was no way the directors could produce a statement along the lines originally envisaged by the Stock Exchange, saying that the company and its subsidiaries were trading satisfactorily. Nor was there any chance of persuading the Stock Exchange authorities to allow trading in the company's shares to resume. The only course of action open to the board was to acknowledge the company's plight.

Just before 10 p.m. Monday 1 October, Polly Peck's board finally issued its statement. It had taken ten days to produce a document of only 835 words. A second statement from Asil Nadir accompanied it. For over 23,000 shareholders, especially the unhappy minority who had received their bills that morning for shares bought during the last accounting period, the sombre paragraphs contained not just a devastating disappointment but serious cause for fresh alarm. 'The collapse of the share price and associated negative publicity, however, precipitated liquidity problems' sounded like something of an understatement. Instead of a new Stock Exchange listing, there was to be a meeting with banks and other lenders the following Friday.

To those inside the company this came as no surprise. They knew that Polly Peck's relations with its banks had frozen up, plunging the company and many of its subsidiaries into grave difficulties as suppliers' credits were interrupted. By the creditors' meeting on 5 October, eleven lenders had already cut off lines of credit totalling £52 million.

On the share-price collapse, the directors said that they were not aware of any business reason for it, and noted the many extraordinary rumours which had circulated on the morning of 20 September. They pointed out the strengths of the group, with its 35,000 employees, well-known brand-names, and 'its capable, dedicated operational and corporate management team'.

As for the allegations about Asil Nadir, the statement fell short of an explicit declaration of confidence by Polly Peck's other directors in their chairman. Apart from Asil Nadir, none of the directors had any connection with South Audley Management, and the board had been informed by its chairman that he denied all allegations of impropriety and was suing the *Sunday Times* and the *Observer*.

The board was co-operating fully with the SFO and had offered to provide any help needed in the investigation and to restore business confidence. It was commissioning Coopers & Lybrand to prepare an independent report on the group's businesses, working with Polly Peck's audit committee, chaired by Larry Tindale. Richard Stone, Coopers & Lybrand's head of corporate finance, who would be made one of Polly Peck's administrators just over three weeks later, and Jim Truscott, another accountant at Coopers, were to head the investigation.

There was one small chink of apparent hope in the statement. 'The chairman has been in touch with the government of Turkey and the board draws considerable encouragement from the degree of interest shown by that government.' In view of the hesitation which the Turkish government had displayed in New York, this was an optimistic way of putting things.

Asil Nadir's statement was, characteristically, much livelier. It was just under 500 words long. 'It is impossible and inappropriate for me to deal, in this statement, with all the unfounded suggestions, or all the calls for information as to a variety of personal matters, that have been made,' he said. He claimed that his personal financial position was still strong, even though the value of his Polly Peck shareholdings had dropped from £400 million to £100 million, but he admitted that, partly because of his recent share purchases, there were some personal liquidity problems. 'These I am urgently addressing,' he declared.

He explained that South Audley Management provided management and administration services to the Nadir family interests and had no connection with Polly Peck. It was owned by a Nadir family trust of which he was a principal beneficiary and life tenant.

As for improper share-dealings, 'Certainly, any suggestions that I have been involved in improper share-dealings are false.' That disposed of the SFO as well. Their enquiries seemed to be related to alleged improper share-dealing, and so were 'in consequence unrelated to matters within my knowledge'.

In a separate statement, he gave details of his share sales. A total of 16.65 million shares held against margin loans had been sold, of which 3.05 million had been disposed of before 10 September. The remainder – 13.6 million shares, worth around £55 million a few weeks earlier – had been sold either during the collapse on 20 September or in the following few days. About 10 million shares had been shed by the banks on the 20th alone, the biggest package being the 7.9 million shares held against loans from Citicorp.

It emerged that Credit Suisse in Basle had sold 300,000 shares as early as 31 August: as the share price had started to fall, loans made relatively recently and secured against Polly Peck shares at the highest prices had been the first to be affected. It had taken Asil Nadir a few days to notify the company about the sales, because, since the shares were held through trusts, he himself was not formally notified until some time afterwards. His own shares in Polly Peck now amounted to 24.22 per cent, worth about £112 million at their final market price.

All in all, there had been four phases to the share-dumping. Between 31 August and 10 September 3.05 million shares had been sold; 255,000 shares had been sold between 24 and 26 September; 575,000 shares had been sold on 16 and 27 September; and finally, a further 12.7 million shares had been off-loaded. Unaware that his bankers were dumping shares, Asil Nadir had himself been in the market as a buyer. These sales, while in no way improper, raised some important questions about how the interests of other shareholders are to be protected when the chairman or chief executive of a company is also its biggest share-holder.

Asil Nadir had used his borrowings to finance a wide range of businesses outside the group, something which was by no means unusual, but it meant that his private business activities, and especially the borrowing that made them possible, could have a powerful impact on the fate of Polly Peck in the markets. When a bank sold off its collateral, it triggered a further fall in the stock price, which would not have happened if the shares had been spread in the market in the usual way between investors who were holding them as investments.

The London Stock Exchange had allowed the statements to go forward, but it did not give any sign that it had approved them. To have gained such approval, the directors would have had to provide information about the group's market position, its forecast profits, future sales and the value of its assets. None of that could be found in what the directors had written; indeed, the appointment of outside accountants to review the state of the group's business seemed to be an admission of uncertainty about Polly Peck's most basic functions.

On the same day, Monday 1 October, the Stock Exchange finally removed Polly Peck from its FT–SE 100 index. The move now looked long overdue, for it was impossible to say when, if ever, trading would be resumed. Polly Peck had been on the index for almost a year, having been finally accepted as one of the UK's top shares in the wake of the Del Monte purchase. One by one, the symbols of its credibility were being dismantled.

Meanwhile, David Fawcus was ringing around the subsidiaries outside Turkey and Cyprus to see how much cash each of them could send to London. Not all their managers were amenable to the idea of pouring money from their businesses into a potentially bottomless pit, and the lines ran hot at times. 'Until I know exactly what the banking situation is doing, I am not releasing a penny,' one far-flung subsidiary told Fawcus. The manager concerned then went home and pulled out all his telephone plugs to ensure that he could not be contacted.

A team from Kidder Peabody, the New York corporate finance specialists, were called in. Perhaps, Asil Nadir's advisers thought, they would know how to stop the banks kicking sand in his face. Nothing came of the visit.

In general, onlookers still thought that if the cash could be found anywhere, it would be in Turkey. 'If, as the company asserts, the government of Turkey is showing interest in its plight, it is high time for Mr Özal to confirm the fact,' wrote Lex in the *Financial Times*.

But Mr Özal would not confirm the fact. None the less, Asil Nadir indicated that there was still a good chance that finance would come from Ankara: 'I have had recent urgent talks with the Turkish government, at the highest level, with a view to arrangements being made, in the near future, that will restore confidence in Polly Peck and financial stability to the market in its shares.' The first step would be a visit to Ankara to take matters forward with the Turkish government to see if more progress could be made on the loan he had asked for but not received in New York the previous weekend.

Asil Nadir's friends in Turgut Özal's entourage had a clear explanation for why the aid package had not been granted in New York. They blamed the British authorities, in particular the Bank of England, for offending Özal's national pride just at the wrong moment. They claimed that the rescue package had been assembled, with state banks and private banks ready to put up the necessary funds, but at the last moment the Foreign and Commonwealth Office had sent to Ankara (more exactly to New York) a reply to Güneş Taner's letter which had infuriated the Turkish president. President Özal has never said anything, either on the record or off it, to confirm the version of events which came from Asil Nadir's allies.

During the following week the contents of the Foreign Office's letter were leaked to two *Financial Times* journalists, and were confirmed by the British authorities. In even blunter language than that of the Turkish letter to which it was replying, the British letter warned that Polly Peck was at the centre of an investigation by the SFO. Its affairs were in considerable disarray. For there to be any chance of saving it from going into administration, an immediate injection of £100 million would be needed by first thing London time on the morning of Monday 1 October. Even if the money were sent, however, it would not necessarily mean that the problems of the company would be resolved.

Although the text had been drafted by bankers and came ultimately from the Bank of England, it was signed by Douglas Hurd, the Foreign Secretary. The Foreign Office later denied that the letter had been an ultimatum, describing it as more a reflection of soundings made in the City by the Bank of England. In Ankara the letter was delivered to the Turkish Foreign Ministry by an embarrassed British Ambassador who knew it would not go down well. It was less than two weeks since he and his wife had attended Ayşegül Nadir's masked ball.

If a direct rescue was out of the question, perhaps there could be a fire-sale of subsidiaries. Among the solutions now being canvassed was another desperate idea: to sell the Turkish subsidiaries but keep Del Monte and Sansui, enabling Polly Peck to survive as a global business group. On the face of it, the idea had a certain plausibility.

Vestel, the Turkish electronics subsidiary, might indeed have had considerable appeal to some of the other Turkish consumer electronics companies in the large conglomerates. Businesses in Turkey could probably be rebuilt in the future, even if terms were inserted into the sale agreement preventing managers and other key staff from returning to employment with Nadir for a fixed period. The drawback was that Turkish buyers would not be easy to find, unless perhaps the 'sale' was simply a cloak for a government-backed rescue loan. Cash on the necessary scale was simply not available from most of the conglomerates, and in any case they knew that administration was looming for Polly Peck and that prices for the same businesses might be a great deal lower in a few months.

One name persistently mentioned as a possible buyer was Sakıp Sabancı, the head of the Sabancı Group, one of Turkey's two main conglomerates. Sabancı, the reasoning went, would not only find Vestel a good business, he might view the deal as part of some sort of political bargain with Özal. But when reporters rang Sabancı, who was staying in the Ankara Hilton on a trip from Istanbul to the Turkish capital, he declared roundly that no one had approached him with such an idea and he was not interested in it.

Nor, apparently, were the owners of the Çukurova Group, another fairly large Turkish industrial empire which included three banks. They were more closely linked with both Özal and Asil Nadir. It was Çukurova who had agreed the previous spring to become partners in a joint venture with Polly Peck to manufacture Peugeot cars in Turkey. Çukurova also had some family links through marriage with Bülent Şemiler, the Turkish Cypriot who was in the entourage of President Özal and a friend of Asil Nadir, but Mehmet Emin Karamehmet, the owner of the group, was believed to be annoyed at the way the motor deal had been handled by Nadir, and reluctant to get involved with him again.

Despite all this, it is to this day widely believed by former senior figures at 42 Berkeley Square and others who were very close to the company that Asil Nadir did in fact find a £100-million line of credit in Turkey. They believe that money was to be channelled through one of the Turkish/Middle Eastern banking joint ventures, but that at the last moment Asil Nadir refused to sign, apparently reluctant to give away any assets as security for the loan. And there are straws in the wind which confirm the idea. When Güneş Taner met representatives of the administrators the following month, he would ask why Asil Nadir had not signed. 'We arranged it all,' he told them. 'Why didn't he sign?'

Before meeting the banks, Asil Nadir flew to Turkey, leaving in his Gulf Stream jet on 3 October. His entire future depended on a bail-out which would ultimately have to come from the Turkish taxpayer. Perhaps this more than anything else had been the reason why President Özal and Güneş Taner had been reluctant to promise him anything in New York.

Turkey's private sector banks, the smaller, livelier part of a financial services industry which was clogged up by bad debts and outdated business practices, had never put up a loan on the scale required – between £50 million and £200 million – for anyone in the past. Neither, for that matter, had the large Turkish state banks, although, with the resources of the Treasury behind them, they could have found the money. When Turkish companies needed funds on this scale, they tended to look abroad for them. One Turkish construction group had indeed raised more than $500 million in the 1980s, but its income was generated in hard currency on international projects outside Turkey, and the money had come from a flow of bank borrowings rather than a single giant syndicated loan.

Polly Peck was even less involved with the Turkish banking system. Meyna, its Turkish fruit and vegetable business, was unusual for the group in that it did rely on Garanti, an Istanbul-based private sector bank, and Finansbank had advised Vestel when it sold shares on the Stock Exchange. That was almost the sum total of the group's banking relationships, although in September, around the time of the Sheraton opening, Asil Nadir had persuaded another well-known private sector

bank to lend him $5 million – a decision which the lender was soon
bitterly to regret.

A public sector rescue would undoubtedly have raised awkward political questions. Why should Asil Nadir be saved by the Turkish government when it had allowed many Turkish companies, some of them run
by genuinely able entrepreneurs, to go to the wall as a direct result of
its own free-market policies? Privileged treatment for an admirer of
Turgut Özal would have aroused so much opposition that the issue
hardly needed to be discussed. There could be legal difficulties, too. 'I
don't think you will find any general manager of a state bank who would
be willing to sign the advance,' said one private sector banker in Istanbul.
Another asked: 'Why should Turkish banks give a guarantee to UK
banks?' Yet Asil Nadir's Turkish advisers thought that the matter might
be resolved very simply, perhaps through export credits from Turkey's
Exim Bank, rather than a formal syndicated loan which would take time
to put together.

How much most Turkish bankers knew or understood about Polly
Peck's balance sheet is doubtful. In some ways the company was even
less clearly understood in Turkey than it was in London. But Turkish
bankers had lived for a decade in a high-risk environment. In 1990 they
knew from recent experience what the collapse of a company could
bring in tow, and they feared that a one-off injection of funds, even if
it had been possible, would not have been the end of the story.

There were no cries of outrage in the Turkish press at the idea of a
bail-out by the Turkish taxpayer for Asil Nadir. Only *Sabah*, Turkey's
largest selling daily and the paper which had most persistently attacked
Asil Nadir over the previous year, mentioned in the opening days of
October that the idea was being mooted in London. In the remainder
of the Turkish press – apart from those papers which were owned by
Asil Nadir himself and which ceaselessly reported his troubles resulting
from the alleged machinations of Greek Cypriots and their allies –
coverage of the Polly Peck affair was relatively subdued and several
papers adopted a notably gentler attitude to Asil Nadir than previously.
The financial scandal in London was largely incomprehensible to Turkish readers, and though other newspapers were unwilling to go as far
as Nadir's own papers did in branding recent events as the work of a
Greek Cypriot and foreign conspiracy, perhaps they thought that there
might be something in the idea.

When a top investigative reporter on one leading Turkish daily wrote
a critical story about some of Polly Peck's subsidiaries, he found his
proprietors unwilling to publish it. 'There seems to be a secret embargo
on the news,' he commented.

One explanation for this reticence might be solidarity between Turkish newspaper proprietors, even those who in the past have been bitter enemies, hang together in times of crisis. Another possibility was that Asil Nadir still had friends in high places in Turkey who wanted a veil to be cast over his misfortunes.

A simpler explanation for the muted and detached tone of Turkish press coverage of Polly Peck's collapse, after years of fierce hostility, may be cautious sympathy and an unwillingness to moralise. In Turkey, a country which has experienced three military coups in the last forty years, a disastrous reversal of a big man's fortunes is usually an essentially political event, brought about by his enemies. Who could stand in judgment and say whether the present case was very different?

So yet again Asil Nadir returned to London with an empty suitcase. But he was still optimistic on 5 October, when Polly Peck's bankers met the company at the Accountants' Hall in the City. He strode into the meeting, as one of the bankers present later put it, like a pop star strutting into a concert hall full of his fans. He was accompanied by David Fawcus and Reg Mogg. Facing him were 300 representatives from more than five dozen banks and one journalist from the *Independent* who had slipped unrecognised through the security net at the entrance. Former Polly Peck executives claim that she ignored a slide asking all non-bankers to leave, but the journalist concerned considers that she behaved in no way improperly. As a result, the figures which the company thought that it was revealing in confidence to its bankers were published in the newspapers the next morning.

Polly Peck conceded that it was facing a severe cash shortage. By the end of the year, the group would have to pay out £200 million in cash to service its bonds and bank debt. Polly Peck had defaulted already on £92.1 million of loans, and £52 million in credit had been withdrawn by eleven lenders. Net borrowings had risen from £864 million to £1.07 billion in the three months ending on 30 September, as cash balances of £404 million held by the group had halved. There was a particularly striking fall in cash balances in Turkey and Cyprus which had dropped from £306 million to £143 million, apparently for seasonal reasons. Late summer and early autumn was the most difficult period of the year for the citrus-exporting business in Turkey and Cyprus – the months when growers expected to get paid in advance – but the crop had not been harvested and exports were not yet under way.

The total Polly Peck group debt to banks was £1.3 billion. Its total assets were thought to be worth about £1.6 billion. So if the worst ever came to the worst and the company and its subsidiaries were put into liquidation, there ought to be enough cash to pay off all creditors, leaving a surplus of £300 million to distribute to the shareholders.

If the group went into immediate receivership rather than administration, the banks would get back only two-thirds of their money. Not surprisingly, the banks decided to wait. Polly Peck's directors were given a further week to try to come up with the money before a fresh meeting on 12 October.

How had the cash shortage arisen in a group which outsiders had until then supposed to be enormously cash-rich, with subsidiaries all over the world generating remarkable profits? Group employees at the UK head office knew from experience that Polly Peck experienced severe cash shortages from time to time. That was not particularly unusual.

Other subsidiaries from the Far East to the Americas did their bit to remit cash. Sansui, a company which had always been strapped for cash, sent $30 million. PPI Del Monte also remitted cash. The Del Monte money was sent to a London branch of Midland Bank which slapped it straight into a Polly Peck account, thus inadvertently breaching the terms of the previous year's ring-fencing agreement between the banks and the company over Del Monte's finances at the time of the purchase. When news of this mistake leaked out, there were many red faces.

The other option was to sell off businesses. There were a few Polly Peck subsidiaries which could go – Shell Company in Hong Kong was one. There might also be some private holdings of Asil Nadir to off-load. Three days after seeing the bankers, Asil Nadir announced that he had sold his 9.3 per cent stake in Turkey Trust, the small investment trust into which he had bought during the summer, for £1.88 million. It seemed a step in the right direction, albeit a small one. However, the sale was to Impex Bank, the Istanbul bank which he himself owned and which was Turkey Trust's financial adviser. Another future cash source would be the remainder of the cash due on the last three of the nine reefer ships which had come with the purchase of PPI Del Monte.

However, even when all possible sources of assistance outside Turkey and Cyprus had been tapped, there was still far less than £100 million in cash available.

On 10 October, Asil Nadir once again flew to Istanbul, indicating that he hoped to be able to release £70 million blocked in accounts in Northern Cyprus. There was also the possibility of selling other assets: perhaps the five main Polly Peck hotels, including the Antalya Sheraton Voyager, could be disposed of. Now that it was up and running, it might fetch well over $65 million.

What was clear was that if cash was to be raised, it had to be through a sale, for any rescue operation by the Turkish government by now looked very unlikely. At a vast party in the ballroom of the Ankara Hilton on 8 October to celebrate the opening of Midland Bank's first branch in Turkey, Güneş Taner, a portly, bespectacled figure who on this occasion showed little of his customary bonhomie, confirmed to the flock of journalists crowding around him that he expected to meet Asil Nadir shortly for talks, but added, 'There is absolutely no question of a government rescue package for Polly Peck International. It is a British private sector company and I do not see why we in Turkey should be expected to come to its rescue.'

The news duly appeared in next morning's *Financial Times*. Perhaps this was the moment at which it became clear that PPI's situation was irretrievable and that the company would go into administration within days.

Taner made another point: 'If the Serious Fraud Office fails to substantiate its charges against the company,' he said, 'there will be a lot of questions about the way this company has been treated.' Even Asil Nadir's critics in Britain conceded this point.

In Turkey, Asil Nadir conferred with his remaining band of allies. State bankers and government officials met him and his representatives behind closed doors. Even for those on the spot, it was extremely difficult to assess what was happening. The heads of all the state banks made it clear that they did not want to lend money to Polly Peck. Turkey's state bankers are by nature reticent and do not like to see their names in the papers, but several state bankers on this occasion let it be known that they had no objection to being quoted by name on this subject.

Nevertheless some of the same men were sighted by reliable witnesses in discussion with Nadir and bankers close to him. Were they perhaps trying to resist government pressure? Around this time, Asil Nadir seems to have met with President Özal again. But the only allies to put forward any money were the banks of the Çukurova Group. Yapi ve Kredi Bankası agreed to put up a one-year credit of around $25 million, but the telex to the creditors mentioned only £12.5 million, and this was to be a second mortgage on the Antalya Sheraton Voyager, an arrangement which would conflict with the claims of other creditors on Polly Peck's assets.

With no sign of help on the horizon, but still radiating confidence Asil Nadir flew from Turkey to Northern Cyprus on Thursday 11 October. The press believed that he was trying to withdraw £20 million from bank accounts on the island, but some newspapers noted that Jason Davies, the former director of South Audley Management who was at the heart of the share-dealing rumours, was also on the island, staying at the Jasmine Court.

In London, the SFO investigation was still attracting as much publicity as the threat of administration. As Taner had indicated, the publicity surrounding the investigations was undoubtedly making life even
more difficult for the company than it would otherwise have been.

On the day of his arrival in Cyprus, Asil Nadir made a bid to neutralise
the effects of the SFO's attention. His lawyers applied to the High
Court for a judicial review of the refusal of Barbara Mills, then the
SFO director, to indicate to him what she was investigating. Asil Nadir
claimed that, since he was innocent of any law-breaking, if he knew
what the allegations were, he would be able to supply the evidence to
disprove them and halt the enquiry.

Edward Bannister, Asil Nadir's counsel, said that of course his client
did not expect to be given any details of evidence against him or to be
shown documents, but he was entitled to a 'rough clue' about what was
alleged so that he could defend himself. Bannister pointed out that SFO
investigations under Section 2 of the 1987 Criminal Justice Act compel
statements to be given, without the person giving them having any idea
of what was being investigated, in contrast with ordinary police investigations, in which suspects have a right to silence and also know what
they are suspected of.

The court was not convinced. On 12 October, Mr Justice Steyn
turned down the application. However, there was leave to appeal and
the case was still being fought – with some success for Asil Nadir –
when he was arrested in mid-December.

In the early morning of 12 October, Asil Nadir flew back to London
and met Polly Peck's creditors again. Two hundred bankers stared ston-
ily at him in the Accountants' Hall as he told them that he did not have
£70 million to offer them, but that £5 million had been found. News of
this figure had arrived during the meeting when a telex message bearing
the good news was thrust into Asil Nadir's hands. The money had
come, he said, from Polly Peck's assets in Northern Cyprus. However, it
eventually emerged that it had come from the sale of Polly Peck's 93
per cent stake in the Salamis Bay Hotel – a hotel in Cyprus owned by
the group – a deal finally announced on 17 October. The hotel was sold
for $12 million, less than the price the group had paid for it earlier in
the year. A day or two earlier, the group had raised £5.5 million by
selling its 24 per cent stake in Shell Electric Holdings in Hong Kong.
But these disposals were tiny compared to the group's cash deficit.

Asil Nadir also spoke bitterly of the fact that Coopers & Lybrand
had chosen to announce themselves under the name of Cork Gully, a
subsidiary company which specialised in insolvency, when they arrived
in Cyprus the previous week. The move could create the impression

that the team might be coming as part of a liquidation operation rather than a rescue bid, exactly the opposite of what was intended. Coopers say they used the Cork Gully name on this visit at the suggestion of Polly Peck.

The meeting stretched on for four hours. Asil Nadir was once again calm and self-confident as he spoke – something which the bankers found mildly annoying. 'He has no idea of the trouble he is in,' commented one banker sourly. By the end of the meeting, though he again managed to persuade the banks to give him another week's grace, the banks made it clear that they wanted him to step down as Polly Peck's chairman. Like some of the group's own directors, they saw Sir Michael Sandberg as a natural candidate to take over, perhaps in the role of titular deputy chairman, though he did not want the role. The bankers did not wish to force Asil Nadir directly into resigning: had they done that, they would have taken on greater responsibility for the company under British insolvency law.

Even among Asil Nadir's allies on the board, there was recognition that the time had come for a change. 'The attacks were not against the company, in the end they were against him. He was such a high-profile chairman. Banks always referred to Asil Nadir's Polly Peck. In other companies, you don't connect the two,' says one former director. Asil Nadir replied to all such criticisms that he had already agreed to resign at the previous meeting, acknowledging that being a Turkish Cypriot was a handicap for his role as the figure-head of a UK public company.

However, the name of another possible new chairman was in fact already circulating. Anthony 'Cob' Stenham, a former finance director of Unilever, and non-executive chairman of Banker's Trust in Europe, was approached around this time, and is thought to have turned down the offer unless a number of stringent preconditions were met, including the placing of Asil Nadir's shares in a blind trust, new non-executive directors and new merchant bank advisers.

Coopers & Lybrand now issued a report on the group's financial situation. They had found £96 million in Polly Peck's subsidiaries in Turkey and Northern Cyprus, but around £200 million supposedly in Cyprus had not yet been tracked down and might be missing. £50 million was supposed to be in accounts with the Industry Bank of Cyprus, the bank which Asil Nadir had established in 1982. Much of this cash was presumably being held for payments to fruit-growers ahead of the season, and perhaps as cash-flow support for the group's hotels. These figures appeared slightly at variance with the reported total foreign currency reserves of Northern Cyprus, which had been around £70 million in June, but until the administrators could look directly at the books, there was no way of telling how much money was held there. Fearful that these funds, and other Polly Peck assets in Cyprus, might be nationalised by the Turkish Cypriots the moment the group went into administration, the bankers decided to wait, and professing deep reluctance, they eventually postponed their decision until 9 November.

Meanwhile, the hunt was on for Elizabeth Forsyth and Jason Davies, from South Audley Management, whose names were being linked with the share-dealing allegations mentioned in the Sunday papers. Neither could be found. SFO officers, hotly pursued by journalists, arrived at Elizabeth Forsyth's home in Grantham, and visited her London flat. Both were empty. The SFO must have been well aware that she had not returned from the holiday which had begun a day or two before the raid on South Audley Management on 19 September. 'We need to speak to her, but now that the balloon has gone up, God only knows what sort of access we shall have,' an investigator told *Today*.

Mrs Forsyth, who denies all accusations of improper conduct, says that she decided to lie low on the advice of her lawyers. The press reported that the SFO had prepared an order which would compel her to answer questions about South Audley Management, Asil Nadir and share-dealings in Polly Peck. From Switzerland, where she had been on holiday at the time of the SFO raid on South Audley Management on 20 September, she flew to Istanbul and then on to Cyprus. Awareness that she was probably on the island drew more British journalists to Northern Cyprus than at any time since the Turkish invasion in 1974. Though many local people must have known that she was staying in the houses belonging to two of Asil Nadir's leading associates on the island, the news did not leak out.

Why was Elizabeth Forsyth taking refuge in Cyprus? In London, Metin Münir had been relaying to his press contacts the message that she was planning to come back to England imminently. So indeed she was, but her lawyers were adamant that she should not return until the SFO guaranteed that she would not be detained.

There were some nervous moments as she tried to elude the press. On a flight through Switzerland, a friend who was due to meet her was unable to turn up. Mrs Forsyth was appalled to hear the loudspeaker system booming: 'Will Mrs Elizabeth Forsyth please come to the information desk?' There was another close squeak at the Istanbul Sheraton where a journalist from the *Financial Times* was staying. Elizabeth Forsyth was in little danger of being spotted, since there seemed to be no press photographs of her. Nevertheless, she was dismayed to find herself walking past the journalist as he interviewed a visitor in the lobby.

Fortunately both he and Forsyth were long-standing customers of the Istanbul Sheraton, and the girls on the hotel's staff, muttering darkly about sinister press conspiracies and Greek spies, knew where the path of discretion lay. They gallantly formed a human wall shielding Mrs Forsyth from the journalist's gaze. She went down the lift to the basement of the hotel, where a waiting car whisked her to the airport and a plane to Cyprus. 'I avoided him by just seconds,' she declared to Mehmet Ali Akpınar when she landed in Nicosia.

Other journalists had even less luck in meeting Forsyth. One British correspondent based in Ankara, acting on a tip-off from left-wing Turkish Cypriot journalists, quietly entered the Ozanköy home of Metin Münir, in the belief that Mrs Forsyth was there. He surprised only an indignant Münir who was having a shower at the time.

On another occasion Mrs Forsyth seems to have come quite close to being tracked down in Cyprus by a man and a woman who claimed to be journalists from London, but who the Turkish Cypriots believed were in fact emissaries of the SFO. The mysterious duo arrived one afternoon at the end of the long track close to the house where Mrs Forsyth was staying.

'We are looking for accommodation,' said the man.

'And also for Elizabeth Forsyth,' added the girl. They were directed elsewhere.

Photographs of the two of them were prominently displayed in the Turkish Cypriot press the next day and they left the island almost immediately. If they were indeed from the SFO, they may have been intending to serve a Section 2 order on Forsyth as soon as they saw her.

On 16 October, trading in Polly Peck shares began once more, not in London but in Zurich. The Zurich Stock Exchange had gone ahead and lifted the suspension, even though it had been strongly urged not to do so by its London counterpart, on the grounds that there were too many uncertainties to permit trading to begin. No member of the London Stock Exchange would be allowed to deal in Polly Peck shares while the London suspension was in force, so the main players would be missing from the Swiss market anyhow. But the Swiss said that many investors, especially those holding the Swiss franc bonds, wanted trading to resume.

In the event there was only one day's trading and, not surprisingly, it was not a great success. Even though trading was confined to matched deals, the price plunged from its opening level of 50p to 36p, after touching 16p at one point.

On 18 October, Noble Raredon, the company controlled by Bilge

Nevzat, Asil Nadir's younger sister, followed Polly Peck by asking for
its shares to be suspended on the market. They had plunged to 26p,
from a high of 102p earlier in the year.

A day later, it was announced that the Mercury Newspaper Group,
the small newspaper company which Asil Nadir had bought through
South Audley Management, would go into receivership with the loss of
fifty jobs. The group, which printed about 150,000 newspapers a week,
had been intended as the seed-bed for a future Nadir newspaper group,
but it had been badly hit by the recession. Its executives told reporters
that the group's financial problems had got completely out of hand when
the flow of money from South Audley Management had dried up a few
weeks earlier. No one wanted to buy the group, so there was no alternative but to put it into liquidation.

By the weekend, the mood of the banks was beginning to change,
and Polly Peck's prospects of staying out of administration until the 9
November creditors' meeting had faded. 'Patience is running out,' as
one banker put it. No cash had been remitted from Cyprus, despite
many reports that it was due to arrive at any moment. Turkish Cypriot
exchange controls were blamed for the delay. But in fact the Yapı ve
Kredi loan appeared to be all that Asil Nadir had been able to secure
in the way of new money, and it was thought to be secured against
company assets, including the Antalya Sheraton Voyager.

On 21 October, Asil Nadir flew back to Cyprus from Istanbul. He had
turned every stone in the search for funds, including some unlikely ones.
Lonrho's chief executive, 'Tiny' Rowland, not generally regarded as one
of Asil Nadir's obvious allies, had been approached. 'It is far too complicated, so we would not want to get involved,' Rowland said. In Turkey, no
buyers for his assets could be found, even though he was leaving no avenue
unexplored. Before leaving Istanbul, he is believed to have lunched with
Dinç Bilgin, the owner of *Sabah*, the largest-selling paper in Turkey and
until very recently the bitterest Nadir critic in the Turkish press. The two
men appear to have discussed the possible sale of some of Asil Nadir's
newspapers and magazines, but no deal was clinched.

Meanwhile, Coopers & Lybrand were pressing ahead with their survey
of the group's companies and their operations. They soon discovered that
they faced stiff opposition in some quarters. Meyna, the Turkish fruit and
vegetable operation, was reluctant to open its records to them. A more
serious blow to their work came unexpectedly on 22 October in the Turkish sector of Nicosia, when a group of seven orange grove farmers applied
successfully to a Turkish Cypriot court in Nicosia for an injunction to
prevent any documents or information from Asil Nadir's nine companies
on the island being shown to third parties. The injunction came into force

just two hours before the Coopers & Lybrand team was to begin examining the books detailing Polly Peck's operations on the island.

The ban seemed to stretch credibility. Turkish Cypriot opposition groups immediately denounced it as a ploy to keep the inspectors away from the documents they needed to see. Asil Nadir, however, was strictly dissociated from the court action. Coopers were assured that he was doing all he could, through Menteş Aziz, the Nadir family lawyer, to get the injunction lifted. The farmers themselves said that they were being damaged by the rumours about Polly Peck and they wanted to ensure that their position was protected.

The court action pitted Menteş Aziz against Kıvanç Riza, the growers' lawyer and an old rival. The obvious personal antagonism between the two men convinced visiting journalists that whatever lay behind the injunction, it was not a straightforward case of a put-up job.

In London, news of the injunction helped the hardliners among Polly Peck's critics who were arguing that the company should be placed in administration without delay. On Tuesday 23 September, one of the smaller creditors, the National Bank of Canada, which was owed a relatively modest £17 million, broke ranks and lodged a petition with the High Court to have the group compulsorily wound up. It was not the first such move – British Land was also pressing to get back £1 million owed to it – but other banks acknowledged that it was National Bank of Canada's action which posed the real threat of insolvency for Polly Peck. If a single bank stepped out of line with the other sixty creditors, any chance of saving the company from administration would disappear. 'If anyone rushes for the lifeboat, it's all over,' the *Guardian* reported one banker saying.

Asil Nadir heard the news of the petition in Cyprus, where he had returned empty-handed after only twenty-four hours away. His arrival in Cyprus coincided with the news of the first redundancies among Polly Peck employees there. More than a hundred workers had been told that their jobs had gone. If Polly Peck went into administration, many other redundancies would follow. The group employed more than 8,000 people on the island, making it the largest single private employer by far.

Meanwhile, Asil Nadir began to introduce the Coopers & Lybrand team to President Rauf Denktaş and other leading Turkish Cypriot officials, in a bid to convince people on the island that they were working with him and not against him. During these days he forged the beginnings of what was to prove, for a while, an outwardly friendly relationship with the Coopers & Lybrand team, especially Richard Stone, which would continue after the group went into administration.

The fuss over Michael Jordan's choice of the name of Cork Gully, his firm of specialist liquidators, rather than the group name of Coopers & Lybrand, had now faded. Coopers seem to have felt that they would not make progress on the island without the active support of Asil Nadir at their side. In July and August 1991, both Michael Jordan and Richard Stone would endorse this.

Although administration was obviously very close, there were still some grounds for hope. National Bank of Canada's action could not be heard before 12 December, and if it did not lift its action, the group would go into liquidation. For the directors of the company, however, there was another issue. If Polly Peck traded while insolvent, they would be liable to prosecution. The point seemed to have arrived where they could go no further without that elusive fresh cash. In fact, by Wednesday 24 October it was clear that unless Asil Nadir somehow produced £30 million for the creditors that very day, the company would go into administration. Polly Peck's board met again at 42 Berkeley Square at 2.30 p.m. The elegant boardroom had seen incessant meetings in the previous two months. This was to be the last of them, and the directors entered the room in sombre mood, knowing that within a few hours the group was bound to be placed in administration. Asil Nadir had not yet returned from Turkey and there was no definite news of whether he had been able to find any money. (In fact, by this time, Asil Nadir was on his way to London.)

The directors assembled with their legal and financial advisers. In Asil Nadir's absence, Larry Tindale was in the chair. There was only one piece of business: the resolution on administration was raised and unanimously approved. Some of the newer directors were struck by the fact that Polly Peck veterans and staunch allies of the chairman, such as Mark Ellis, voted with them unhesitatingly. As a mark of respect, they then left the meeting open until the chairman arrived, growing more impatient as the hours passed.

Late in the afternoon, the endless, desultory conversation was interrupted by a piece of news. Just before flying out of Istanbul, Asil Nadir had put out a defiant statement in Turkish in which he pledged himself to defend the group's Turkish and Turkish Cypriot subsidiaries from foreign interference. The statement was not couched in the sort of tones usually heard from chairmen of London public companies, but its message was clear enough.

'My operations in Turkey and the Turkish Republic of Northern Cyprus, and the need to ensure a healthy future for them, have always come before all else for me. Just as all my efforts until now have been aimed at continuing my group and personal investments in Turkey and Northern Cyprus in the most healthy fashion, so will they continue to be.'

This statement gave little practical reassurance to his employees in Turkey and Cyprus, however, many of whom were destined to lose their jobs in the months that followed, and it was taken as a rebuff by Polly Peck creditors in London.

News of the statement, which appeared to recognise the inevitability of Polly Peck going into administration while hinting that it might not be enforced in the Eastern Mediterranean, reached the directors in the boardroom at Berkeley Square at 5 p.m. Bankers predictably concluded that Asil Nadir was more concerned about protecting the Turkish businesses than ensuring the survival of the group. Possibly the directors made the same inference.

About an hour later, the black front door of 42 Berkeley Square banged. Asil Nadir had arrived. He was in a highly emotional state and visibly tired after two weeks of more or less continual shuttling between London, Istanbul, and Cyprus. He went up to his office for a moment before descending the stairs to the boardroom and his final meeting with the directors. On the stairs he turned round and said, almost to himself, 'This isn't necessary. This isn't necessary. They [the directors] just don't understand. They will never understand.' And then he went on down.

In the boardroom, Asil Nadir looked across the table but said little other than to confirm that he had been unable to find new finance. The rest of the business was conducted rapidly, for the decision to go into administration had already been taken. The next step was the formal application to the court for the company to be placed in administration. A brief statement said that the directors believed that taking this step would be the only way for the company and its operations to survive as going concerns.

Afterwards, Asil Nadir stayed in his office for a short while before his driver took him home. Later in the evening, still sounding a little overwrought, he spoke to the newspapers.

'It has been a rotten day. I am going to have a hot bath and relax,' he said. He was now interpreting the collapse of his company as part of an international plot to unseat President Rauf Denktaş in Northern Cyprus. He said he had the documents which would prove this, and would show them to journalists in the next few days, as well as demonstrating a series of 'cock-ups' by the British investigators. But the documents were never revealed.

Even in defeat, however, he found one cause for congratulation. He had, he said, set up a new record for press column inches devoted to a single individual in the UK. Previously the record had been held by Churchill, he said, now the distinction had passed to him. It was not altogether clear what research this claim was based on.

In just over six weeks, one of the UK's best-known companies, with a market value over more than £2 billion, had crumbled into rubble. Many small investors, who had trusted Asil Nadir and believed in his magical ability to produce astonishing profits, had lost all their money. The fall of Polly Peck was not the only mega-corporate collapse in Britain that year. Five months earlier, British and Commonwealth, another high-flying group of the Thatcher years, had also gone bust. But in that case, the reasons seemed to be clear enough: the company had been pushed over the edge by the losses of its leasing subsidiary. In Polly Peck's case, there was no such explanation. Indeed, all its subsidiaries, with a few relatively minor exceptions such as Russell Hobbs Tower, were supposed to be growing vigorously and generating unusually large profits.

The question the shareholders asked was how such a sudden collapse had been possible. There was a host of different answers, ranging from Nadir's view (accepted in Turkey to this day) that there had been a conspiracy masterminded by the Greek Cypriots to the dismissive explanations offered by those in the City who regarded Polly Peck as an overgrown 'spiv stock'. But no one seemed to be able to produce the facts which would have clinched the explanation.

There were also some glaring questions about the conduct of the banks, 'sharks attacking a wounded whale' as Nadir liked to refer to them. A few days later, when Brent Walker, the leisure group, got into financial difficulties, the banks showed much more willingness to try to find ways out. With a little discreet prodding from the Bank of England behind the scenes, a rescue package was arranged. Why had the banks not done the same with Asil Nadir and Polly Peck? The explanation seemed to lie at least partly in the distrust engendered by the news of the SFO's raid on South Audley Management.

In *The Times* David Brewerton wrote: 'The behaviour of the bankers in this instance has been totally inconsistent. Only months ago, they were queuing up to lend hundreds of millions to the company. Yet last week, the chairman was forced to fly around the world, to scour Asia Minor, looking for a paltry £30m or face liquidation. The difference is that, in between, Asil Nadir was interviewed by the Serious Fraud Office in connection with events that seem to involve a family company. Interviewed. Not charged. The worst that could arise from that visit is that Nadir would have been taken out of active service. The group would have had to function without him.

'If the bankers did really lend, collectively, more than a billion pounds against the skills of one businessman, they are stupid. What would they have done if Nadir had had a helicopter crash, a heart attack, or met the proverbial double-decker bus?' he asked.

Perhaps the main explanation for the behaviour of the banks towards Polly Peck is that Asil Nadir had been careful to build up a wide range of multiple banking relationships, rather than concentrating on a few lenders who knew the company well. The banks also knew little about who else was lending to Polly Peck or how much. Bankers at Standard Chartered, by far the largest lender, are said to have learned who else was on the list of creditors only when the terminal crisis of Polly Peck was well under way, and to have been deeply dismayed to discover how long the list was.

When things started going wrong, none of the banks was close enough to the company to be fully certain what its overall position truly was – and because most of them had lent relatively small amounts to Polly Peck, the company's collapse was a tolerable misfortune. In this way, Nadir's policy of playing off the banks against each other, and borrowing widely in small amounts, eventually rebounded upon him.

While Polly Peck was going through the throes of its final boardroom meeting in London, the Nicosia court met again to discuss whether or not the injunction should be lifted which denied Coopers & Lybrand access to the Polly Peck documents on Cyprus. The timing of the session seemed unlikely to be coincidental, and it was no surprise when the court ordered the injunction to remain in force.

In Turkey, Güneş Taner, the minister who had turned down Asil Nadir's request for state aid, professed surprise at news of the collapse. 'As I understand it, they were about to get a bank loan,' Taner said, with perhaps calculated vagueness.

Early in the morning of 25 October, Mr Justice Morritt heard the director's petition for Polly Peck to be placed in administration. David Fawcus, the deputy chief executive, and Reg Mogg, the new finance director, put in the application at 10.30 a.m. They found themselves being opposed by National Bank of Canada, which wanted the group wound up, but the court was told by the directors that unless Polly Peck went into administration, staff could not be paid. £390,000 in wages was due to be paid that same day. The hearing was adjourned after a quarter of an hour to allow National Bank of Canada time to read the submission.

When it resumed at 2.00 p.m., the court was told that Polly Peck had liabilities of £300 million more than its assets, as the group's auditors had been told at their first meeting nearly three weeks before. National Bank of Canada agreed to withdraw its winding-up petition, provided that one of the administrators appointed was independent of Coopers & Lybrand.

By 3.00 p.m. the hearing was over. Mr Justice Morritt ruled that as both directors and creditors were agreed that the only way of saving the company was to place it in administration, he would dismiss the winding-up petition. The group had run into what the judge called 'extreme cash-flow problems'.

The names of two of the administrators were predictable. Michael Jordan and Richard Stone were the natural candidates, in view of the role that Coopers & Lybrand were already playing as the independent auditor. In any case, they already knew the company well, having carried out many of the feasibility studies before each expansion of the group's activities over the previous decade.

The third administrator was Christopher Morris of Touche Ross. His job would be to represent the shareholders and investigate whether they might have any claims against the directors. This was likely to be a crucial appointment, National Bank of Canada having objected to the originally envisaged candidate coming from Coopers & Lybrand. As Coopers had acted as Asil Nadir's tax advisers and had also audited Capetronics, the Taiwan-based Polly Peck electronics subsidiary headed by Norbert Wirsching, for three years, there could well have been a possible conflict of interest. Nevertheless, the appointment made some of the directors faintly uneasy.

An hour later, the administrators were at 42 Berkeley Square holding their first meeting with Asil Nadir. They found him, they said, a deeply shaken man, still in shock from the previous day's events. But he undertook to co-operate fully with them and to help in tracing group assets.

At six o'clock that evening, in the headquarters of Cork Gully not far from St Paul's, the three administrators looked out at a room full of journalists, under the full glare of the television cameras. It was to be the first of many meetings with the press, and also the start of what was at that time the largest and most complex administration in British commercial history.

Notwithstanding, the three men struck a cautiously optimistic note. They were not liquidators – even though they were holding the meeting at Cork Gully – and they aimed to save the group, not wind it up or even sell off its subsidiaries on a piecemeal basis. Michael Jordan, the chief administrator, said that he believed the whole or a large part of the group could be saved. 'Most of the debt is concentrated in the UK parent company. The subsidiaries are not debt-laden and one of our first tasks will be to establish how profitably they are trading.'

Only a small amount of cash – between £10 million and £15 million – was needed to keep the group running until Christmas, but when bonds and commercial papers were taken into account, the total debt of the parent company was between £900 million and £950 million. Richard Stone said that so far he had not come across any evidence of fraud or false accounting.

Calls for a formal government enquiry into Polly Peck, through the DTI, were declined by Mr Peter Lilley, the Trade and Industry Secretary, who merely told the administrators on the afternoon of their appointment that they should keep him informed if they found anything to justify a DTI investigation. Asil Nadir himself made it clear that he would have welcomed such an investigation. But so far none has been forthcoming.

The administration was not the only bitter pill which Asil Nadir had to swallow that day. He arrived at 42 Berkeley Square at 8.30 a.m. surrounded as always by his bodyguards, and looking unusually wretched. In the afternoon, within half an hour of the administrators being named, an attempt was made to serve a personal bankruptcy petition against him from Barclays de Zoete Wedd, who had been joint brokers to Polly Peck. He was being sued over an unpaid debt of £3.6 million for Polly Peck shares purchased in September. He had to shelter in the boardroom until Aisling Daly, his secretary, told him the man trying to serve the order had left the building.

This new spectre of personal bankruptcy contrasted starkly with the great personal wealth which Asil Nadir had been supposed to enjoy in the very recent past. His holding in Polly Peck alone had been worth £400 million in July, while he had been claiming early in October that his personal net worth was over £1 billion. The descent from being one of the UK's thirty-six wealthiest individuals to defendant in a bankruptcy action had occurred over just a few weeks, and could have easily been avoided. It was the result of his repeated purchases of Polly Peck shares during the autumn as the share price tumbled. Taken all together, his last-ditch purchases totalled between £40 million and £50 million, and on top of this were liabilities to the Inland Revenue believed to be about £20 million.

If it seems remarkable that Asil Nadir would have made purchases on this scale while his empire was tottering around him, it may seem even more astonishing that the securities houses with whom he traded allowed themselves to become involved in risky transactions on this scale when a moment's reflection would have warned them of what might lie ahead. Yet in the City things sometimes happen at such speed that impulse drives out calculation. Earlier in the year, for example, Kitcat and Aitken, a medium-sized city stockbroker, took an order over the lunch hour which left it with a large debt and many months of legal wrangling.

Against the growing mountain of his personal debts, Asil Nadir could
list his press empire in Turkey, which had cost him around £55 million
but was currently heavily in the red; land in Turkey and Northern
Cyprus including Zeytin Island, the holiday home he had bought the
previous spring; Baggrave Hall in Leicestershire, his country home, and
Burley-on-the-Hill, the country house near Rutland Water which he
had bought with a view to turning it into a conference centre.

It was an impressive, if varied, list. Time would show whether these
assets could be turned into sufficient cash to save Nadir from being
declared bankrupt. Those who knew him well said that he would hang on
to the Turkish newspapers even if everything else had to go. Moves to sell
Baggrave Hall, on the other hand, got under way in the next few days.

Meanwhile, he did not forget his obligations to charity. On Thursday,
the day the administrators were appointed, the Harley Street charity ball
was due to take place. Asil Nadir and Prince Edward were to have been
the star guests, but neither showed up. Apparently Prince Edward had
been told by the Queen to stay at home in Buckingham Palace for a
banquet in honour of the Italian president, then on a state visit.

The collapse of Asil Nadir's business empire threatened £5 million
which Asil Nadir had pledged for the centre at Milton Keynes to help
young victims of cerebral palsy. Bill Grosvenor, public relations adviser
to Asil Nadir and company spokesman for Polly Peck, addressed the
ballroom at large. 'Asil has telephoned me this evening. He has said
very emphatically that he has every intention of fulfilling his pledge.'
There was a moment's silence, then thunderous applause.

Moral support was no longer what Asil Nadir needed, however. Two
days later, Barclays de Zoete Wedd began to prepare a petition for
Nadir's personal bankruptcy, claiming he owed them £6 million.

On Monday 29 October, 42 Berkeley Square settled down to the first
day's work under the administration. As yet there was little discontinuity.
Coopers' men had been in the building for some weeks. So, too, had
been a team of accountants from the SFO, who were being given access
to the company papers.

The first step the administrators took that day was to set up an
informal steering committee to design a rescue plan for the company.
Michael Jordan, Richard Stone and Christopher Morris, met Asil Nadir
and explained the committee's role in raising new finance. It was agreed
that Asil Nadir would be in attendance when the administrators travelled
to Cyprus the following Thursday, 1 November. He promised to give
them his full assistance, though it would be helpful if he could have just
a few days to make arrangements on the island for the visit. 'You will
be fully satisfied, when you see things over there,' he said.

Richard Stone referred to Asil Nadir's close links with the governments of Northern Cyprus and Turkey and to the fact that without his active co-operation, there seemed to be little chance of gaining access to the group's records and cash deposits in Northern Cyprus. If they remained blocked, many people thought that the administration would quickly give way to an outright liquidation.

This assumption eventually proved wrong. The secrets of the company's holdings in Northern Cyprus were to remain almost entirely closed to the administrators for the following year. However, on the Turkish mainland, things were different. Asil Nadir's operations there were divided between Fahri Görgülü and Vestel, which was headed by Tahsin Karan. 'I will comply with whatever is legally required,' Mr Karan said the same day, 29 October. He would work with the administrators because they were the representatives of the company shareholders.

Meyna took longer to bring under the administrators' control. Unlike Vestel and Sunzest, the citrus business in Cyprus, Meyna was relatively little known and its premises were hard to visit. For several weeks the administrators were kept from entering its offices, on grounds which were never made entirely clear. Mr Fahrettin Otluoğlu, the general manager, told journalists that a news blackout had been imposed on the company. All interviews and visits were forbidden. Even the administrators had difficulty getting access.

In Turkey and Northern Cyprus, heads were beginning to roll within Asil Nadir's private businesses and press empire. The first to go had been Metin Münir, who in less than a year had made Asil Nadir's quality daily, *Güneş*, into possibly the best paper in the country, modelling it along the lines of the *Independent* in the UK. Bruce Matthews, Asil Nadir's former press consultant, had been proved right in selecting Münir as editor, although admittedly the improvement in *Güneş* had been partly achieved by pouring money into it to hire the best-known names in the Turkish press. The paper's circulation had risen from around 40,000 to just under 100,000 – a respectable figure by the standards of the quality press in Turkey. Break-even point had not yet arrived, but it might not be far away. Perhaps the best indicator of *Güneş*'s success was that its rivals, particularly *Cumhuriyet* – Turkey's equivalent of *Le Monde* – also began to improve markedly under the pressure of competition.

On the evening of the 24th, as Polly Peck went into administration, Münir had received a call from Asil Nadir requesting him to leave the newspaper and come immediately to London, apparently to act as some kind of press spokesman. If Münir had done so, it would have been a shrewd move, for he had many friends in the media in London and was in his element when talking to journalists. However, he refused and was fired from *Güneş* on the spot.

Over the next few days, employees in the press subsidiaries in Turkey and Cyprus began to realise that a drastic change in their fortunes had occurred. Up to now, there had been little need to count the cost of the press operations.

Now the cash flow to *Güneş*, *Günaydın* and the other Nadir newspapers suddenly dried up. Salaries were paid late, production costs were slashed, and the laying-off of staff began. In Turkey the top talent hired to produce the papers was quickly laid off and more homespun original figures returned to the helm. In Cyprus, Mehmet Ali Akpınar, the former Reuters correspondent, was also ousted.

Polly Peck's Eastern Mediterranean operations also saw upheavals. İlker Nevzat, the slightly Quixotic former London solicitor whose younger brother was married to Asil's sister Bilge, resigned abruptly as head of Polly Peck's operations on the island. According to the Turkish press, there had been a dispute about the signature of documents. According to the papers, Nevzat had refused to do as he was asked, choosing instead to leave the company. He withdrew, an unhappy and troubled man, to his home in Ozanköy village in the olive groves above Kyrenia. He had run the fruit business on the island ever since the death of İrfan Nadir. His decency and sense of honour were renowned. On Cyprus, people clucked their tongues and spoke of him sadly.

On Tuesday 30 October, Polly Peck received another bad jolt when the SFO raided 42 Berkeley Square, thus making it clear for the first time that the company itself came within the framework of its investigations. The raid began around 8.00 a.m., with the arrival of sixteen investigators and six uniformed officers. It followed much the same pattern as that on South Audley Management. It lasted throughout the day and well into the night. The SFO had only one warrant to enter the building and its officers were reluctant to leave until they were sure they had left nothing undiscovered.

Polly Peck staff arriving for duty were startled by the SFO's action, which affected the newly appointed administrators as well as the existing staff. They were told to stay in the Yellow Room, where in better times visitors had waited to see Asil Nadir. Most of the staff were then sent home, after being searched as they left the building. Evidently Asil Nadir himself learned of the raid at home, for he did not show up at the office that day.

A locksmith was called in to open cupboards and filing cabinets, but although the raid went on into the small hours, no documents were taken from the building. Even a building society passbook which had belonged to Raif Denktaş, the younger son of President Denktaş who had died in a car crash in the mid-1980s, was left behind. It had been found in a drawer in Asil Nadir's desk, where apparently it had been kept for sentimental reasons. Those who saw it say that the account contained only a couple of hundred pounds.

Accountants from KPMG Peat Marwick McLintock had already been working inside the company for the previous three weeks on behalf of the SFO, but with the company's consent. Now they helped in the investigation. This raid came at a point when it could do Polly Peck no further practical damage, but its timing – the day before Richard Stone of Coopers & Lybrand was due to fly to Cyprus – did not improve chances of persuading the subsidiaries on the island to open up to the administrators.

One puzzle was why the SFO had insisted on a raid, and all its attendant theatricality, on a building where its representatives were already working. Asil Nadir furiously denounced it as 'symptomatic of a new desperation' in the SFO, but, despite the vehemence of his own language, he guaranteed that he would continue to co-operate with the investigators, and repeated that he had not been involved in any illegal share deals.

Was the SFO in fact desperate? A report in the *Sunday Times* not long afterwards claimed that the SFO had taken what the paper said was the unusual step of enlisting the aid of an unnamed investigative journalist to help them with their enquiries in Switzerland. 'The journalist, who wishes to remain anonymous, was asked by SFO detectives to help identify mysterious individuals behind the deals,' the paper reported.

While the emotions stirred up by the SFO raid were still running high, Richard Stone arrived in Cyprus. He was told by Derviş Eroğlu, the prime minister of the Turkish Cypriot state, that the administrators were free to come and go, but they would have to get permission from the government to conduct any investigation. Perhaps this stipulation was not unreasonable. Turkish Cypriots had endured more than a decade of non-recognition by the outside world. Now they had a chance to assert their importance as the *de facto* government in the north.

Nazif Borman, the finance minister, went further. On 26 October, two days after the decision to place Polly Peck in administration, he said: 'If any London creditor bank wants to take away Polly Peck assets here, the government and the central bank will intervene immediately. The Polly Peck subsidiaries will be protected.'

Rauf Denktaş warned that he would not allow the subsidiaries to be dismantled, adding: 'Asil Nadir will always be welcome here.'

In the wake of Polly Peck's descent into administration, former admirers and sceptics alike looked in bafflement at a situation in which a company which had reported record profits for a decade, could collapse in just a few weeks. The explanation seemed to be that the company's extraordinary profits had always been partly a mirage.

For years everyone interested had known that part of the explanation also lay in Polly Peck's Turkish and Turkish Cypriot profits which were made in Turkish lira, a currency afflicted by inflation which ran at an annual rate of never less than 20 per cent in the 1980s, and sometimes nearer 60 per cent. Richard Strong, a friend of Asil Nadir for many years, and a Polly Peck director in the mid-1980s, believes the consequences of this should have been clearly understood by bankers and investors. 'Everybody who knew anything about it at all knew that he had massive currency losses in the balance sheets. The assets were written up in Turkey and the provision was in the back [notes] of the balance sheets for currency depreciation. So it was there for everybody to see that the money was made in Turkish lira but not made in hard currency. The high margins were made in Turkish lira, but how the finance director in the early 1980s interpreted them into sterling I am not qualified to say.'

Until the autumn of 1990, however, very few people seemed eager to address this problem – even if those in the know understood the accounting problems involved. After the crash of Polly Peck, some people would argue that the market had always taken the foreign exchange losses into account and that this was why the group's shares traded on a low p/e ratio. But this was not a point that was much heard at the time.

More than a few of the company's admirers believed that Polly Peck actually made substantial foreign currency gains by holding large TL cash balances in Turkey and earning stratospheric interest on them which outstripped losses on currency depreciation. However, a little investigation would have showed them that although headline TL interest rates might look very high by London standards, real rates on TL bank deposits were not large. Also, they usually hovered close to the inflation rate and from time to time dropped beneath it. In any case, the vast cash balance did not exist. The Turkish subsidiaries consumed cash at least as fast as they generated it.

On the eve of the meeting with Polly Peck's bankers, attention fastened on an analyst's note from James Capel, the London stockbrokers, which explained succinctly how standard accounting policies understated the costs of operating in a high-inflation country.

Polly Peck had never had many links with Turkish banks, other than with a few specialists who handled operations such as the Vestel flotation. In Turkey, where inflation was usually well above 40 per cent in the second half of the 1980s, the local currency depreciated rapidly against other currencies. Foreign investors in Turkey and other high-inflation countries were familiar with the problem: once injected into the Turkish economy and converted into Turkish, a unit of capital would begin to melt away as the TL depreciated. Just to retain its original value, a very high rate of return would be needed. On the other hand, because of Turkey's raging inflation, the results when expressed in TL would show enormously rapid growth.

Polly Peck's subsidiaries largely bypassed the Turkish banking system when borrowing money. If they had borrowed locally, they would have found themselves paying interest at net rates of between 80 and 120 per cent much of the time. Instead, they relied on financing from abroad, bringing foreign exchange into the country with a much lower rate of interest, which gave them considerable advantages in the local markets, enabling them to pay well in advance (thereby securing a lower price) and offer extended credit.

If this was followed by a strong export performance, all might still be fine. The export earnings would be in foreign currency and there might be no foreign exchange loss. This result was harder to achieve if the sales were made in the Turkish domestic market rather than abroad.

Either way, accounting conventions allowed the company to show any exchange losses not in the profit and loss account but by deducting them from its reserves. This made the accounts look much more appealing, but it also exposed the company to the temptation of trying to finance its working capital needs from further borrowing rather than profits generated by operations.

In its final five years, Polly Peck had raised £1.67 billion mainly from banks and shareholders, taking its total debt from a modest £44 million in 1985 to well over £1.1 billion at the end of 1989. Even so, the group claimed to have cash and bank balances of £249 million at the end of 1989, although less than 3 per cent of this was held by the London-based parent company.

At the same time, losses on exchange rate variations on net overseas investments were shown in the notes to the accounts. IBCA, the London bank-rating agency, published a report in January 1991 which spelt out very clearly the full implications of this. According to IBCA, in the five years between 1984 and 1989, total exchange losses by Polly Peck reached £396 million – while total net profits were £439 million and pre-tax profits £522 million.

In some years, if the losses caused by the depreciation of the TL had been shown in the profit and loss account, Polly Peck's profits would have shrunk dramatically, indeed in 1988 – Polly Peck's sixteen-month-long accounting year – there had been a loss of £38 million. Using the same accounting method, Polly Peck would have made a pre-tax profit of just £2 million in 1987, though it would still have reported a strong showing of £114 million in pre-tax profits in 1989.

None of this was illegal, or even deeply disguised. Anyone who cared to could disinter the evidence from the notes to the annual accounts. Because banks and investors alike had confidence in the miraculous profitability of the company, some banks were always willing to lend to it, and indeed Asil Nadir followed a shrewd policy of raising small amounts of cash from a large number of banks. Standard Chartered's £50 million and Lloyds' £20 million in loans to Polly Peck were glaring exceptions. 'He let the banks come to him, giving them the impression that if they didn't make the approach, they would possibly lose the business to a competitor. Banks fall for that very easily and they came to him cap in hand,' says one banker.

Even so, not surprisingly there were periodic cash-flow difficulties inside the group, particularly between 1986 and 1988, and the subsidiaries, all eager to expand rapidly in their own markets, tended to be greedy consumers of cash from the centre. This could usually only be supplied by fresh borrowing, and this of course depended on confidence among lenders. Once the lenders had lost confidence and the flow of cash was interrupted, the entire edifice began to crack and tremble. That seemed to be the point Polly Peck had finally reached at the end of September 1990.

None of this, it should be stressed yet again, was in any way illegal or improper. Accounting conventions allow foreign exchange losses to be taken out of reserves, and the fact that this was being done could have been discovered by anyone who read the accounts carefully enough. Many bankers evidently overlooked this point. Polly Peck's accounts, with their short balance sheets and profit and loss statements, followed by pages of technical notes to the accounts, were simply following an established trend in the accountancy world.

If anyone is to blame for failing to spot the consequences of the losses on foreign exchange variations, it is surely those outside the company who followed its affairs for a decade and developed sophisticated explanations (such as hypothetical TL bank deposits generating interest income at impossibly high levels) for the profitability of the Turkish operations.

Those investors who did spot the snags did not get much of a hearing. After the crash one Swiss shareholder in Polly Peck recalled that when he raised the question of the treatment of foreign exchange losses at the company's annual general meetings, he was simply laughed down by other investors.

In the USA these things are done differently. One reason why the much-mooted Del Monte flotation in New York never took place, was that if it had, Polly Peck would have had to publish a set of its own accounts, presented according to US auditing standards. That would have meant taking foreign exchange losses out of the profit and loss account and showing that in some years the group had made little or no profit – a move which would have attracted considerable attention in the UK. Whatever the explanation, all hopes and dreams had now vanished. As far as journalists writing in the City pages of the newspapers were concerned, Polly Peck was simply a collapsed company.

15 · An Indomitable Spirit

With Polly Peck in administration, a new and drastically different period in Asil Nadir's life suddenly began. The years of building up and running a business empire were, at least temporarily, over. His days were spent battling to hold back a sea of troubles.

The challenges which confront him now range from personal bankruptcy to a set of criminal charges so long that it instantly found a place in the *Guinness Book of Records*. At one point in 1991, one of his assistants claimed that no fewer than fifty solicitors were thought to be working on the various legal actions in which he was involved.

Throughout his life, Asil Nadir's friends and family have marvelled at his tenacity and persistence. Perhaps persistence is, above all, the quality most needed for success in business life. If so, few people have been more abundantly endowed with it from birth than Asil Nadir or continue to display it in the most depressing circumstances. 'It's astonishing. You would think that we would be trying to cheer him up. But when we meet, it is always the other way round. He boosts our morale,' says one of his relatives.

In the mid-1970s, Asil Nadir showed equally steady nerves during the months where Wearwell was teetering on the edge of liquidation and only two of his family stood by him. The scale of his problems in 1991 and 1992 is vastly greater than in the case of Wearwell. Yet he still pursues his two familiar rules of conduct in difficult situations: stay calm and cheerful and look for ways out of the problem.

The two months immediately after Polly Peck was handed over to the administrators on 26 October brought a series of developments which made it clear how complete the change in Asil Nadir's fortunes had been, and how bleak the next two years would be for him. His first priorities at this stage had to be to try and remove the shadow of the SFO investigation. Challenges against a prosecuting authority, especially one like the SFO which is armed with extraordinary powers, might seem hopeless, but Asil Nadir decided to take the SFO on. For a time, against all expectation, he appeared to be winning. Throughout November and December 1990, his lawyers pressed ahead with a court petition to force the SFO to tell him why it was investigating him. In early November, a surprise decision in the High Court gave him leave to seek a judicial review.

On the day of this High Court victory for Asil Nadir, Richard Stone, the administrator now in charge of Polly Peck's corporate finance, flew from London to Istanbul, the first of many journeys to Turkey and Cyprus by the administrators and their staff over the next two years.

In London, the collapse of Polly Peck and the fortunes of its chairman continued to attract huge publicity.

For most of the 1980s, Asil Nadir had shrunk from public appearances, leaving even the announcement of the company's results to Mark Ellis. But in November and December 1990, Asil Nadir gave television interviews in both Turkey and Britain, seeking the support of the general public for the first time. On 6 November, talking on Turkish television, he likened himself to a wounded whale being attacked by sharks – the banks. He said his chief mistake had been to fail to grasp the part that politics could play in business. 'I will not accept the words that Asil Nadir is finished. Asil Nadirs are never finished,' he said. Polly Peck, he assured viewers, would regain its former position in another six months or so.

By now Asil Nadir spent most of his day at his home in 3 Aldford Street or at South Audley Management's offices nearby. He came into 42 Berkeley Square less often. Polly Peck was beginning to change rapidly. Control of the company was no longer in the chairman's hands. Michael Jordan and Richard Stone now took the main decisions. Two of the old board, Reg Mogg and Peter Compson, the finance and personnel directors, would eventually be left in charge of the day-to-day running of the company, but a great deal of painful surgery lay ahead. On 1 November, seventy of the 140 people working at 42 Berkeley Square and Commercial Road lost their jobs. It was the first of many waves of redundancies that lay ahead.

There was also the delicate question of the future of the board. The directors remained in office but they had lost their powers. Apart from Compson and Mogg, most of the other executive directors no longer had a role to play in the day-to-day life of the company.

Even in the earliest days of the administration in November 1990, when the administrators were talking about possibly overcoming the company's financial problems and eventually relaunching it on the market with the permission of the court and its creditors, some of the more astute directors privately feared that the company was doomed to eventual liquidation after its more profitable subsidiaries had been sold off. If Del Monte, Sansui and the fruit operations failed to generate enough profits to pay off the claimants, and large amounts of cash could not be unlocked in Turkey and Cyprus, then the profitable parts of the group would have to be sold and the rest would face possible liquidation.

The administrators' first task in the early weeks was to keep Polly Peck operating despite its cash problems. This meant trimming costs and raising some fresh money either from the banks or through sales. Joseph Le Shark, the small textile company which Nadir had bought in 1989, went almost immediately. Preparations were made to sell Russell Hobbs, the American businesses built up by Mark Ellis and the European fruit distribution companies. Many other subsidiaries would need some management attention and perhaps more cash before they could be sold if there was to be any chance of getting a good price for them.

An informal creditors' committee was formed on 15 November and it readily agreed to allow the administrators both time and some cash to see the company through the first six months of the administration. Standard Chartered, the bank that was owed £50 million, went along with the proposal that a little more cash be put up. It was the bank which knew the group best and it still had some faith in it.

The most obvious candidate for a sale was the glittering collection of antiques and furniture at 42 Berkeley Square. Two weeks after the administration got under way, Phillips the auctioneers were called in to start preparing a catalogue. It had taken Gülderen Tekvar four years to assemble the collection; it was to be dispersed in a day.

Asil Nadir's other pressing problem through late 1990 and 1991 was his mountain of personal debts. By now the press knew that he owed around £30 million, mostly to the four stockbrokers from whom he had bought Polly Peck shares during the autumn. In fact new claims were coming in almost every day and his total debts were over £80 million when his tax and other liabilities were included. On 2 November, Lehman Brothers, the owners of L. Messel, the company which had acted as Polly Peck's brokers throughout the 1980s, announced that they would be suing him for £18.5 million spent on 6.25 million Polly Peck shares during September and October.

A vast amount of money had to be raised fast to stave off bankruptcy. Baggrave Hall, Asil Nadir's stunningly beautiful Leicestershire country home, was sold for £4 million, along with its farms and its herds of prize cattle. The Shamley Dominant, a magnificent long-haired Aberdeen Angus bull which had won prize after prize for Nadir in county shows, left the Nadir Empire. Baggrave had perhaps been bought for a future when he might have a title and would want to spend part of his time as an English country gentleman. Burley-on-the-Hill, the Rutland country house which he had bought to develop as an international conference centre, also went back on to the market.

This did not stop the proceedings in the bankruptcy courts, but it helped gain time for Asil Nadir. The creditors hoped that he would raise funds through the sale of his Turkish newspapers and magazines and of Impex Bank of Istanbul. So there was obviously a strong case for returning to Turkey and Northern Cyprus to see what could be sorted out among his surviving business interests there, though in the circumstances it would not have been surprising if Asil Nadir did not also yearn to be back in a world where he was treated with adulation.

His passports – British, Turkish Cypriot and Turkish – had been among the documents seized by the SFO when it raided 42 Berkeley Square, but they were returned to him a day or two later. He talked of flying to Cyprus with Richard Stone, with whom he was now on very good terms, but at the end of the first week in November Stone left without him. According to the press Stone was seeking £200 million in cash from Polly Peck accounts on the island. He also believed that he would not find it difficult to reach an agreement with President Denktaş and the Turkish Cypriot authorities, backed by Asil Nadir and his fellow-director in many of the Cyprus businesses, Menteş Aziz, the Nadir family lawyer.

On 16 November 1990, two days after his first bankruptcy hearing and ten days after Stone's visit to Cyprus, Asil Nadir flew out from Stanstead on what proved to be his last journey to the Near East for a while. The UK bankers who were now probing everything that went on at Polly Peck asked him why he could not take a scheduled flight. One large UK bank recalls that he looked at them coolly. 'I have a reputation in Turkey to consider,' he told them. 'If I turn up on a normal airline flight, I shall be finished.' He went in the older of his two executive jets, the JetStar which he had bought five years earlier on Ayşegül's recommendation. Normally he would have gone in the Gulfstream jet which he much preferred. But that plane now stood forlornly at Luton Airport with its bills unpaid and a notice on a piece of string dangling from its windscreen, saying 'Not to be used by Asil Nadir'.

He spent much of his first day back in Cyprus at the Jasmine Court Hotel, Polly Peck's luxury hotel just outside Kyrenia, chatting to John Murray Brown of the *Financial Times* and Tom Carver of the BBC. On his hotel balcony, as he tucked into a chicken sandwich, Asil Nadir directed his visitors' attention to the dazzling spectacle of the Mediterranean sea and sky beyond the hotel. 'It's beautiful, isn't it?' he said, with the satisfaction of a man who had come home.

There was plenty of work to be done in Cyprus. The administrators were still vainly trying to get access to Polly Peck's records and bank deposits on the island. Asil Nadir promised to help them.

There was also a great deal of personal business to attend to, much of it consisting of reassuring friends and followers. Just under one job in three in the north of the island came from Asil Nadir's companies, and the first redundancies were already being announced. Fahrettin Tunalıer, a Turkish Cypriot who had effectively taken over as the head of the group's operations on the island after the resignations of İlker Nevzat, and Menteş Aziz, the family lawyer, worked by his side. Despite the gloom among managers and employees in Polly Peck and his other companies, Asil Nadir urged everyone not to be depressed. His problems were, he said, caused by the Serious Fraud Office, but they would pass and meanwhile the businesses were all sound and doing well.

Nothing had been heard of Elizabeth Forsyth since the SFO's raid on South Audley Management in September, but on 25 November, she surfaced unexpectedly in the pages of the *Sunday Telegraph*, to deny all the accusations of illegal share-dealing which had been made against her and Jason Davies. 'I'm a strong personality,' she said, 'but the innuendo has been awful.'

The same week Jason Davies spoke at length in Switzerland to the administrators of Polly Peck and asked for the fifty-page transcript of the conversation to be passed on to the SFO. Both he and Elizabeth Forsyth hoped to be able to return home soon. They strongly denied having done anything unlawful.

In Cyprus, Asil Nadir was spending much of his time with the orange growers who were now very alarmed about whether or not they would be paid for their crop that season. He addressed a rally of 2,000 farmers on the last Tuesday of November. He even seemed to have persuaded the growers to drop their injunction preventing Richard Stone and the Polly Peck administrators from getting access to company records and bank accounts on the island.

The accountants working for Richard Stone had quickly found that a large amount of company money, thought to be around £160 million, had been spent on buying land in Northern Cyprus and Turkey. The money had gone on advance payments for hotel projects, holiday villages and other leisure developments and it had absorbed a great deal of cash which could have gone to the group's creditors or to support businesses such as Sansui. Discussion of the sales was high on the agenda of the next meeting between Asil Nadir and the administrators, due to take place just after the middle of the month.

*

In London there was fresh excitement on 12 December. The *Sun* carried the news that the Assistant Commissioner of Metropolitan Police, Wyn Jones, the number three in Scotland Yard in charge of personnel and training, was being investigated by the Home Office for possible links with Asil Nadir. In fact the two men had never met: Jones was a friend of Bruce Matthews, the former deputy chief executive of News International who had worked out of South Audley Management's offices the previous year. But the Assistant Commissioner's name had been found at South Audley Management by the SFO during their raid on 19 September. A report was sent to the Home Secretary and an investigation began. In May 1991, Jones was cleared by the investigation, but he has not yet been reinstated and has begun an action against the Metropolitan Police. The preliminary hearing got under way eighteen months later, on 6 May 1992.

Asil Nadir returned to Istanbul, in the second week of December, and his lawyers announced the sale of Impex Bank, the small trade finance and merchant bank which he owned personally. The sale price was believed to be around $25 million. This was a much smaller amount than the sum he owed his creditors, but it did look as if he had finally managed to raise substantial funds in Turkey. His creditors decided to relent for a few more weeks. They now hoped that if Asil Nadir raised more cash by selling off the newspapers and other assets, such as the small island he had bought in the Aegean the previous spring, they might come within striking distance of getting most of their money back.

Asil Nadir might have few friends and admirers left in London, but public opinion in Turkey had swung firmly behind him, partly out of natural sympathy at his fall and partly because the media suspected he had been the victim of an anti-Turkish plot. Other than *Sabah*, the mainland Turkish papers which he did not own now shed most of their reservations about him. His television interviews had undoubtedly helped him, but so did the Turkish political establishment in Ankara. The Motherland Party government and the Foreign Ministry both pitched in to defend him.

Throughout the months of Polly Peck's crisis, Nadir's papers in Turkey continued to back him with a shrillness which onlookers often found amusing. By November, the newspapers and magazines were suffering severe cash problems and many of their employees were working without pay, so their disgruntlement was easy to understand. *Günaydın*, the tabloid in the Nadir group, was particularly outspoken in its owner's defence, hailing every small victory as a triumph and paying minimal attention to any of his reverses. One ridiculous suggestion, apparently seriously made by some Istanbul journalists, was that all Asil Nadir's troubles stemmed ultimately from the fact that the grandfather of Barbara Mills, the director of the SFO, had been killed fighting the Ottoman army at Gallipoli in World War II. There is absolutely no foundation to the claim.

By mid-December Asil Nadir had been out of England for almost a month and the length of his absence abroad was beginning to attract private comment. Was he perhaps afraid to return? Since its raid on 42 Berkeley Square in late October, there had been no further public moves from the SFO against Asil Nadir or anyone else at Polly Peck or South Audley Management. But no such hesitations figured in Asil Nadir's own mind. He had decided to return to England a week and a half before Christmas.

Knowing of his intentions, Ayşegül rang him on Thursday 13 December, to warn him that she had heard rumours that he might be arrested if he came back to England. She was not the only one to do so. Aisling Daly, Asil's secretary in Polly Peck, made a similar call the same day, and so did other friends and relatives.

To each of them, Asil Nadir replied imperturbably: 'I haven't done anything wrong. Nobody can arrest me. Why should they arrest me?'

'I don't know why they want to arrest you, all I know is that they are going to arrest you, so please don't come back. For God's sake, please stay away,' said Ayşegül.

'No, no, I am coming on Saturday,' said Asil, unruffled.

The next day, less than twenty-four hours before he was due to set off, Aysegül again heard, from a totally different and highly placed source this time, that Asil might be arrested if he returned, and she became even more alarmed. She decided to call him once more. 'I rang him again in Istanbul on Saturday and said, "Don't you dare get on that plane." But he refused. He said, "Who on earth should I be afraid of? Why should they arrest me?"'

Even the administrators, who tactfully suggested that Asil Nadir might like to hold his next meeting with them in Istanbul, found him insisistent that he would prefer to meet them in London. And so it was arranged. He would see Michael Jordan and Richard Stone on the afternoon of Sunday 16 December, at 42 Berkeley Square.

Asil Nadir travelled back with his brother-in-law, Fehim Nevzat, and a Turkish Cypriot construction engineer from Polly Peck. The JetStar was still over Europe when the pilot received news on his radio that there was fog at Stanstead and the flight was being diverted to Heathrow instead. A ripple of comment ran through the plane, but Asil Nadir was apparently unworried.

When the plane touched down at Heathrow, it was told to taxi into a siding and there could no longer be any mistake about what was going on. Asil Nadir said later that armed police burst into the plane as if he was Che Guevara at his most dangerous, yelling, 'You're all under arrest.' The JetStar was then thoroughly searched. Asil Nadir and his companions were driven away to a night of custody in Holborn Police station.

In Britain, the news of his arrest broke late on the evening of Saturday 15 December. The Sunday newspapers, his oldest enemies in the British press, nevertheless managed to get the news into their late editions the next morning. All through Sunday, he was questioned by police until, after twenty-eight hours of interrogation, he was finally charged. The others detained with him had been released without charge hours earlier.

News of the charges was broken to journalists by Detective Superintendent David Staff. 'Mr Asil Nadir who was arrested at Heathrow Airport on 15 December has tonight been charged with 18 offences of theft and false accounting in respect of the affairs of Polly Peck International.' There were eight theft charges involving £20.2 million of Polly Peck company money. A further six theft charges covered £27.75 million of money from Unipac, the cardboard box company in Famagusta, but some of the charges apparently overlapped: the total sum involved was £25 million. The four charges of false accounting all had to do with alleged tampering with Polly Peck cash books.

On Monday morning, Asil Nadir was taken to the Magistrates' Court at Bow Street, opposite the Royal Opera House. A crowd of friends and family and Turkish Cypriot well-wishers waited in the dingy anteroom to the court for the doors to open. Sir David Hopkin, the Chief Metropolitan Magistrate, set bail at the record figure of £3.5 million – £2 million in an irrevocable cash deposit and a further five sureties totalling £1.5 million. The sureties proved fairly easy to raise. The cash deposit was much harder to find and it was largely because of its size that Asil Nadir spent the next few days in prison.

The huge bail demanded of Asil Nadir raised some eyebrows. Eighteen months later, when Kevin and Ian Maxwell were charged at Bow Street Magistrates' Court for alleged offences committed with their father, they were asked to raise less than one-tenth of the bail demanded of Asil Nadir. The sums involved in the two cases both ran into tens of millions and it is not obvious why Asil Nadir's bail terms were so much stiffer.

Asil Nadir was no longer in court when the discussion of his bail got under way. He was waiting in a cellroom below. Outside the court his friends and family rang friends on portable telephones searching for the money. Ayşegül Nadir pledged £500,000 immediately from the sale of jewels. It took three further days of hard work by lawyers and family before the whole £3.5 million could be raised and guaranteed in a satisfactory manner to the court.

Asil Nadir spent Monday and Tuesday nights in different prisons. There was a grim first night in Brixton jail, where he was taunted by the other prisoners and suffered a rictus, and a more cheerful one in Wormwood Scrubs, where the lags in his cell viewed him with some awe. A prison chaplain who saw him that night pronounced him in fine spirits. Nevertheless his health seemed precarious, perhaps because of the shock of his arrest, and after he complained of chest pains, his doctor was allowed to make several visits, both at Holborn police station and in prison.

Asil Nadir's fourth night in captivity was made necessary by the failure of documents pledging £2 million to reach the court before 6 p.m. on Tuesday. As the days dragged on, there was a serious risk that the bail guarantees would not be in place before the end of the week. Monday was Christmas Eve and the court would not be sitting, so he might end up spending the following weekend, and perhaps the Christmas holiday, in prison. On the Wednesday, the money missed the deadline by minutes.

Bilge Nevzat, after hours of phoning around, had identified a Turkish Cypriot businessman who was able to put up £1 million bail. Ramadan Güney, the owner of a 460-acre cemetery in Brookwood, Surrey, had been a friend and distant relative of İrfan Nadir, but he scarcely knew Asil. He was none the less honoured by Bilge's appeal for help and readily put up his million.

Some of the rest of the bail money came from Turkey. Part was put up by friends of Asil Nadir, but there was also a contribution from sources backed by the Turkish government. On Tuesday, at his weekly briefing in Ankara with local journalists, the Turkish Foreign Ministry spokesman declared that Turkish banks were making a significant effort to help with Asil Nadir's bail and that the government supported them in this. The banks which put up this money have never been publicly identified. It is a striking coincidence that the general manager of Ziraat, Turkey's largest bank, happened to be in London the day of Asil Nadir's arrest, but he has always firmly denied being involved in the bail operation.

Despite all this support, the middle of the week arrived without the court's requirements being satisfied. The danger that Asil would have to spend Christmas in prison was growing stronger. When his lawyers were finally able to announce to the court that all the bail conditions had been met, his papers were faxed to the prison rather than delivered by hand, to ensure that he was released before the holiday.

Asil Nadir left Wormwood Scrubs at 3 p.m. on Thursday 20 December, by a side door to avoid a crowd of journalists and cameramen. He was driven home to Aldford Street where Ayşegül and other relatives were waiting for him. Vizards, his solicitors, issued a brief statement saying that he was grateful for the support of family and friends.

The general public was more impressed by Asil Nadir's own statement, delivered when he arrived at the door of his home late on Thursday afternoon. After five days in prison, he appeared not only cheerful, but dapper. He was wearing, reporters noticed, the same suit, white shirt and red tie he had worn in court on Monday. After three days in the Scrubs, he still looked immaculate. 'I'm sorry it's so cold and raining on you,' he told the small crowd waiting outside in the bleak December afternoon. He reappeared a few minutes later. 'I wish everyone a very happy Christmas,' he said.

His own New Year holidays were overshadowed by the proceedings against him. He now had both a trial and possible bankruptcy proceedings to contest. The terms of the bail alone were sufficient to turn his life upside down, even without the £3.5 million in pledges and the court's request that he surrender all his passports, sleep every night in Aldford Street, and refrain from buying even a railway ticket.

He could no longer speak to anyone who had worked for Polly Peck or who might be called as a witness against him. For a time, the restriction appeared to include even the administrators of Polly Peck, his mother Safiye and his sister Bilge Nevzat. At one stroke he was cut off from most of his immediate past life.

In Turkey there was fury at the news of his arrest, and a fierce and rather curious squabble developed in the national press. *Günaydın* and *Güneş*, the two main Nadir papers, attacked *Sabah*, by then the largest circulation paper in the country, for allegedly informing on Asil Nadir to the SFO and so carrying out the wishes of the Greek Cypriots. The suggestion was that *Sabah* had somehow printed a special edition of the paper and conveyed it to the SFO in order to cause Asil Nadir's arrest. This nonsensical allegation was, it almost goes without saying, a fabrication. The link between Turkey's largest and strongest daily newspaper and its national enemies was alleged to be one of the *Financial Times* journalists covering the Polly Peck affair. What, if anything, *Günaydın* was referring to remains very unclear. Its views were not those of Asil Nadir himself, who soon afterwards described them as ridiculous in a telephone interview and dissociated himself from them.

During the week when Asil Nadir was in jail, Elizabeth Forsyth quietly slipped back into Britain after three months in Switzerland and Cyprus and travelled to her Georgian home in Grantham. Her lawyers announced that she would be visiting the SFO for an interview early in the New Year. She had been planning since September to return to England, but had not done so partly on the advice of her lawyers, but also because she was waiting for the hue and cry from the media to die down. She had not turned against Asil Nadir and had no intention of becoming a hostile witness. To this day, she remains firmly loyal to him and strongly believes it is only a matter of time until he is cleared of all the charges against him and can embark on a new business career.

On 8 January Elizabeth Forsyth travelled to Elm Street for an interview with the SFO, but she declared firmly that she had not been involved in share purchases of any sort, let alone illegal share-price operations. After that she was on her own, without a job and unable to communicate with her former master.

On 13 February, Jason Davies was interviewed in Lausanne on behalf of the SFO by M. Jacques Antenen, a Swiss magistrate, about his alleged dealings in Polly Peck shares through nominee companies. Davies had spoken to Christopher Morris on behalf of the Polly Peck administration in December. Through his lawyer, Davies once again reiterated that he was innocent of any wrong-doing.

At the end of the first week in January, many new faces and a few old ones toured 42 Berkeley Square, inspecting the antiques collection. The premises now housed only a few executives – there was no longer a board of directors to enjoy the splendid furnishings. Asil Nadir remained chairman of Polly Peck in name only until he was declared bankrupt at the end of November. The other executive directors, except for Reg Mogg and Peter Compson, departed, as did all but two of the non-executives. The resignations of Mark Ellis, the corporate development director who had been one of Asil Nadir's closest followers, David Fawcus, the deputy chief executive and finance director, and Radar Reshad, the food division chief, were announced early in the New Year. Compson and Mogg now ran the company, and its headquarters returned to the Commercial Road offices. By mid-summer, the eighteenth-century building at 42 Berkeley Square stood empty and remains so to this day.

On 19 February 1991, the antiques went under the auctioneer's hammer. Many of Asil Nadir's friends and relatives were in the packed-out sales-room. The sale attracted a great deal of publicity and even some former Polly Peck employees returned to buy themselves small mementos.

A Hong Kong millionaire bought many of the items, but otherwise the sale was a little disappointing. By February 1991 Britain was in the grip of the Gulf War recession, and in any case, antiques seldom benefit from a quick reappearance on the market. The collection had cost £5.5 million but, with value added tax included, the sale fetched only £4.46 million, raising about £3.5 million for the administration. Souvenir items, such as cushions, tended to sell for better than expected prices.

While Polly Peck was travelling back towards its East End origins, Asil Nadir's own life remained firmly rooted in the West End. Throughout 1991, he continued to work out in offices in Berkeley Square, using the premises of South Audley Management at number 24. He was surrounded by a few faithful Turkish retainers, though as time went by several deserted him, and a band of adoring women.

This was not a fate which another group of ladies, the South Audley Management's directors, had envisaged for their company. They were mostly young women who had worked with Elizabeth Forsyth during Asil Nadir's heyday but were now eager to set the whole South Audley Management episode behind them. Just after the New Year, they let it be known that they planned to hold a meeting of creditors and directors on 30 January to wind up the company and appoint liquidators. Some of the directors had also put in claims for compensation for loss of office and breach of contract, which would be taken into account during the winding-up. Notices were sent out. But then things took a radically different turn.

In March, S. J. Berwin, Asil Nadir's lawyers, called in a second accountant to examine the proposals, apparently on behalf of the Nadir family trust which ultimately owned South Audley Management. The conclusion seems to have been that some of the claims might be excessive, at least when measured against the professional qualifications of those making them. The second accountant proposed a different arrangement, whereby all the creditors apart from the Nadir family trusts would be paid in full. The Nadir family trust, the largest creditor, converted its debts into shares in South Audley Management and got control of the company. Thanks to this adroit legal and accounting manoeuvre, South Audley was not shut down but survived as a vehicle of the Trust and Asil Nadir.

This outcome did not please Christopher Morris, the administrator charged with investigating possible offences by the directors of Polly Peck. He launched an application for a winding-up petition against South Audley Management in May. It failed. South Audley Management remained in existence until May 1992 when it went into liquidation after its lease expired with debts of £300,000.

Inside his sanctum at South Audley Management, Asil Nadir could be visited by distinguished guests from Turkey and receive his professional advisers. Most of his energies were spent fighting his legal battles. By the end of 1991, he was contesting not one massive legal action but three.

The main one was the SFO prosecution. The SFO's case went through ten hearings at Bow Street Magistrates' Court and was eventually transferred to the Crown Court. The full trial is expected to get under way sometime after the beginning of March 1993. Very little could be said in the press about the hearings since reporting restrictions were not lifted. A sense of high drama hung over Bow Street on the days the case was heard. Outside the court, the Turkish Cypriot community in London showed its continuing loyalty to its most famous figure. A crowd demonstrated in the street waving banners and placards calling on British justice to assert itself. Court-room spectators would arrive as much as an hour early to be sure of a place, and family and friends, Turkish and British journalists would form a tight but always good-natured scrimmage outside the door until it opened.

Anthony Scrivener QC, one of the finest British lawyers of his generation and the ex-chairman of the Bar Council, has represented Asil Nadir since the end of January 1991. The bail terms were slightly eased to allow Asil Nadir to talk to Polly Peck directors or employees without SFO permission if he did so in the presence of one of Polly Peck's three administrators.

However, the bail restriction which Asil Nadir most wanted to have lifted was the ban on foreign travel. He argued that he could not make any progress with his business affairs or be of effective assistance to the administrators unless he was allowed a visit to Cyprus. He also very much wanted to see his mother Safiye again at her home in Famagusta. In July 1991 it seemed he might be close to achieving this, for two of the three administrators declared that it was essential for him to return to Northern Cyprus to examine company documents there. But the request was then rejected at the hearing on 1 August.

For months there were signs that the SFO was contemplating fresh charges. On 12 September 1991, the blow arrived. Asil Nadir was summoned to Holborn police station for two days of questioning which lasted a total of twenty hours. At the court hearing on 22 October, a further fifty-eight charges of theft, involving £130 million, were added to the list. The total number of charges he now faced was seventy-six, covering £150 million of company funds. Not long afterwards, John Turner, the Polly Peck group chief accountant, was also arrested and joined his former chairman in the dock on 7 November. He was charged with ten counts of false accounting, totalling £7.4 million.

But the pendulum has a habit of swinging rather wildly in Asil Nadir's life. On 8 June 1992, after a special application by his lawyers, forty-six of the theft charges, involving £119.5 million pounds, were thrown out by the judge a good nine months before the trial was scheduled to begin. Nevertheless, Asil Nadir still faced twenty charges of theft and false accounting totalling £30 million. When the case comes to the Crown Court, he is likely to face a much smaller number of charges.

The SFO prosecution did not represent his most immediate danger of going to prison, however. That came from his personal creditors who throughout the autumn of 1991 sought to have him sent to jail for contempt of court. The reason behind their anger went back to December 1990 when Asil Nadir had sold Impex Bank for $27 million. Around the same time he had been locked in negotiations with his creditors who were unaware of the sale. They claimed that he had undertaken not to get rid of any assets without their permission.

Meetings with his creditors came and went over the New Year. In the City, Asil Nadir's critics daily expected news of his bankruptcy to be announced. They were confounded. On 5 February 1991 it was announced that he and his creditors had reached agreement and the petition for his bankruptcy was being withdrawn. Once again, the Nadir magic seemed to have worked.

Among the creditors was the Inland Revenue, with whom the agreement contained in the settlement was in its way historic. It had been the Inland Revenue's investigations – started in 1989 – which generated the rumours in the City and the Sunday press which preceded the collapse of Polly Peck. Peter Knight at Vizards, Asil Nadir's lawyers, told reporters: 'The investigation has been resolved to the satisfaction of both parties, following an approach by the Inland Revenue to ourselves.'

Meanwhile, the creditors wanted their security: the titles to Asil Nadir's Turkish newspapers and magazines were lodged with the Istanbul branch of a French bank. The terms of the deal were never made public, but Asil Nadir seems to have agreed to produce $12 million in March 1991 and a further $15 million in June. In the event the months rolled by and the creditors never got their money. Impex Bank changed hands again after a fierce battle in Turkey over its ownership.

By June, when the date for the second payment to the creditors had come and gone, they decided to take action. The newspaper titles were placed on the market in mid-July. The first intimation Asil Nadir had of this move seems to have been when the press rang him at South Audley Management to ask if he had seen the advertisement in the

Financial Times. In fact selling off the newspapers was largely a symbolic gesture. By the summer of 1991, most of the Nadir press empire in Istanbul was a shrunken and tattered remnant of what it had been the previous year.

The creditors did not let things rest there, however. They could not resume their bankruptcy action against Asil Nadir. Instead, they launched a complicated legal action against him in the High Court, alleging that he had committed contempt of court by breaching his undertaking to them in December 1990. Unusually, they demanded that he be imprisoned for his alleged contempt. Asil Nadir fought unsuccessfully to have the action thrown out, but it dragged on in the High Court until July 1992 when the creditors agreed to withdraw it. Their reasons for doing so were not made public.

In November 1991, quite suddenly, personal bankruptcy finally arrived for Asil Nadir, a full year after Polly Peck had been placed in administration. On 26 November Den Norsk Bank sued him for a guarantee on a £1.5 million guarantee loan to a relative. The other creditors, learning of the new action, seized the opportunity to add their names to it.

Bankruptcy meant that Asil Nadir had to give up his remaining UK directorships. For months he had been chairman and director of Polly Peck in name only. Now he lost even the title.

His Turkish directorships were also slipping from him, though not for the same reason. Under Turkish law a company director must attend a board meeting at least once a year. Asil Nadir was of course no longer able to fulfil that condition. In November 1991, Richard Stone of Coopers & Lybrand replaced him on the board of Vestel, the most significant of the remaining Polly Peck subsidiaries in the Eastern Mediterranean.

Bankruptcy also meant that Asil Nadir could no longer pay Vizards and S. J. Berwin, the solicitors who had acted for him over the previous two years. He had taken them on at the time of his attempt to buy Polly Peck and they had remained with him through all that followed. His barrister, Anthony Scrivener, indicated that he was willing to continue. Roger Pannone, of Pannone March Pearson, a Manchester law firm which positively relished taking a high profile, stepped in to act as his solicitors. The fact that Nadir was able to retain any legal advisers at all raised some eyebrows. Surely these eminent professional figures must expect to be remunerated somehow? He was also able to retain the services of the Morgan Partnership, a small upmarket PR company.

Another disagreeable consequence of the bankruptcy was the sale of Asil Nadir's home at 3 Aldford Street. He moved to the flat in Eaton

Square, rented from the Grosvenor estate, where Ayşegül had lived for the previous few years.

The third and most complex of his legal battles was with Christopher Morris and the administrators of Polly Peck. Although Morris had been hinting at possible legal action for months, the first Asil Nadir knew of it came on 22 October 1991 as he left Bow Street Magistrates' Court where he had just heard the SFO place further criminal charges against him. As he stepped into the street, he was served with a writ on behalf of the administrators.

A day later, Morris's writs, prepared by Alsop Wilkinson, the City law firm, were made public. He had served writs on Asil Nadir, Safiye Nadir and five others including the Central Bank of the Turkish Republic of Northern Cyprus. Two others escaped having their assets frozen, but Asil Nadir, Safiye Nadir and the Central Bank were subjected to a worldwide freezing order. The writs covered claims totalling about £1 billion which was supposed to have come from Polly Peck funds. The injunction against Asil Nadir claimed just over £378 million. Another figure named in the writ was Menteş Aziz, Asil Nadir's lawyer and family friend.

Menteş Aziz, a London-trained barrister and a close associate of President Denktaş, who is also a wealthy businessman in Cyprus, has had a chequered relationship with the administrators. He began as their ally, representing them in their action against the Turkish Cypriot court injunction which prevented them gaining access to Polly Peck records on the island. He was paid £50,000 for acting as an adviser to the administrators during 1991. But eventually the working relationship became less cordial. The administrators tried to remove Aziz and Fahri Tunalıer from their directorships on Voyager, the Isle of Man company which was the direct legal owner of the Polly Peck companies in Cyprus.

Menteş Aziz's reaction to the injunction was furious and eloquent. 'One day you are working for the administrators. The next day you find yourself in a litigation suit with them. Am I the Prophet Mohammed? Should I just take the slap in the face? Naturally I shall defend myself. All I have is a carob tree in the village. They can have it. And my trousers and shoes,' he declared.

The immediate effect of the actions brought by Morris was to generate a set of counter-actions in the High Court by the defendants. Most of these appeals failed, but one of them scored a notable success against the administration's lawyers. The Central Bank of the Turkish Republic of Northern Cyprus, an unrecognised body because the state to which it belongs has no international diplomatic recognition outside Turkey, managed to get its injunction freezing £29 million in funds held in

London converted into a very much weaker order affecting only £10 million.

In December 1991 came news of a further court action as the administrators of Polly Peck served a writ on Stoy Hayward, the accountancy house which had audited first Wearwell and later Polly Peck through the 1970s and 1980s, alleging serious shortcomings in the company's audited accounts for 1985. The case against them was brought just before the time limit for taking legal action on that year's accounts expired. Stoys promised to contest it vigorously and reiterated all their earlier claims that full normal tests and procedures had been carried out, in the Near East as well as in London, when auditing Polly Peck. The case has not yet come to court, nor is it clear whether the administrators intend to bring similar actions over the Polly Peck accounts for 1986 and subsequent years.

By the summer of 1992, while the court cases looked set to drag on for months and years, Polly Peck itself had almost melted away. The eighteen months of administration, including endless shuttling between Nicosia and London by Richard Stone and his men, had not produced a relaunch of the company. Rather, they had taken it to a point where the stronger subsidiaries looked like going it alone, while the weaker ones had long since been sold off or disappeared. Control of Sansui, driven into a heavy loss in 1990 when it was forced to write off good will on its balance sheet after the collapse of Polly Peck, had been sold to a Hong Kong company. PPI Del Monte was also on the market after plans to float it on the New York Stock Exchange had finally been abandoned.

The Cyprus businesses, of course, were still outside the control of the administration and they were still pursuing their claims in the Turkish Cypriot courts in hope of gaining access to bank accounts and company records. Vestel, the Turkish consumer electronics business, had made a fairish adaptation to changed circumstances, but it was no longer the market leader in Turkey and sooner or later it was expected to announce a tie-up with a new backer. Meyna, the fruit business on the Turkish mainland which had been the group's cash-cow, was still something of a puzzle to the administrators. They declared simply that it was trading at a greatly reduced level.

The creditors were now promised not 50p or even 20p in the pound, but, according to a letter sent to them in early June, probably only a pitiful 3p. The shareholders, of course, would get nothing back. To make matters more confused, a possible dispute between different types of creditor had to be resolved. A lucky few would get over 50p in the pound. Most would not.

The administrators were among the few groups involved who could be satisfied with the way things had turned out. The costs of the administration, according to the same letter to creditors, were £13 million plus a further £7 million on lawyers' fees.

By this time Richard Stone and Michael Jordan were fighting an action themselves, though not in the High Court. They faced an investigation by the Institute of Chartered Accountants on the grounds that they had allegedly infringed the rules of their profession because of a possible conflict of interest. Their firm, Coopers & Lybrand, had worked for Asil Nadir and Polly Peck in the three years immediately before it collapsed. The investigation meant that both men could find themselves being censured or even having their licences removed. However, they were confident, on the advice of leading counsel, that they had not broken the guidelines.

Asil Nadir is still living in the Eaton Square flat and works in Mayfair offices which he has shared with his younger sister, Bilge Nevzat, since the closure of South Audley Management in May 1992.

The women around him remain, as always, ready to make any sacrifice. Not so the men. Bora Paran, the London correspondent of *Günaydın*, who was Nadir's right-hand man throughout much of 1991, finally left him early in 1992 and wrote up his memoirs in *Sabah*, Asil Nadir's worst enemy in the Turkish press. Among his stories was the suggestion that Asil Nadir had retained the services of a magician from Nigeria called Matthew to restore his fortunes. Turkish readers scratched their heads and wondered whether or not to believe this.

It is too early for any but the most preliminary judgments on Asil Nadir and his business career, a career which may indeed be resumed some day. Yet some things stand out.

His strengths include his almost uncanny negotiating skills, brilliance as a commodities dealer, and an intuitive grasp of strategic opportunities in setting up industrial ventures. Many strokes of undeniable vision and originality can be discerned throughout his business career, stretching back to the Wearwell cash-and-carry operation, and continuing with the idea of building a package factory in Famagusta for Cyprus oranges, to the acquisition of PPI Del Monte and the merger of Capetronics and Sansui. The idea behind Meyna, of building up an ultra-modern Turkish fruit exporting industry which could match that of Spain and Israel, was also an appealing one.

The trouble was that the vision could not often be translated into reality. Polly Peck's management was that of a small or medium-sized company, not a super-efficient global corporation. Nadir's penchant for improvisation and for encouraging competition between his subordinates only made matters worse, fostering deep rivalries.

In the final year before administration, Asil Nadir seems to have been working with Peter Compson, his personnel director, to beef up the board and the top management, but it was too late. If the company had not collapsed and Compson and Fawcus's plans for a corporate restructuring had taken effect, Polly Peck might have evolved into a much stronger and more soundly based international group by the mid-1990s. He was also engaged in early 1990 in a refinancing operation with the banks, which, if it had been completed in time, would have made the financial collapse that autumn impossible.

Asil Nadir was perhaps also a victim of the legend of his own success. His ventures into Turkish publishing in particular brought him into contact with a sycophantic environment whose flattery perhaps encouraged him to pour money into ventures which a tough board of directors of any large corporation would never have approved. The penny-pinching East End factory owner became the fabulously generous Maecenas of Istanbul, a sort of Gatsby figure forever chasing dreams on the edge of attainability and willing to borrow heavily to achieve them.

When the dreams did not work out, those who had pinned their hopes to him suffered havoc. Yet do they have any real reason to blame him more than themselves for their losses and disappointment? The more hard-headed among his friends always tempered their affection by keeping a prudent distance. 'Nobody has any reason to blame Asil. Polly Peck was a glamour stock and investors and bankers were greedy,' says one of his old friends.

Asil Nadir's followers, now a tiny group in Britain but a much larger one in Northern Cyprus, believe that it is only a matter of time until he steps back into the business arena, though perhaps not in the UK. Before he can think of that, of course, he must resolve his difficulties with the SFO and the administrators.

Meanwhile, only one reminder of Polly Peck remains on the London scene. In New Road and Commercial Road the rag trade shops are still there. These days, they are more likely to be owned by Bangladeshis and Indians than by the Jews who were their proprietors in the early 1960s. Thirty years ago, İrfan Nadir and his teenage son Asilkan stood outside them for hours in the rain waiting to buy cloth, dreaming of better times.

101 Commercial Road is a small and very narrow building used as offices. It betrays no hint of its distant origins as a church. Amidst the

seething street-life of the East End, the building stands out for one thing. Above its doorway flutters a large banner with a blue and red logo on a white background. Almost everything else the company ever possessed has gone, and the flag itself is old and grey-looking, but, at least for a little longer, the Polly Peck standard still flies in the streets of London, almost as jauntily as it did in the good times.

Index